EUCHARISTIC DOCUMENTS FOR THE NEW MILLENNIUM

DOCUMENTOS EUCARÍSTICOS PARA EL NUEVO MILENIO

ECCLESIA DE EUCHARISTIA

REDEMPTIONIS SACRAMENTUM

Printed in the United States of America.

Library of Congress Control Number:
2004106883

ISBN 1-56854-559-2

BEUDOC

CONTENTS

ENCYCLICAL LETTER
ECCLESIA DE EUCHARISTIA

OF HIS HOLINESS
POPE JOHN PAUL II
TO THE BISHOPS
PRIESTS AND DEACONS
MEN AND WOMEN IN THE CONSECRATED LIFE
AND ALL THE LAY FAITHFUL
ON THE EUCHARIST
IN ITS RELATIONSHIP TO THE CHURCH

OUTLINE

INTRODUCTION

1. The Church draws her life from the Eucharist. This truth does not simply express a daily experience of faith, but recapitulates *the heart of the mystery of the Church.* In a variety of ways she joyfully experiences the constant fulfillment of the promise: "Lo, I am with you always, to the close of the age" (Matthew 28:20), but in the Holy Eucharist, through the changing of bread and wine into the body and blood of the Lord, she rejoices in this presence with unique intensity. Ever since Pentecost, when the Church, the People of the New Covenant, began her pilgrim journey towards her heavenly homeland, the Divine Sacrament has continued to mark the passing of her days, filling them with confident hope.

The Second Vatican Council rightly proclaimed that the Eucharistic sacrifice is "the source and summit of the Christian life."[1] "For the most holy Eucharist contains the Church's entire spiritual wealth: Christ himself, our passover and living bread. Through his own flesh, now made living and life-giving by the Holy Spirit, he offers life to men."[2] Consequently the gaze of the Church is constantly turned to her Lord, present in the Sacrament of the Altar, in which she discovers the full manifestation of his boundless love.

2. During the Great Jubilee of the Year 2000 I had an opportunity to celebrate the Eucharist in the Cenacle of Jerusalem where, according to tradition, it was first celebrated by Jesus himself. *The Upper Room was where this most holy Sacrament was instituted.* It is there that Christ took bread, broke it and gave it to his disciples, saying: "Take this, all of you, and eat it: this is my body which will be given up for you" (cf. Mark 26:26; Luke 22:19; 1 Corinthians 11:24). Then he took the cup of wine and said to them: "Take this, all of you and drink from it: this is the cup of

my blood, the blood of the new and everlasting covenant. It will be shed for you and for all, so that sins may be forgiven" (cf. Matthew 14:24; Luke 22:20; 1 Corinthians 11:25). I am grateful to the Lord Jesus for allowing me to repeat in that same place, in obedience to his command: "Do this in memory of me" (Luke 22:19), the words which he spoke two thousand years ago.

Did the Apostles who took part in the Last Supper understand the meaning of the words spoken by Christ? Perhaps not. Those words would only be fully clear at the end of the *Triduum sacrum,* the time from Thursday evening to Sunday morning. Those days embrace the *mysterium paschale;* they also embrace the *mysterium eucharisticum.*

3. The Church was born of the paschal mystery. For this very reason the Eucharist, which is in an outstanding way the sacrament of the paschal mystery, *stands at the center of the Church's life.* This is already clear from the earliest images of the Church found in the Acts of the Apostles: "They devoted themselves to the Apostles' teaching and fellowship, to the breaking of bread and the prayers" (2:42). The "breaking of the bread" refers to the Eucharist. Two thousand years later, we continue to relive that primordial image of the Church. At every celebration of the Eucharist, we are spiritually brought back to the paschal Triduum: to the events of the evening of Holy Thursday, to the Last Supper and to what followed it. The institution of the Eucharist sacramentally anticipated the events which were about to take place, beginning with the agony in Gethsemane. Once again we see Jesus as he leaves the Upper Room, descends with his disciples to the Kidron valley and goes to the Garden of Olives. Even today that Garden shelters some very ancient olive trees. Perhaps they witnessed what happened beneath their shade that evening, when Christ in prayer was filled with anguish "and his sweat became like drops of blood falling down upon the ground" (cf. Luke 22:44). The blood which shortly before he had given to the Church as the drink of salvation in the sacrament of the Eucharist, *began to be shed;* its outpouring would then be completed on Golgotha to become the means of our redemption: "Christ . . . as high priest of the good things to come . . . entered once for all into the Holy Place, taking not the blood of goats and calves but his own blood, thus securing an eternal redemption" (Hebrews 9:11–12).

4. *The hour of our redemption.* Although deeply troubled, Jesus does not flee before his "hour." "And what shall I say? 'Father, save me from this hour?' No, for this purpose I have come to this hour" (John 12:27). He wanted his disciples to keep him company, yet he had to experience loneliness and abandonment: "So, could you not watch with me one hour? Watch and pray that you may not enter into temptation" (Matthew 26:40–41). Only John would remain at the foot of the Cross, at the side of Mary and the faithful women. The agony in Gethsemane was the introduction to the agony of the Cross on Good Friday. *The holy hour,* the hour of the redemption of the world. Whenever the Eucharist is celebrated at the tomb of Jesus in Jerusalem, there is an almost tangible return to his "hour," the hour of his Cross and glorification. Every priest who celebrates Holy Mass, together with the Christian community which takes part in it, is led back in spirit to that place and that hour.

"He was crucified, he suffered death and was buried; he descended to the dead; on the third day he rose again." The words of the profession of faith are echoed by the words of contemplation and proclamation: *"This is the wood of the Cross, on which hung the Savior of the world. Come, let us worship."* This is the invitation which the Church extends to all in the afternoon hours of Good Friday. She then takes up her song during the Easter season in order to proclaim: *"The Lord is risen from the tomb; for our sake he hung on the Cross, Alleluia."*

5. *"Mysterium fidei!—The Mystery of Faith!"* When the priest recites or chants these words, all present acclaim: "We announce your death, O Lord, and we proclaim your resurrection, until you come in glory."

In these or similar words the Church, while pointing to Christ in the mystery of his passion, *also reveals her own mystery: Ecclesia de Eucharistia.* By the gift of the Holy Spirit at Pentecost the Church was born and set out upon the pathways of the world, yet a decisive moment in her taking shape was certainly the institution of the Eucharist in the Upper Room. Her foundation and wellspring is the whole *Triduum paschale,* but this is as it were gathered up, foreshadowed and "concentrated" for ever in the gift of the Eucharist. In this gift Jesus Christ entrusted to his Church the perennial making present of the paschal mystery. With it he brought about a mysterious "oneness in time" between that *Triduum* and the passage of the centuries.

The thought of this leads us to profound amazement and gratitude. In the paschal event and the Eucharist which makes it present throughout the centuries, there is a truly enormous "capacity" which embraces all of history as the recipient of the grace of the redemption. This amazement should always fill the Church assembled for the celebration of the Eucharist. But in a special way it should fill the minister of the Eucharist. For it is he who, by the authority given him in the sacrament of priestly ordination, effects the consecration. It is he who says with the power coming to him from Christ in the Upper Room: "This is my body which will be given up for you This is the cup of my blood, poured out for you. . . ." The priest says these words, or rather *he puts his voice at the disposal of the One who spoke these words in the Upper Room* and who desires that they should be repeated in every generation by all those who in the Church ministerially share in his priesthood.

6. I would like to rekindle this Eucharistic "amazement" by the present Encyclical Letter, in continuity with the Jubilee heritage which I have left to the Church in the Apostolic Letter *Novo Millennio Ineunte* and its Marian crowning, *Rosarium Virginis Mariae.* To contemplate the face of Christ, and to contemplate it with Mary, is the "program" which I have set before the Church at the dawn of the third millennium, summoning her to put out into the deep on the sea of history with the enthusiasm of the new evangelization. To contemplate Christ involves being able to recognize him wherever he manifests himself, in his many forms of presence, but above all in the living sacrament of his body and his blood. *The Church draws her life from Christ in the Eucharist;* by him she is fed and by him she is enlightened. The Eucharist is both a mystery of faith and a "mystery of light."[3] Whenever the Church celebrates the Eucharist, the faithful can in some way relive the experience of the two disciples on the road to Emmaus: "their eyes were opened and they recognized him" (Luke 24:31).

7. From the time I began my ministry as the Successor of Peter, I have always marked Holy Thursday, the day of the Eucharist and of the priesthood, by sending a letter to all the priests of the world. This year, the twenty-fifth of my Pontificate, I wish to involve the whole Church more fully in this Eucharistic reflection, also as a way of thanking the Lord for the gift of the Eucharist and the priesthood: "Gift and Mystery."[4] By proclaiming the Year of the Rosary, I wish to put this, my twenty-fifth anniversary, *under the*

aegis of the contemplation of Christ at the school of Mary. Consequently, I cannot let this Holy Thursday 2003 pass without halting before the "Eucharistic face" of Christ and pointing out with new force to the Church the centrality of the Eucharist.

From it the Church draws her life. From this "living bread" she draws her nourishment. How could I not feel the need to urge everyone to experience it ever anew?

8. When I think of the Eucharist, and look at my life as a priest, as a Bishop and as the Successor of Peter, I naturally recall the many times and places in which I was able to celebrate it. I remember the parish church of Niegowi, where I had my first pastoral assignment, the collegiate church of Saint Florian in Krakow, Wawel Cathedral, Saint Peter's Basilica and so many basilicas and churches in Rome and throughout the world. I have been able to celebrate Holy Mass in chapels built along mountain paths, on lakeshores and seacoasts; I have celebrated it on altars built in stadiums and in city squares . . . This varied scenario of celebrations of the Eucharist has given me a powerful experience of its universal and, so to speak, cosmic character. Yes, cosmic! Because even when it is celebrated on the humble altar of a country church, the Eucharist is always in some way celebrated *on the altar of the world.* It unites heaven and earth. It embraces and permeates all creation. The Son of God became man in order to restore all creation, in one supreme act of praise, to the One who made it from nothing. He, the Eternal High Priest who by the blood of his Cross entered the eternal sanctuary, thus gives back to the Creator and Father all creation redeemed. He does so through the priestly ministry of the Church, to the glory of the Most Holy Trinity. Truly this is the *mysterium fidei* which is accomplished in the Eucharist: the world which came forth from the hands of God the Creator now returns to him redeemed by Christ.

9. The Eucharist, as Christ's saving presence in the community of the faithful and its spiritual food, is the most precious possession which the Church can have in her journey through history. This explains the *lively concern* which she has always shown for the Eucharistic mystery, a concern which finds authoritative expression in the work of the Councils and the Popes. How can we not admire the doctrinal expositions of the Decrees on the Most Holy Eucharist and on the Holy Sacrifice of the Mass promulgated by the Council of Trent? For centuries those Decrees

guided theology and catechesis, and they are still a dogmatic reference-point for the continual renewal and growth of God's People in faith and in love for the Eucharist. In times closer to our own, three Encyclical Letters should be mentioned: the Encyclical *Mirae Caritatis* of Leo XIII (28 May 1902),[5] the Encyclical *Mediator Dei* of Pius XII (20 November 1947)[6] and the Encyclical *Mysterium Fidei* of Paul VI (3 September 1965).[7]

The Second Vatican Council, while not issuing a specific document on the Eucharistic mystery, considered its various aspects throughout its documents, especially the Dogmatic Constitution on the Church *Lumen Gentium* and the Constitution on the Sacred Liturgy *Sacrosanctum Concilium.*

I myself, in the first years of my apostolic ministry in the Chair of Peter, wrote the Apostolic Letter *Dominicae Cenae* (24 February 1980),[8] in which I discussed some aspects of the Eucharistic mystery and its importance for the life of those who are its ministers. Today I take up anew the thread of that argument, with even greater emotion and gratitude in my heart, echoing as it were the word of the Psalmist: "What shall I render to the Lord for all his bounty to me? I will lift up the cup of salvation and call on the name of the Lord" (Psalm 116:12–13).

10. The Magisterium's commitment to proclaiming the Eucharistic mystery has been matched by interior growth within the Christian community. Certainly *the liturgical reform inaugurated by the Council* has greatly contributed to a more conscious, active and fruitful participation in the Holy Sacrifice of the Altar on the part of the faithful. In many places, *adoration of the Blessed Sacrament* is also an important daily practice and becomes an inexhaustible source of holiness. The devout participation of the faithful in the Eucharistic procession on the Solemnity of the Body and Blood of Christ is a grace from the Lord which yearly brings joy to those who take part in it.

Other positive signs of Eucharistic faith and love might also be mentioned.

Unfortunately, alongside these lights, *there are also shadows.* In some places the practice of Eucharistic adoration has been almost completely abandoned. In various parts of the Church abuses have occurred, leading to confusion with regard to sound faith and Catholic doctrine concerning this wonderful sacrament. At times one encounters an extremely reductive understanding of the Eucharistic mystery. Stripped of its sacrificial meaning, it is celebrated as if it were simply a fraternal banquet. Furthermore, the necessity of the ministerial priesthood, grounded in apostolic succession, is at times obscured and the sacramental nature of the Eucharist is reduced to its mere effectiveness as a form of proclamation. This has led here and there to ecumenical initiatives which, albeit well-intentioned, indulge in Eucharistic practices contrary to the discipline by which the Church expresses her faith. How can we not express profound grief at all this? The Eucharist is too great a gift to tolerate ambiguity and depreciation.

It is my hope that the present Encyclical Letter will effectively help to banish the dark clouds of unacceptable doctrine and practice, so that the Eucharist will continue to shine forth in all its radiant mystery.

CHAPTER I
THE MYSTERY OF FAITH

11. "The Lord Jesus on the night he was betrayed" (1 Corinthians 11:23) instituted the Eucharistic Sacrifice of his body and his blood. The words of the Apostle Paul bring us back to the dramatic setting in which the Eucharist was born. The Eucharist is indelibly marked by the event of the Lord's passion and death, of which it is not only a reminder but the sacramental re-presentation. It is the sacrifice of the Cross perpetuated down the ages.[9] This truth is well expressed by the words with which the assembly in the Latin rite responds to the priest's proclamation of the "Mystery of Faith": *"We announce your death, O Lord."*

The Church has received the Eucharist from Christ her Lord not as one gift—however precious—among so many others, but as *the gift par excellence,* for it is the gift of himself, of his person in his sacred humanity, as well as the gift of his saving work. Nor does it remain confined to the past, since "all that Christ is—all that he did and suffered for all men—participates in the divine eternity, and so transcends all times."[10]

When the Church celebrates the Eucharist, the memorial of her Lord's death and resurrection, this central event of salvation becomes really present and "the work of our redemption is carried out."[11] This sacrifice is so decisive for the salvation of the human race that Jesus Christ offered it and returned to the Father only *after he had left us a means of sharing in it* as if we had been present there. Each member of the faithful can thus take part in it and inexhaustibly gain its fruits. This is the faith from which generations of Christians down the ages have lived. The Church's Magisterium has constantly reaffirmed this faith with joyful gratitude for its inestimable gift.[12] I wish once more to recall this truth and to join you, my dear brothers and sisters, in adoration before this mystery: a great mystery, a mystery of mercy. What more could Jesus have done for us? Truly, in the Eucharist, he shows us a love which goes "to the end" (cf. John 13:1), a love which knows no measure.

12. This aspect of the universal charity of the Eucharistic Sacrifice is based on the words of the Savior himself. In instituting it, he did not merely say: "This is my body," "this is my blood," but went on to add: "which is given for you," "which is poured out for you" (Luke 22:19–20). Jesus did not simply state that what he was giving them to eat and drink was his body and his blood; he also expressed *its sacrificial meaning* and made sacramentally present his sacrifice which would soon be offered on the Cross for the salvation of all. "The Mass is at the same time, and inseparably, the sacrificial memorial in which the sacrifice of the Cross is perpetuated and the sacred banquet of communion with the Lord's body and blood."[13]

The Church constantly draws her life from the redeeming sacrifice; she approaches it not only through faith-filled remembrance, but also through a real contact, since *this sacrifice is made present ever anew,* sacramentally perpetuated, in every community which offers it at the hands of the consecrated minister. The Eucharist thus applies to men and women today the reconciliation won once for all by Christ for mankind in every age. "The sacrifice of Christ and the sacrifice of the Eucharist are *one single sacrifice.*"[14] Saint John Chrysostom put it well: "We always offer the same Lamb, not one today and another tomorrow, but always the same one. For this reason the sacrifice is always only one . . . Even now we offer that victim who was once offered and who will never be consumed."[15]

The Mass makes present the sacrifice of the Cross; it does not add to that sacrifice nor does it multiply it.[16] What is repeated is its memorial celebration, its "commemorative representation" (*memorialis demonstratio*),[17] which makes Christ's one, definitive redemptive sacrifice always present in time. The sacrificial nature of the Eucharistic mystery cannot therefore be understood as something separate, independent of the Cross or only indirectly referring to the sacrifice of Calvary.

13. By virtue of its close relationship to the sacrifice of Golgotha, the Eucharist is *a sacrifice in the strict sense,* and not only in a general way, as if it were simply a matter of Christ's offering himself to the faithful as their spiritual food. The gift of his love and obedience to the point of giving his life (cf. John 10:17–18) is in the first place a gift to his Father. Certainly it is a gift given for our sake, and indeed that of all humanity (cf. Matthew 26:28; Mark 14:24; Luke 22:20; John 10:15), yet it is *first and foremost a gift to the Father:* "a sacrifice that the Father accepted, giving, in return for this total self-giving by his Son, who 'became obedient unto death' (Philippians 2:8), his own paternal gift, that is to say the grant of new immortal life in the resurrection."[18]

In giving his sacrifice to the Church, Christ has also made his own the spiritual sacrifice of the Church, which is called to offer herself in union with the sacrifice of Christ. This is the teaching of the Second Vatican Council concerning all the faithful: "Taking part in the Eucharistic Sacrifice, which is the source and summit of the whole Christian life, they offer the divine victim to God, and offer themselves along with it."[19]

14. Christ's passover includes not only his passion and death, but also his resurrection. This is recalled by the assembly's acclamation following the consecration: *"We proclaim your resurrection."* The Eucharistic Sacrifice makes present not only the mystery of the Savior's passion and death, but also the mystery of the resurrection which crowned his sacrifice. It is as the living and risen One that Christ can become in the Eucharist the "bread of life" (John 6:35, 48), the "living bread" (John 6:51). Saint Ambrose reminded the newly-initiated that the Eucharist applies the event of the resurrection to their lives: "Today Christ is yours, yet each day he rises again for you."[20] Saint Cyril of Alexandria also makes clear that sharing in the sacred mysteries "is a true confession and a remembrance that the Lord died and returned to life for us and on our behalf."[21]

15. The sacramental re-presentation of Christ's sacrifice, crowned by the resurrection, in the Mass involves a most special presence which—in the words of Paul VI—"is called 'real' not as

a way of excluding all other types of presence as if they were 'not real,' but because it is a presence in the fullest sense: a substantial presence whereby Christ, the God-Man, is wholly and entirely present."[22] This sets forth once more the perennially valid teaching of the Council of Trent: "the consecration of the bread and wine effects the change of the whole substance of the bread into the substance of the body of Christ our Lord, and of the whole substance of the wine into the substance of his blood. And the holy Catholic Church has fittingly and properly called this change transubstantiation."[23] Truly the Eucharist is a *mysterium fidei*, a mystery which surpasses our understanding and can only be received in faith, as is often brought out in the catechesis of the Church Fathers regarding this divine sacrament: "Do not see—Saint Cyril of Jerusalem exhorts—in the bread and wine merely natural elements, because the Lord has expressly said that they are his body and his blood: faith assures you of this, though your senses suggest otherwise."[24]

Adoro te devote, latens Deitas, we shall continue to sing with the Angelic Doctor. Before this mystery of love, human reason fully experiences its limitations. One understands how, down the centuries, this truth has stimulated theology to strive to understand it ever more deeply.

These are praiseworthy efforts, which are all the more helpful and insightful to the extent that they are able to join critical thinking to the "living faith" of the Church, as grasped especially by the Magisterium's "sure charism of truth" and the "intimate sense of spiritual realities"[25] which is attained above all by the saints. There remains the boundary indicated by Paul VI: "Every theological explanation which seeks some understanding of this mystery, in order to be in accord with Catholic faith, must firmly maintain that in objective reality, independently of our mind, the bread and wine have ceased to exist after the consecration, so that the adorable body and blood of the Lord Jesus from that moment on are really before us under the sacramental species of bread and wine."[26]

16. The saving efficacy of the sacrifice is fully realized when the Lord's body and blood are received in communion. The Eucharistic Sacrifice is intrinsically directed to the inward union of the faithful with Christ through communion; we receive the very One who offered himself for us, we receive his body which he

gave up for us on the Cross and his blood which he "poured out for many for the forgiveness of sins" (Matthew 26:28). We are reminded of his words: "As the living Father sent me, and I live because of the Father, so he who eats me will live because of me" (John 6:57). Jesus himself reassures us that this union, which he compares to that of the life of the Trinity, is truly realized. *The Eucharist is a true banquet,* in which Christ offers himself as our nourishment. When for the first time Jesus spoke of this food, his listeners were astonished and bewildered, which forced the Master to emphasize the objective truth of his words: "Truly, truly, I say to you, unless you eat the flesh of the Son of Man and drink his blood, you have no life within you" (John 6:53). This is no metaphorical food: "My flesh is food indeed, and my blood is drink indeed" (John 6:55).

17. Through our communion in his body and blood, Christ also grants us his Spirit. Saint Ephrem writes: "He called the bread his living body and he filled it with himself and his Spirit . . . .

He who eats it with faith, eats Fire and Spirit . . . . Take and eat this, all of you, and eat with it the Holy Spirit. For it is truly my body and whoever eats it will have eternal life."[27] The Church implores this divine Gift, the source of every other gift, in the Eucharistic epiclesis. In the *Divine Liturgy* of Saint John Chrysostom, for example, we find the prayer: "We beseech, implore and beg you: send your Holy Spirit upon us all and upon these gifts . . . that those who partake of them may be purified in soul, receive the forgiveness of their sins, and share in the Holy Spirit."[28] And in the *Roman Missal* the celebrant prays: "grant that we who are nourished by his body and blood may be filled with his Holy Spirit, and become one body, one spirit in Christ."[29] Thus by the gift of his body and blood Christ increases within us the gift of his Spirit, already poured out in Baptism and bestowed as a "seal" in the sacrament of Confirmation.

18. The acclamation of the assembly following the consecration appropriately ends by expressing the eschatological thrust which marks the celebration of the Eucharist (cf. 1 Corinthians 11:26): *"until you come in glory."* The Eucharist is a straining towards the goal, a foretaste of the fullness of joy promised by Christ (cf. John 15:11); it is in some way the anticipation of heaven, the "pledge of future glory."[30] In the Eucharist, everything speaks of confident waiting "in joyful hope for the coming of our Savior,

Jesus Christ."[31] Those who feed on Christ in the Eucharist need not wait until the hereafter to receive eternal life: *they already possess it on earth,* as the first-fruits of a future fullness which will embrace man in his totality. For in the Eucharist we also receive the pledge of our bodily resurrection at the end of the world: "He who eats my flesh and drinks my blood has eternal life, and I will raise him up at the last day" (John 6:54). This pledge of the future resurrection comes from the fact that the flesh of the Son of Man, given as food, is his body in its glorious state after the resurrection. With the Eucharist we digest, as it were, the "secret" of the resurrection. For this reason Saint Ignatius of Antioch rightly defined the Eucharistic Bread as "a medicine of immortality, an antidote to death."[32]

19. The eschatological tension kindled by the Eucharist *expresses and reinforces our communion with the Church in heaven.* It is not by chance that the Eastern Anaphoras and the Latin Eucharistic Prayers honor Mary, the ever-Virgin Mother of Jesus Christ our Lord and God, the angels, the holy apostles, the glorious martyrs and all the saints. This is an aspect of the Eucharist which merits greater attention: in celebrating the sacrifice of the Lamb, we are united to the heavenly "liturgy" and become part of that great multitude which cries out: "Salvation belongs to our God who sits upon the throne, and to the Lamb!" (Revelation 7:10). The Eucharist is truly a glimpse of heaven appearing on earth. It is a glorious ray of the heavenly Jerusalem which pierces the clouds of our history and lights up our journey.

20. A significant consequence of the eschatological tension inherent in the Eucharist is also the fact that it spurs us on our journey through history and plants a seed of living hope in our daily commitment to the work before us. Certainly the Christian vision leads to the expectation of "new heavens" and "a new earth" (Revelation 21:1), but this increases, rather than lessens, *our sense of responsibility for the world today.*[33] I wish to reaffirm this forcefully at the beginning of the new millennium, so that Christians will feel more obliged than ever not to neglect their duties as citizens in this world. Theirs is the task of contributing with the light of the Gospel to the building of a more human world, a world fully in harmony with God's plan.

Many problems darken the horizon of our time. We need but think of the urgent need to work for peace, to base relationships between peoples on solid premises of justice and solidarity, and to defend human life from conception to its natural end. And what should we say of the thousand inconsistencies of a "globalized" world where the weakest, the most powerless and the poorest appear to have so little hope! It is in this world that Christian hope must shine forth! For this reason too, the Lord wished to remain with us in the Eucharist, making his presence in meal and sacrifice the promise of a humanity renewed by his love. Significantly, in their account of the Last Supper, the Synoptics recount the institution of the Eucharist, while the Gospel of John relates, as a way of bringing out its profound meaning, the account of the "washing of the feet," in which Jesus appears as the teacher of communion and of service (cf. John 13:1–20). The Apostle Paul, for his part, says that it is "unworthy" of a Christian community to partake of the Lord's Supper amid division and indifference towards the poor (cf. 1 Corinthians 11:17–22, 27–34).[34]

Proclaiming the death of the Lord "until he comes" (1 Corinthians 11:26) entails that all who take part in the Eucharist be committed to changing their lives and making them in a certain way completely "Eucharistic." It is this fruit of a transfigured existence and a commitment to transforming the world in accordance with the Gospel which splendidly illustrates the eschatological tension inherent in the celebration of the Eucharist and in the Christian life as a whole: "Come, Lord Jesus!" (Revelation 22:20).

CHAPTER II
THE EUCHARIST BUILDS THE CHURCH

21. The Second Vatican Council teaches that the celebration of the Eucharist is at the center of the process of the Church's growth. After stating that "the Church, as the Kingdom of Christ already present in mystery, grows visibly in the world through the power of God."[35] Then, as if in answer to the question: "How does the Church grow?," the Council adds: "as often as the sacrifice of the Cross by which 'Christ our pasch is sacrificed' (1 Corinthians 5:7) is celebrated on the altar, the work of our redemption is carried out. At the same time in the sacrament of the Eucharistic bread, the unity of the faithful, who form one body in Christ (cf. 1 Corinthians 10:17), is both expressed and brought about."[36]

A causal influence of the Eucharist is present at the Church's very origins. The Evangelists specify that it was the Twelve, the Apostles, who gathered with Jesus at the Last Supper (cf. Matthew

26:20; Mark 14:17; Luke 22:14). This is a detail of notable importance, for the Apostles "were both the seeds of the new Israel and the beginning of the sacred hierarchy."[37] By offering them his body and his blood as food, Christ mysteriously involved them in the sacrifice which would be completed later on Calvary. By analogy with the Covenant of Mount Sinai, sealed by sacrifice and the sprinkling of blood,[38] the actions and words of Jesus at the Last Supper laid the foundations of the new messianic community, the People of the New Covenant.

The Apostles, by accepting in the Upper Room Jesus' invitation: "Take, eat," "Drink of it, all of you" (Matthew 26:26–27), entered for the first time into sacramental communion with him. From that time forward, until the end of the age, the Church is built up through sacramental communion with the Son of God who was sacrificed for our sake: "Do this is remembrance of me . . . . Do this, as often as you drink it, in remembrance of me" (1 Corinthians 11:24–25; cf. Luke 22:19).

22. Incorporation into Christ, which is brought about by Baptism, is constantly renewed and consolidated by sharing in the Eucharistic Sacrifice, especially by that full sharing which takes place in sacramental communion. We can say not only that *each of us receives Christ,* but also that *Christ receives each of us.* He enters into friendship with us: "You are my friends" (John 15:14). Indeed, it is because of him that we have life: "He who eats me will live because of me" (John 6:57). Eucharistic communion brings about in a sublime way the mutual "abiding" of Christ and each of his followers: "Abide in me, and I in you" (John 15:4).

By its union with Christ, the People of the New Covenant, far from closing in upon itself, becomes a "sacrament" for humanity,[39] a sign and instrument of the salvation achieved by Christ, the light of the world and the salt of the earth (cf. Matthew 5:13–16), for the redemption of all.[40] The Church's mission stands in continuity with the mission of Christ: "As the Father has sent me, even so I send you" (John 20:21). From the perpetuation of the sacrifice of the Cross and her communion with the body and blood of Christ in the Eucharist, the Church draws the spiritual power needed to carry out her mission. The Eucharist thus appears as both *the source* and *the summit* of all evangelization, since its goal is the communion of mankind with Christ and in him with the Father and the Holy Spirit.[41]

23. Eucharistic communion also confirms the Church in her unity as the body of Christ. Saint Paul refers to this *unifying power* of participation in the banquet of the Eucharist when he writes to the Corinthians: "The bread which we break, is it not a communion in the body of Christ? Because there is one bread, we who are many are one body, for we all partake of the one bread" (1 Corinthians 10:16–17). Saint John Chrysostom's commentary on these words is profound and perceptive: "For what is the bread? It is the body of Christ. And what do those who receive it become? The Body of Christ—not many bodies but one body. For as bread is completely one, though made of up many grains of wheat, and these, albeit unseen, remain nonetheless present, in such a way that their difference is not apparent since they have been made a perfect whole, so too are we mutually joined to one another and together united with Christ."[42] The argument is compelling: our union with Christ, which is a gift and grace for each of us, makes it possible for us, in him, to share in the unity of his body which is the Church. The Eucharist reinforces the incorporation into Christ which took place in Baptism though the gift of the Spirit (cf. 1 Corinthians 12:13, 27).

The joint and inseparable activity of the Son and of the Holy Spirit, which is at the origin of the Church, of her consolidation and her continued life, is at work in the Eucharist. This was clearly evident to the author of the *Liturgy of Saint James:* in the epiclesis of the Anaphora, God the Father is asked to send the Holy Spirit upon the faithful and upon the offerings, so that the body and blood of Christ "may be a help to all those who partake of it . . . for the sanctification of their souls and bodies."[43] The Church is fortified by the divine Paraclete through the sanctification of the faithful in the Eucharist.

24. The gift of Christ and his Spirit which we receive in Eucharistic communion superabundantly fulfils the yearning for fraternal unity deeply rooted in the human heart; at the same time it elevates the experience of fraternity already present in our common sharing at the same Eucharistic table to a degree which far surpasses that of the simple human experience of sharing a meal. Through her communion with the body of Christ the Church comes to be ever more profoundly "in Christ in the nature of a sacrament, that is, a sign and instrument of intimate unity with God and of the unity of the whole human race."[44]

The seeds of disunity, which daily experience shows to be so deeply rooted in humanity as a result of sin, are countered by *the unifying power* of the body of Christ. The Eucharist, precisely by building up the Church, creates human community.

25. The *worship of the Eucharist outside of the Mass* is of inestimable value for the life of the Church. This worship is strictly linked to the celebration of the Eucharistic Sacrifice. The presence of Christ under the sacred species reserved after Mass—a presence which lasts as long as the species of bread and of wine remain[45]—derives from the celebration of the sacrifice and is directed towards communion, both sacramental and spiritual.[46] It is the responsibility of Pastors to encourage, also by their personal witness, the practice of Eucharistic adoration, and exposition of the Blessed Sacrament in particular, as well as prayer of adoration before Christ present under the Eucharistic species.[47]

It is pleasant to spend time with him, to lie close to his breast like the Beloved Disciple (cf. John 13:25) and to feel the infinite love present in his heart. If in our time Christians must be distinguished above all by the "art of prayer,"[48] how can we not feel a renewed need to spend time in spiritual converse, in silent adoration, in heartfelt love before Christ present in the Most Holy Sacrament? How often, dear brother and sisters, have I experienced this, and drawn from it strength, consolation and support!

This practice, repeatedly praised and recommended by the Magisterium,[49] is supported by the example of many saints. Particularly outstanding in this regard was Saint Alphonsus Liguori, who wrote: "Of all devotions, that of adoring Jesus in the Blessed Sacrament is the greatest after the sacraments, the one dearest to God and the one most helpful to us."[50] The Eucharist is a priceless treasure: by not only celebrating it but also by praying before it outside of Mass we are enabled to make contact with the very wellspring of grace. A Christian community desirous of contemplating the face of Christ in the spirit which I proposed in the Apostolic Letters *Novo Millennio Ineunte* and *Rosarium Virginis Mariae* cannot fail also to develop this aspect of Eucharistic worship, which prolongs and increases the fruits of our communion in the body and blood of the Lord.

CHAPTER III
THE APOSTOLICITY OF THE EUCHARIST AND OF THE CHURCH

26. If, as I have said, the Eucharist builds the Church and the Church makes the Eucharist, it follows that there is a profound relationship between the two, so much so that we can apply to the Eucharistic mystery the very words with which, in the Nicene-Constantinopolitan Creed, we profess the Church to be "one, holy, catholic and apostolic." The Eucharist too is one and catholic. It is also holy, indeed, the Most Holy Sacrament. But it is above all its apostolicity that we must now consider.

27. The Catechism of the Catholic Church, in explaining how the Church is apostolic—founded on the Apostles—sees *three meanings* in this expression. First, "she was and remains built on 'the foundation of the Apostles' (Ephesians 2:20), the witnesses chosen and sent on mission by Christ himself."[51] The Eucharist too has its foundation in the Apostles, not in the sense that it did not originate in Christ himself, but because it was entrusted by Jesus to the Apostles and has been handed down to us by them and by their successors. It is in continuity with the practice of the Apostles, in obedience to the Lord's command, that the Church has celebrated the Eucharist down the centuries.

The second sense in which the Church is apostolic, as the *Catechism* points out, is that "with the help of the Spirit dwelling in her, the Church keeps and hands on the teaching, the 'good deposit,' the salutary words she has heard from the Apostles."[52] Here too the Eucharist is apostolic, for it is celebrated in conformity with the faith of the Apostles. At various times in the two-thousand-year history of the People of the New Covenant, the Church's Magisterium has more precisely defined her teaching on the Eucharist, including its proper terminology, precisely in order to safeguard the apostolic faith with regard to this sublime mystery. This faith remains unchanged and it is essential for the Church that it remain unchanged.

28. Lastly, the Church is apostolic in the sense that she "continues to be taught, sanctified and guided by the Apostles until Christ's return, through their successors in pastoral office: the college of Bishops assisted by priests, in union with the Successor of Peter, the Church's supreme pastor."[53] Succession to the Apostles

in the pastoral mission necessarily entails the sacrament of Holy Orders, that is, the uninterrupted sequence, from the very beginning, of valid episcopal ordinations.[54] This succession is essential for the Church to exist in a proper and full sense.

The Eucharist also expresses this sense of apostolicity. As the Second Vatican Council teaches, "the faithful join in the offering of the Eucharist by virtue of their royal priesthood,"[55] yet it is the ordained priest who, "acting in the person of Christ, brings about the Eucharistic Sacrifice and offers it to God in the name of all the people."[56] For this reason, the *Roman Missal* prescribes that only the priest should recite the Eucharistic Prayer, while the people participate in faith and in silence.[57]

29. The expression repeatedly employed by the Second Vatican Council, according to which "the ministerial priest, acting in the person of Christ, brings about the Eucharistic Sacrifice."[58] was already firmly rooted in papal teaching.[59] As I have pointed out on other occasions, the phrase *in persona Christi* "means more than offering 'in the name of' or 'in the place of' Christ. *In persona* means in specific sacramental identification with the eternal High Priest who is the author and principal subject of this sacrifice of his, a sacrifice in which, in truth, nobody can take his place."[60] The ministry of priests who have received the sacrament of Holy Orders, in the economy of salvation chosen by Christ, makes clear that the Eucharist which they celebrate is *a gift which radically transcends the power of the assembly* and is in any event essential for validly linking the Eucharistic consecration to the sacrifice of the Cross and to the Last Supper. The assembly gathered together for the celebration of the Eucharist, if it is to be a truly Eucharistic assembly, absolutely requires the presence of an ordained priest as its president. On the other hand, the community is by itself incapable of providing an ordained minister. This minister is a gift which the assembly *receives through episcopal succession going back to the Apostles.* It is the Bishop who, through the Sacrament of Holy Orders, makes a new presbyter by conferring upon him the power to consecrate the Eucharist. Consequently, "the Eucharistic mystery cannot be celebrated in any community except by an ordained priest, as the Fourth Lateran Council expressly taught."[61]

30. The Catholic Church's teaching on the relationship between priestly ministry and the Eucharist and her teaching on the Eucharistic Sacrifice have both been the subject in recent decades of a

fruitful dialogue *in the area of ecumenism.* We must give thanks to the Blessed Trinity for the significant progress and convergence achieved in this regard, which lead us to hope one day for a full sharing of faith. Nonetheless, the observations of the Council concerning the Ecclesial Communities which arose in the West from the sixteenth century onwards and are separated from the Catholic Church remain fully pertinent: "The Ecclesial Communities separated from us lack that fullness of unity with us which should flow from Baptism, and we believe that especially because of the lack of the sacrament of Orders they have not preserved the genuine and total reality of the Eucharistic mystery. Nevertheless, when they commemorate the Lord's death and resurrection in the Holy Supper, they profess that it signifies life in communion with Christ and they await his coming in glory."[62]

The Catholic faithful, therefore, while respecting the religious convictions of these separated brethren, must refrain from receiving the communion distributed in their celebrations, so as not to condone an ambiguity about the nature of the Eucharist and, consequently, to fail in their duty to bear clear witness to the truth. This would result in slowing the progress being made towards full visible unity. Similarly, it is unthinkable to substitute for Sunday Mass ecumenical celebrations of the word or services of common prayer with Christians from the aforementioned Ecclesial Communities, or even participation in their own liturgical services. Such celebrations and services, however praiseworthy in certain situations, prepare for the goal of full communion, including Eucharistic communion, but they cannot replace it.

The fact that the power of consecrating the Eucharist has been entrusted only to Bishops and priests does not represent any kind of belittlement of the rest of the People of God, for in the communion of the one body of Christ which is the Church this gift redounds to the benefit of all.

31. If the Eucharist is the center and summit of the Church's life, it is likewise the center and summit of priestly ministry. For this reason, with a heart filled with gratitude to our Lord Jesus Christ, I repeat that the Eucharist "is the principal and central *raison d'être* of the sacrament of priesthood, which effectively came into being at the moment of the institution of the Eucharist."[63]

Priests are engaged in a wide variety of pastoral activities. If we also consider the social and cultural conditions of the modern world it is easy to understand how priests face the very real *risk of losing their focus* amid such a great number of different tasks. The Second Vatican Council saw in pastoral charity the bond which gives unity to the priest's life and work. This, the Council adds, "flows mainly from the Eucharistic Sacrifice, which is therefore the center and root of the whole priestly life."[64] We can understand, then, how important it is for the spiritual life of the priest, as well as for the good of the Church and the world, that priests follow the Council's recommendation to celebrate the Eucharist daily: "for even if the faithful are unable to be present, it is an act of Christ and the Church."[65] In this way priests will be able to counteract the daily tensions which lead to a lack of focus and they will find in the Eucharistic Sacrifice—the true center of their lives and ministry—the spiritual strength needed to deal with their different pastoral responsibilities. Their daily activity will thus become truly Eucharistic.

The centrality of the Eucharist in the life and ministry of priests is the basis of its centrality in the *pastoral promotion of priestly vocations.* It is in the Eucharist that prayer for vocations is most closely united to the prayer of Christ the Eternal High Priest. At the same time the diligence of priests in carrying out their Eucharistic ministry, together with the conscious, active and fruitful participation of the faithful in the Eucharist, provides young men with a powerful example and incentive for responding generously to God's call. Often it is the example of a priest's fervent pastoral charity which the Lord uses to sow and to bring to fruition in a young man's heart the seed of a priestly calling.

32. All of this shows how distressing and irregular is the situation of a Christian community which, despite having sufficient numbers and variety of faithful to form a parish, does not have a priest to lead it. Parishes are communities of the baptized who express and affirm their identity above all through the celebration of the Eucharistic Sacrifice. But this requires the presence of a presbyter, who alone is qualified to offer the Eucharist *in persona Christi.* When a community lacks a priest, attempts are rightly made somehow to remedy the situation so that it can continue its Sunday celebrations, and those religious and laity who lead their brothers and sisters in prayer exercise in a praiseworthy way the common priesthood of all the faithful based on the grace of Baptism. But such solutions must be considered merely temporary, while the community awaits a priest.

The sacramental incompleteness of these celebrations should above all inspire the whole community to pray with greater fervor that the Lord will send laborers into his harvest (cf. Matthew 9:38). It should also be an incentive to mobilize all the resources needed for an adequate pastoral promotion of vocations, without yielding to the temptation to seek solutions which lower the moral and formative standards demanded of candidates for the priesthood.

33. When, due to the scarcity of priests, non-ordained members of the faithful are entrusted with a share in the pastoral care of a parish, they should bear in mind that—as the Second Vatican Council teaches—"no Christian community can be built up unless it has its basis and center in the celebration of the most Holy Eucharist."[66] They have a responsibility, therefore, to keep alive in the community a genuine "hunger" for the Eucharist, so that no opportunity for the celebration of Mass will ever be missed, also taking advantage of the occasional presence of a priest who is not impeded by Church law from celebrating Mass.

CHAPTER IV
THE EUCHARIST AND ECCLESIAL COMMUNION

34. The Extraordinary Assembly of the Synod of Bishops in 1985 saw in the concept of an "ecclesiology of communion" the central and fundamental idea of the documents of the Second Vatican Council.[67] The Church is called during her earthly pilgrimage to maintain and promote communion with the Triune God and communion among the faithful. For this purpose she possesses the word and the sacraments, particularly the Eucharist, by which she "constantly lives and grows"[68] and in which she expresses her very nature. It is not by chance that the term *communion* has become one of the names given to this sublime sacrament.

The Eucharist thus appears as the culmination of all the sacraments in perfecting our communion with God the Father by identification with his only-begotten Son through the working of the Holy Spirit. With discerning faith a distinguished writer of the Byzantine tradition voiced this truth: in the Eucharist "unlike any other sacrament, the mystery [of communion] is so perfect that it brings us to the heights of every good thing: here is the ultimate goal of every human desire, because here we attain God and God joins himself to us in the most perfect union."[69] Precisely for this reason it is good to *cultivate in our hearts a constant desire for the sacrament of the Eucharist.* This was the origin of the practice of "spiritual communion," which has happily been established in the Church for centuries and recommended by saints who were masters of the spiritual life. Saint Teresa of Jesus wrote: "When you do not receive communion and you do not attend Mass, you can make a spiritual communion, which is a most beneficial practice; by it the love of God will be greatly impressed on you."[70]

35. The celebration of the Eucharist, however, cannot be the starting-point for communion; it presupposes that communion already exists, a communion which it seeks to consolidate and bring to perfection. The sacrament is an expression of this bond of communion both in its *invisible* dimension, which, in Christ and through the working of the Holy Spirit, unites us to the Father and among ourselves, and in its *visible* dimension, which entails communion in the teaching of the Apostles, in the sacraments and in the Church's hierarchical order. The profound relationship between the invisible and the visible elements of ecclesial communion is constitutive of the Church as the sacrament of salvation.[71] Only in this context can there be a legitimate celebration of the Eucharist and true participation in it. Consequently it is an intrinsic requirement of the Eucharist that it should be celebrated in communion, and specifically maintaining the various bonds of that communion intact.

36. Invisible communion, though by its nature always growing, presupposes the life of grace, by which we become "partakers of the divine nature" (2 Peter 1:4), and the practice of the virtues of faith, hope and love. Only in this way do we have true communion with the Father, the Son and the Holy Spirit. Nor is faith sufficient; we must persevere in sanctifying grace and love, remaining within the Church "bodily" as well as "in our heart";[72] what is required, in the words of Saint Paul, is "faith working through love" (Galatians 5:6).

Keeping these invisible bonds intact is a specific moral duty incumbent upon Christians who wish to participate fully in the Eucharist by receiving the body and blood of Christ. The Apostle Paul appeals to this duty when he warns: "Let a man examine himself, and so eat of the bread and drink of the cup" (1 Corinthians 11:28). Saint John Chrysostom, with his stirring eloquence, exhorted the faithful: "I too raise my voice, I beseech, beg and implore that no one draw near to this sacred table with a sullied and corrupt conscience. Such an act, in fact, can never be called 'communion,' not even were we to touch the Lord's body a thousand times over, but 'condemnation,' 'torment' and 'increase of punishment.'"[73]

Along these same lines, the Catechism of the Catholic Church rightly stipulates that "anyone conscious of a grave sin must receive the sacrament of Reconciliation before coming to communion."[74] I therefore desire to reaffirm that in the Church there remains in force, now and in the future, the rule by which the Council of Trent gave concrete expression to the Apostle Paul's stern warning when it affirmed that, in order to receive the Eucharist in a worthy manner, "one must first confess one's sins, when one is aware of mortal sin."[75]

37. The two sacraments of the Eucharist and Penance are very closely connected. Because the Eucharist makes present the redeeming sacrifice of the Cross, perpetuating it sacramentally, it naturally gives rise to a continuous need for conversion, for a personal response to the appeal made by Saint Paul to the Christians of Corinth: "We beseech you on behalf of Christ, be reconciled to God" (2 Corinthians 5:20). If a Christian's conscience is burdened by serious sin, then the path of penance through the sacrament of Reconciliation becomes necessary for full participation in the Eucharistic Sacrifice.

The judgment of one's state of grace obviously belongs only to the person involved, since it is a question of examining one's conscience. However, in cases of outward conduct which is seriously, clearly and steadfastly contrary to the moral norm, the Church, in her pastoral concern for the good order of the community and out of respect for the sacrament, cannot fail to feel directly involved. The *Code of Canon Law* refers to this situation of a manifest lack of proper moral disposition when it states that those who "obstinately persist in manifest grave sin" are not to be admitted to Eucharistic communion.[76]

38. Ecclesial communion, as I have said, is likewise *visible*, and finds expression in the series of "bonds" listed by the Council when it teaches: "They are fully incorporated into the society of the Church who, possessing the Spirit of Christ, accept her whole structure and all the means of salvation established within her,

and within her visible framework are united to Christ, who governs her through the Supreme Pontiff and the Bishops, by the bonds of profession of faith, the sacraments, ecclesiastical government and communion."[77]

The Eucharist, as the supreme sacramental manifestation of communion in the Church, demands to be celebrated in *a context where the outward bonds of communion are also intact.* In a special way, since the Eucharist is "as it were the summit of the spiritual life and the goal of all the sacraments,"[78] it requires that the bonds of communion in the sacraments, particularly in Baptism and in priestly Orders, be real. It is not possible to give communion to a person who is not baptized or to one who rejects the full truth of the faith regarding the Eucharistic mystery. Christ is the truth and he bears witness to the truth (cf. John 14:6; 18:37); the sacrament of his body and blood does not permit duplicity.

39. Furthermore, given the very nature of ecclesial communion and its relation to the sacrament of the Eucharist, it must be recalled that "the Eucharistic Sacrifice, while always offered in a particular community, is never a celebration of that community alone. In fact, the community, in receiving the Eucharistic presence of the Lord, receives the entire gift of salvation and shows, even in its lasting visible particular form, that it is the image and true presence of the one, holy, catholic and apostolic Church."[79] From this it follows that a truly Eucharistic community cannot be closed in upon itself, as though it were somehow self-sufficient; rather it must persevere in harmony with every other Catholic community.

The ecclesial communion of the Eucharistic assembly is a communion with its own *Bishop* and with the *Roman Pontiff.* The Bishop, in effect, is the *visible* principle and the foundation of unity within his particular Church.[80] It would therefore be a great contradiction if the sacrament *par excellence* of the Church's unity were celebrated without true communion with the Bishop. As Saint Ignatius of Antioch wrote: "That Eucharist which is celebrated under the Bishop, or under one to whom the Bishop has given this charge, may be considered certain."[81] Likewise, since "the Roman Pontiff, as the successor of Peter, is the perpetual and visible source and foundation of the unity of the Bishops and of the multitude of the faithful,"[82] communion with him is intrinsically required for the celebration of the Eucharistic Sacrifice. Hence the great truth expressed which the Liturgy expresses in a variety of ways: "Every celebration of the Eucharist is performed in union not only with the proper Bishop, but also with the Pope, with the episcopal order, with all the clergy, and with the entire people. Every valid celebration of the Eucharist expresses this universal communion with Peter and with the whole Church, or objectively calls for it, as in the case of the Christian Churches separated from Rome."[83]

40. The Eucharist *creates communion* and *fosters communion.* Saint Paul wrote to the faithful of Corinth explaining how their divisions, reflected in their Eucharistic gatherings, contradicted what they were celebrating, the Lord's Supper. The Apostle then urged them to reflect on the true reality of the Eucharist in order to return to the spirit of fraternal communion (cf. 1 Corinthians 11:17–34). Saint Augustine effectively echoed this call when, in recalling the Apostle's words: "You are the body of Christ and individually members of it" (1 Corinthians 12:27), he went on to say: "If you are his body and members of him, then you will find set on the Lord's table your own mystery. Yes, you receive your own mystery."[84] And from this observation he concludes: "Christ the Lord . . . hallowed at his table the mystery of our peace and unity. Whoever receives the mystery of unity without preserving the bonds of peace receives not a mystery for his benefit but evidence against himself."[85]

41. The Eucharist's particular effectiveness in promoting communion is one of the reasons for the importance of Sunday Mass. I have already dwelt on this and on the other reasons which make Sunday Mass fundamental for the life of the Church and of individual believers in my Apostolic Letter on the sanctification of Sunday *Dies Domini,*[86] There I recalled that the faithful have the obligation to attend Mass, unless they are seriously impeded, and that Pastors have the corresponding duty to see that it is practical and possible for all to fulfill this precept.[87] More recently, in my Apostolic Letter *Novo Millennio Ineunte,* in setting forth the pastoral path which the Church must take at the beginning of the third millennium, I drew particular attention to the Sunday Eucharist, emphasizing its effectiveness for building communion. "It is"—I wrote—"the privileged place where communion is ceaselessly proclaimed and nurtured. Precisely through sharing in the Eucharist, *the Lord's Day* also becomes *the Day of the Church,* when she can effectively exercise her role as the sacrament of unity."[88]

42. The safeguarding and promotion of ecclesial communion is a task of each member of the faithful, who finds in the Eucharist, as the sacrament of the Church's unity, an area of special concern. More specifically, this task is the particular responsibility of the Church's Pastors, each according to his rank and ecclesiastical office. For this reason the Church has drawn up norms aimed both at fostering the frequent and fruitful access of the faithful to the Eucharistic table and at determining the objective conditions under which communion may not be given. The care shown in promoting the faithful observance of these norms becomes a practical means of showing love for the Eucharist and for the Church.

43. In considering the Eucharist as the sacrament of ecclesial communion, there is one subject which, due to its importance, must not be overlooked: I am referring to the *relationship of the Eucharist to ecumenical activity.* We should all give thanks to the Blessed Trinity for the many members of the faithful throughout the world who in recent decades have felt an ardent desire for unity among all Christians. The Second Vatican Council, at the beginning of its Decree on Ecumenism, sees this as a special gift of God.[89] It was an efficacious grace which inspired us, the sons and daughters of the Catholic Church and our brothers and sisters from other Churches and Ecclesial Communities, to set forth on the path of ecumenism.

Our longing for the goal of unity prompts us to turn to the Eucharist, which is the supreme sacrament of the unity of the People of God, in as much as it is the apt expression and the unsurpassable source of that unity.[90] In the celebration of the Eucharistic Sacrifice the Church prays that God, the Father of mercies, will grant his children the fullness of the Holy Spirit so that they may become one body and one spirit in Christ.[91] In raising this prayer to the Father of lights, from whom comes every good endowment and every perfect gift (cf. James 1:17), the Church believes that she will be heard, for she prays in union with Christ her Head and Spouse, who takes up this plea of his Bride and joins it to that of his own redemptive sacrifice.

44. Precisely because the Church's unity, which the Eucharist brings about through the Lord's sacrifice and by communion in his body and blood, absolutely requires full communion in the bonds of the profession of faith, the sacraments and ecclesiastical governance, it is not possible to celebrate together the same

Eucharistic liturgy until those bonds are fully re-established. Any such concelebration would not be a valid means, and might well prove instead to be *an obstacle, to the attainment of full communion*, by weakening the sense of how far we remain from this goal and by introducing or exacerbating ambiguities with regard to one or another truth of the faith. The path towards full unity can only be undertaken in truth. In this area, the prohibitions of Church law leave no room for uncertainty,[92] in fidelity to the moral norm laid down by the Second Vatican Council.[93]

I would like nonetheless to reaffirm what I said in my Encyclical Letter *Ut Unum Sint* after having acknowledged the impossibility of Eucharistic sharing: "And yet we do have a burning desire to join in celebrating the one Eucharist of the Lord, and this desire itself is already a common prayer of praise, a single supplication. Together we speak to the Father and increasingly we do so 'with one heart.'"[94]

45. While it is never legitimate to concelebrate in the absence of full communion, the same is not true with respect to the administration of the Eucharist *under special circumstances, to individual persons* belonging to Churches or Ecclesial Communities not in full communion with the Catholic Church. In this case, in fact, the intention is to meet a grave spiritual need for the eternal salvation of an individual believer, not to bring about an *intercommunion* which remains impossible until the visible bonds of ecclesial communion are fully re-established.

This was the approach taken by the Second Vatican Council when it gave guidelines for responding to Eastern Christians separated in good faith from the Catholic Church, who spontaneously ask to receive the Eucharist from a Catholic minister and are properly disposed.[95] This approach was then ratified by both Codes, which also consider—with necessary modifications—the case of other non-Eastern Christians who are not in full communion with the Catholic Church.[96]

46. In my Encyclical *Ut Unum Sint* I expressed my own appreciation of these norms, which make it possible to provide for the salvation of souls with proper discernment: "It is a source of joy to note that Catholic ministers are able, in certain particular cases, to administer the sacraments of the Eucharist, Penance and Anointing of the Sick to Christians who are not in full communion with the Catholic Church but who greatly desire to receive

these sacraments, freely request them and manifest the faith which the Catholic Church professes with regard to these sacraments. Conversely, in specific cases and in particular circumstances, Catholics too can request these same sacraments from ministers of Churches in which these sacraments are valid."[97]

These conditions, from which no dispensation can be given, must be carefully respected, even though they deal with specific individual cases, because the denial of one or more truths of the faith regarding these sacraments and, among these, the truth regarding the need of the ministerial priesthood for their validity, renders the person asking improperly disposed to legitimately receiving them. And the opposite is also true: Catholics may not receive communion in those communities which lack a valid sacrament of Orders.[98]

The faithful observance of the body of norms established in this area[99] is a manifestation and, at the same time, a guarantee of our love for Jesus Christ in the Blessed Sacrament, for our brothers and sisters of different Christian confessions—who have a right to our witness to the truth—and for the cause itself of the promotion of unity.

CHAPTER V
THE DIGNITY OF THE EUCHARISTIC CELEBRATION

47. Reading the account of the institution of the Eucharist in the Synoptic Gospels, we are struck by the simplicity and the "solemnity" with which Jesus, on the evening of the Last Supper, instituted this great sacrament. There is an episode which in some way serves as its prelude: *the anointing at Bethany.* A woman, whom John identifies as Mary the sister of Lazarus, pours a flask of *costly ointment* over Jesus' head, which provokes from the disciples—and from Judas in particular (cf. Matthew 26:8; Mark 14:4; John 12:4)—an indignant response, as if this act, in light of the needs of the poor, represented an intolerable "waste." But Jesus' own reaction is completely different. While in no way detracting from the duty of charity towards the needy, for whom the disciples must always show special care—"the poor you will always have with you" (Matthew 26, 11; Mark 14:7; cf. John 12:8)—he looks towards his imminent death and burial, and sees this act of anointing as an anticipation of the honor which

his body will continue to merit even after his death, indissolubly bound as it is to the mystery of his person.

The account continues, in the Synoptic Gospels, with Jesus' charge to the disciples to *prepare carefully the "large upper room"* needed for the Passover meal (cf. Mark 14:15; Luke 22:12) and with the narration of the institution of the Eucharist. Reflecting at least in part the *Jewish rites* of the Passover meal leading up to the singing of the Hallel (cf. Matthew 26:30; Mark 14:26), the story presents with sobriety and solemnity, even in the variants of the different traditions, the words spoken by Christ over the bread and wine, which he made into concrete expressions of the handing over of his body and the shedding of his blood. All these details are recorded by the Evangelists in the light of a praxis of the "breaking of the bread" already well-established in the early Church. But certainly from the time of Jesus on, the event of Holy Thursday has shown visible traces of a liturgical "sensibility" shaped by Old Testament tradition and open to being reshaped in Christian celebrations in a way consonant with the new content of Easter.

48. Like the woman who anointed Jesus in Bethany, *the Church has feared no "extravagance,"* devoting the best of her resources to expressing her wonder and adoration before the *unsurpassable gift of the Eucharist.* No less than the first disciples charged with preparing the "large upper room," she has felt the need, down the centuries and in her encounters with different cultures, to celebrate the Eucharist in a setting worthy of so great a mystery. In the wake of Jesus' own words and actions, and building upon the ritual heritage of Judaism, the *Christian liturgy was born.* Could there ever be an adequate means of expressing the acceptance of that self-gift which the divine Bridegroom continually makes to his Bride, the Church, by bringing the Sacrifice offered once and for all on the Cross to successive generations of believers and thus becoming nourishment for all the faithful? Though the idea of a "banquet" naturally suggests familiarity, the Church has never yielded to the temptation to trivialize this "intimacy" with her Spouse by forgetting that he is also her Lord and that the "banquet" always remains a sacrificial banquet marked by the blood shed on Golgotha. *The Eucharistic Banquet is truly a "sacred" banquet,* in which the simplicity of the signs conceals the unfathomable holiness of God: *O sacrum convivium, in quo Christus sumitur!* The bread which is broken on our altars, offered to us as

wayfarers along the paths of the world, is *panis angelorum*, the bread of angels, which cannot be approached except with the humility of the centurion in the Gospel: "Lord, I am not worthy to have you come under my roof" (Matthew 8:8; Luke 7:6).

49. With this heightened sense of mystery, we understand how the faith of the Church in the mystery of the Eucharist has found historical expression not only in the demand for an interior disposition of devotion, but also *in outward forms* meant to evoke and emphasize the grandeur of the event being celebrated. This led progressively to the development of *a particular form of regulating the Eucharistic liturgy*, with due respect for the various legitimately constituted ecclesial traditions. On this foundation *a rich artistic heritage* also developed. Architecture, sculpture, painting and music, moved by the Christian mystery, have found in the Eucharist, both directly and indirectly, a source of great inspiration.

Such was the case, for example, with architecture, which witnessed the transition, once the historical situation made it possible, from the first places of Eucharistic celebration in the *domus* or "homes" of Christian families to the solemn *basilicas* of the early centuries, to the imposing *cathedrals* of the Middle Ages, and to the *churches*, large and small, which gradually sprang up throughout the lands touched by Christianity. The designs of altars and tabernacles within Church interiors were often not simply motivated by artistic inspiration but also by a clear understanding of the mystery. The same could be said for *sacred music*, if we but think of the inspired Gregorian melodies and the many, often great, composers who sought to do justice to the liturgical texts of the Mass. Similarly, can we overlook the enormous quantity of *artistic production*, ranging from fine craftsmanship to authentic works of art, in the area of Church furnishings and vestments used for the celebration of the Eucharist?

It can be said that the Eucharist, while shaping the Church and her spirituality, has also powerfully affected "culture," and the arts in particular.

50. In this effort to adore the mystery grasped in its ritual and aesthetic dimensions, a certain "competition" has taken place between Christians of the West and the East. How could we not give particular thanks to the Lord for the contributions to Christian art made by the great architectural and artistic works of the Greco-Byzantine tradition and of the whole geographical area marked

by Slav culture? In the East, sacred art has preserved a remarkably powerful sense of mystery, which leads artists to see their efforts at creating beauty not simply as an expression of their own talents, but also as *a genuine service to the faith.* Passing well beyond mere technical skill, they have shown themselves docile and open to the inspiration of the Holy Spirit.

The architectural and mosaic splendors of the Christian East and West are a patrimony belonging to all believers; they contain a hope, and even a pledge, of the desired fullness of communion in faith and in celebration. This would presuppose and demand, as in Rublëv's famous depiction of the Trinity, *a profoundly Eucharistic Church* in which the presence of the mystery of Christ in the broken bread is as it were immersed in the ineffable unity of the three divine Persons, making of the Church herself an "icon" of the Trinity.

Within this context of an art aimed at expressing, in all its elements, the meaning of the Eucharist in accordance with the Church's teaching, attention needs to be given to the norms regulating *the construction and decor of sacred buildings.* As history shows and as I emphasized in my Letter to Artists,[100] the Church has always left ample room for the creativity of artists. But sacred art must be outstanding for its ability to express adequately the mystery grasped in the fullness of the Church's faith and in accordance with the pastoral guidelines appropriately laid down by competent Authority. This holds true both for the figurative arts and for sacred music.

51. The development of sacred art and liturgical discipline which took place in lands of ancient Christian heritage is also taking place *on continents where Christianity is younger.* This was precisely the approach supported by the Second Vatican Council on the need for sound and proper "inculturation." In my numerous Pastoral Visits I have seen, throughout the world, the great vitality which the celebration of the Eucharist can have when marked by the forms, styles and sensibilities of different cultures. By adaptation to the changing conditions of time and place, the Eucharist offers sustenance not only to individuals but to entire peoples, and it shapes cultures inspired by Christianity.

It is necessary, however, that this important work of adaptation be carried out with a constant awareness of the ineffable mystery against which every generation is called to measure itself.

The "treasure" is too important and precious to risk impoverishment or compromise through forms of experimentation or practices introduced without a careful review on the part of the competent ecclesiastical authorities. Furthermore, the centrality of the Eucharistic mystery demands that any such review must be undertaken in close association with the Holy See. As I wrote in my Post-Synodal Apostolic Exhortation Ecclesia in Asia, "such cooperation is essential because the Sacred Liturgy expresses and celebrates the one faith professed by all and, being the heritage of the whole Church, cannot be determined by local Churches in isolation from the universal Church."[101]

52. All of this makes clear the great responsibility which belongs to priests in particular for the celebration of the Eucharist. It is their responsibility to preside at the Eucharist *in persona Christi* and to provide a witness to and a service of communion not only for the community directly taking part in the celebration, but also for the universal Church, which is a part of every Eucharist. It must be lamented that, especially in the years following the post-conciliar liturgical reform, as a result of a misguided sense of creativity and adaptation there have been a number of *abuses* which have been a source of suffering for many. A certain reaction against "formalism" has led some, especially in certain regions, to consider the "forms" chosen by the Church's great liturgical tradition and her Magisterium as non-binding and to introduce unauthorized innovations which are often completely inappropriate.

I consider it my duty, therefore to appeal urgently that the liturgical norms for the celebration of the Eucharist be observed with great fidelity. These norms are a concrete expression of the authentically ecclesial nature of the Eucharist; this is their deepest meaning. Liturgy is never anyone's private property, be it of the celebrant or of the community in which the mysteries are celebrated. The Apostle Paul had to address fiery words to the community of Corinth because of grave shortcomings in their celebration of the Eucharist resulting in divisions (*schismata*) and the emergence of factions (*haireseis*) (cf. 1 Corinthians 11:17–34). Our time, too, calls for a renewed awareness and appreciation of liturgical norms as a reflection of, and a witness to, the one universal Church made present in every celebration of the Eucharist. Priests who faithfully celebrate Mass according to the liturgical norms, and communities which conform to those norms, quietly but eloquently demonstrate their love for the Church. Precisely to bring out more clearly this deeper meaning of liturgical norms, I have asked the competent offices of the Roman Curia to prepare a more specific document, including prescriptions of a juridical nature, on this very important subject. No one is permitted to undervalue the mystery entrusted to our hands: it is too great for anyone to feel free to treat it lightly and with disregard for its sacredness and its universality.

CHAPTER VI
AT THE SCHOOL OF MARY, "WOMAN OF THE EUCHARIST"

53. If we wish to rediscover in all its richness the profound relationship between the Church and the Eucharist, we cannot neglect Mary, Mother and model of the Church. In my Apostolic Letter *Rosarium Virginis Mariae,* I pointed to the Blessed Virgin Mary as our teacher in contemplating Christ's face, and among the mysteries of light I included *the institution of the Eucharist.*[102] Mary can guide us towards this most holy sacrament, because she herself has a profound relationship with it.

At first glance, the Gospel is silent on this subject. The account of the institution of the Eucharist on the night of Holy Thursday makes no mention of Mary. Yet we know that she was present among the Apostles who prayed "with one accord" (cf. Acts 1:14) *in the first community which gathered after the Ascension in expectation of Pentecost.* Certainly Mary must have been present at the Eucharistic celebrations of the first generation of Christians, who were devoted to "the breaking of bread" (Acts 2:42).

But in addition to her sharing in the Eucharistic banquet, an indirect picture of Mary's relationship with the Eucharist can be had, beginning with her interior disposition. *Mary is a "woman of the Eucharist" in her whole life.* The Church, which looks to Mary as a model, is also called to imitate her in her relationship with this most holy mystery.

54. *Mysterium fidei!* If the Eucharist is a mystery of faith which so greatly transcends our understanding as to call for sheer abandonment to the word of God, then there can be no one like Mary to act as our support and guide in acquiring this disposition. In repeating what Christ did at the Last Supper in obedience to his command: "Do this in memory of me!" we also accept Mary's

invitation to obey him without hesitation: "Do whatever he tells you" (John 2:5). With the same maternal concern which she showed at the wedding feast of Cana, Mary seems to say to us: "Do not waver; trust in the words of my Son. If he was able to change water into wine, he can also turn bread and wine into his body and blood, and through this mystery bestow on believers the living memorial of his passover, thus becoming the 'bread of life.'"

55. In a certain sense Mary lived her *Eucharistic faith* even before the institution of the Eucharist, by the very fact that *she offered her virginal womb for the Incarnation of God's Word.* The Eucharist, while commemorating the passion and resurrection, is also in continuity with the incarnation. At the Annunciation Mary conceived the Son of God in the physical reality of his body and blood, thus anticipating within herself what to some degree happens sacramentally in every believer who receives, under the signs of bread and wine, the Lord's body and blood.

As a result, there is a profound analogy between the *Fiat* which Mary said in reply to the angel, and the *Amen* which every believer says when receiving the body of the Lord. Mary was asked to believe that the One whom she conceived "through the Holy Spirit" was "the Son of God" (Luke 1:30–35). In continuity with the Virgin's faith, in the Eucharistic mystery we are asked to believe that the same Jesus Christ, Son of God and Son of Mary, becomes present in his full humanity and divinity under the signs of bread and wine.

"Blessed is she who believed" (Luke 1:45). Mary also anticipated, in the mystery of the incarnation, the Church's Eucharistic faith. When, at the Visitation, she bore in her womb the Word made flesh, she became in some way a "tabernacle"—the first "tabernacle" in history—in which the Son of God, still invisible to our human gaze, allowed himself to be adored by Elizabeth, radiating his light as it were through the eyes and the voice of Mary. And is not the enraptured gaze of Mary as she contemplated the face of the newborn Christ and cradled him in her arms that unparalleled model of love which should inspire us every time we receive Eucharistic communion?

56. Mary, throughout her life at Christ's side and not only on Calvary, made her own *the sacrificial dimension of the Eucharist.* When she brought the child Jesus to the Temple in Jerusalem "to present him to the Lord" (Luke 2:22), she heard the aged Simeon

announce that the child would be a "sign of contradiction" and that a sword would also pierce her own heart (cf. Luke 2:34–35). The tragedy of her Son's crucifixion was thus foretold, and in some sense Mary's *Stabat Mater* at the foot of the Cross was foreshadowed. In her daily preparation for Calvary, Mary experienced a kind of "anticipated Eucharist"—one might say a "spiritual communion"—of desire and of oblation, which would culminate in her union with her Son in his passion, and then find expression after Easter by her partaking in the Eucharist which the Apostles celebrated as the memorial of that passion.

What must Mary have felt as she heard from the mouth of Peter, John, James and the other Apostles the words spoken at the Last Supper: "This is my body which is given for you" (Luke 22:19)? The body given up for us and made present under sacramental signs was the same body which she had conceived in her womb! For Mary, receiving the Eucharist must have somehow meant welcoming once more into her womb that heart which had beat in unison with hers and reliving what she had experienced at the foot of the Cross.

57. "Do this in remembrance of me" (Luke 22:19). In the "memorial" of Calvary all that Christ accomplished by his passion and his death is present. Consequently *all that Christ did with regard to his Mother* for our sake is also present. To her he gave the beloved disciple and, in him, each of us: "Behold, your Son!" To each of us he also says: "Behold your mother!" (cf. John 19:26–27).

Experiencing the memorial of Christ's death in the Eucharist also means continually receiving this gift. It means accepting—like John—the one who is given to us anew as our Mother. It also means taking on a commitment to be conformed to Christ, putting ourselves at the school of his Mother and allowing her to accompany us. Mary is present, with the Church and as the Mother of the Church, at each of our celebrations of the Eucharist. If the Church and the Eucharist are inseparably united, the same ought to be said of Mary and the Eucharist. This is one reason why, since ancient times, the commemoration of Mary has always been part of the Eucharistic celebrations of the Churches of East and West.

58. In the Eucharist the Church is completely united to Christ and his sacrifice, and makes her own the spirit of Mary. This truth can be understood more deeply by *re-reading the Magnificat* in a Eucharistic key. The Eucharist, like the Canticle of Mary, is first

and foremost praise and thanksgiving. When Mary exclaims: "My soul magnifies the Lord and my spirit rejoices in God my Savior," she already bears Jesus in her womb. She praises God "through" Jesus, but she also praises him "in" Jesus and "with" Jesus. This is itself the true "Eucharistic attitude."

At the same time Mary recalls the wonders worked by God in salvation history in fulfillment of the promise once made to the fathers (cf. Luke 1:55), and proclaims the wonder that surpasses them all, the redemptive incarnation. Lastly, the *Magnificat* reflects the eschatological tension of the Eucharist. Every time the Son of God comes again to us in the "poverty" of the sacramental signs of bread and wine, the seeds of that new history wherein the mighty are "put down from their thrones" and "those of low degree are exalted" (cf. Luke 1:52), take root in the world. Mary sings of the "new heavens" and the "new earth" which find in the Eucharist their anticipation and in some sense their program and plan. The *Magnificat* expresses Mary's spirituality, and there is nothing greater than this spirituality for helping us to experience the mystery of the Eucharist. The Eucharist has been given to us so that our life, like that of Mary, may become completely a *Magnificat*!

CONCLUSION

59. *Ave, verum corpus natum de Maria Virgine!* Several years ago I celebrated the fiftieth anniversary of my priesthood. Today I have the grace of offering the Church this Encyclical on the Eucharist on the Holy Thursday which falls *during the twenty-fifth year of my Petrine ministry.* As I do so, my heart is filled with gratitude. For over a half century, every day, beginning on 2 November 1946, when I celebrated my first Mass in the Crypt of Saint Leonard in Wawel Cathedral in Krakow, my eyes have gazed in recollection upon the host and the chalice, where time and space in some way "merge" and the drama of Golgotha is re-presented in a living way, thus revealing its mysterious "contemporaneity." Each day my faith has been able to recognize in the consecrated bread and wine the divine Wayfarer who joined the two disciples on the road to Emmaus and opened their eyes to the light and their hearts to new hope (cf. Luke 24:13–35).

Allow me, dear brothers and sisters, to share with deep emotion, as a means of accompanying and strengthening your faith, my own testimony of faith in the Most Holy Eucharist. *Ave verum corpus natum de Maria Virgine, vere passum, immolatum, in cruce pro homine!* Here is the Church's treasure, the heart of the world, the pledge of the fulfillment for which each man and woman, even unconsciously, yearns. A great and transcendent mystery, indeed, and one that taxes our mind's ability to pass beyond appearances. Here our senses fail us: *visus, tactus, gustus in te fallitur,* in the words of the hymn *Adoro Te Devote;* yet faith alone, rooted in the word of Christ handed down to us by the Apostles, is sufficient for us. Allow me, like Peter at the end of the Eucharistic discourse in John's Gospel, to say once more to Christ, in the name of the whole Church and in the name of each of you: "Lord to whom shall we go? You have the words of eternal life" (John 6:68).

60. At the dawn of this third millennium, we, the children of the Church, are called to undertake with renewed enthusiasm the journey of Christian living. As I wrote in my Apostolic Letter *Novo Millennio Ineunte,* "it is not a matter of inventing a 'new program.' The program already exists: it is the plan found in the Gospel and in the living Tradition; it is the same as ever. Ultimately, it has its center in Christ himself, who is to be known, loved and imitated, so that in him we may live the life of the Trinity, and with him transform history until its fulfillment in the heavenly Jerusalem."[103] The implementation of this program of a renewed impetus in Christian living passes through the Eucharist.

Every commitment to holiness, every activity aimed at carrying out the Church's mission, every work of pastoral planning, must draw the strength it needs from the Eucharistic mystery and in turn be directed to that mystery as its culmination. In the Eucharist we have Jesus, we have his redemptive sacrifice, we have his resurrection, we have the gift of the Holy Spirit, we have adoration, obedience and love of the Father. Were we to disregard the Eucharist, how could we overcome our own deficiency?

61. The mystery of the Eucharist—sacrifice, presence, banquet—*does not allow for reduction or exploitation;* it must be experienced and lived in its integrity, both in its celebration and in the intimate converse with Jesus which takes place after receiving communion or in a prayerful moment of Eucharistic adoration apart from Mass. These are times when the Church is firmly built up and it becomes clear what she truly is: one, holy, catholic and

apostolic; the people, temple and family of God; the body and bride of Christ, enlivened by the Holy Spirit; the universal sacrament of salvation and a hierarchically structured communion.

The path taken by the Church in these first years of the third millennium is also a *path of renewed ecumenical commitment.* The final decades of the second millennium, culminating in the Great Jubilee, have spurred us along this path and called for all the baptized to respond to the prayer of Jesus *"ut unum sint"* (John 17:11). The path itself is long and strewn with obstacles greater than our human resources alone can overcome, yet we have the Eucharist, and in its presence we can hear in the depths of our hearts, as if they were addressed to us, the same words heard by the Prophet Elijah: "Arise and eat, else the journey will be too great for you" (1 Kings 19:7). The treasure of the Eucharist, which the Lord places before us, impels us towards the goal of full sharing with all our brothers and sisters to whom we are joined by our common Baptism. But if this treasure is not to be squandered, we need to respect the demands which derive from its being the sacrament of communion in faith and in apostolic succession.

By giving the Eucharist the prominence it deserves, and by being careful not to diminish any of its dimensions or demands, we show that we are truly conscious of the greatness of this gift. We are urged to do so by an uninterrupted tradition, which from the first centuries on has found the Christian community ever vigilant in guarding this "treasure." Inspired by love, the Church is anxious to hand on to future generations of Christians, without loss, her faith and teaching with regard to the mystery of the Eucharist. There can be no danger of excess in our care for this mystery, for "in this sacrament is recapitulated the whole mystery of our salvation."[104]

62. Let us take our place, dear brothers and sisters, *at the school of the saints,* who are the great interpreters of true Eucharistic piety. In them the theology of the Eucharist takes on all the splendor of a lived reality; it becomes "contagious" and, in a manner of speaking, it "warms our hearts." Above all, let us *listen to Mary Most Holy,* in whom the mystery of the Eucharist appears, more than in anyone else, as *a mystery of light.* Gazing upon Mary, we come to *know the transforming power present in the Eucharist.* In her we see the world renewed in love. Contemplating her, assumed body and soul into heaven, we see opening up before us

those "new heavens" and that "new earth" which will appear at the second coming of Christ. Here below, the Eucharist represents their pledge, and in a certain way, their anticipation: *"Veni, Domine Iesu!"* (Revelation 22:20).

In the humble signs of bread and wine, changed into his body and blood, Christ walks beside us as our strength and our food for the journey, and he enables us to become, for everyone, witnesses of hope. If, in the presence of this mystery, reason experiences its limits, the heart, enlightened by the grace of the Holy Spirit, clearly sees the response that is demanded, and bows low in adoration and unbounded love.

Let us make our own the words of Saint Thomas Aquinas, an eminent theologian and an impassioned poet of Christ in the Eucharist, and turn in hope to the contemplation of that goal to which our hearts aspire in their thirst for joy and peace:

Bone pastor, panis vere,
Iesu, nostri Miserere . . .

Come then, good Shepherd, bread divine,
Still show to us thy mercy sign;
Oh, feed us, still keep us thine;
So we may see thy glories shine
in fields of immortality.

O thou, the wisest, mightiest, best,
Our present food, our future rest,
Come, make us each thy chosen guest,
Co-heirs of thine, and comrades blest
With saints whose dwelling is with thee.

Given in Rome, at Saint Peter's, on 17 April, Holy Thursday, in the year 2003, the twenty-fifth of my Pontificate, the Year of the Rosary.

Ioannes Paulus II

NOTES

1. Second Vatican Ecumenical Council, Dogmatic Constitution on the Church *Lumen Gentium,* 11.
2. Second Vatican Ecumenical Council, Decree on the Ministry and Life of Priests *Presbyterorum Ordinis,* 5.
3. Cf. John Paul II, Apostolic Letter *Rosarium Virginis Mariae* (16 October 2002), 21: AAS 95 (2003), 19.
4. This is the title which I gave to an autobiographical testimony issued for my fiftieth anniversary of priestly ordination.
5. *Leonis XIII P.M. Acta,* XXII (1903), 115–136.
6. AAS 39 (1947), 521–595.
7. AAS 57 (1965), 753–774.
8. AAS 72 (1980), 113–148.
9. Cf. Second Vatican Ecumenical Council, Constitution *Sacrosanctum Concilium,* 47: ". . . our Savior instituted the Eucharistic Sacrifice of his body and blood, in order to perpetuate the sacrifice of the Cross throughout time, until he should return."
10. Catechism of the Catholic Church, 1085.
11. Second Vatican Ecumenical Council, Dogmatic Constitution on the Church *Lumen Gentium,* 3.
12. Cf. Paul VI, *Solemn Profession of Faith,* 30 June 1968, 24: AAS 60 (1968), 442; John Paul II, Apostolic Letter *Dominicae Cenae* (24 February 1980), 12: AAS 72 (1980), 142.
13. *Catechism of the Catholic Church,* 1382.
14. *Catechism of the Catholic Church,* 1367.
15. *In Epistolam ad Hebraeos Homiliae, Hom.* 17,3: PG 63, 131.
16. Cf. Ecumenical Council of Trent, Session XXII, *Doctrina de ss. Missae Sacrificio,* Chapter 2: DS 1743: "It is one and the same victim here offering himself by the ministry of his priests, who then offered himself on the Cross; it is only the manner of offering that is different."
17. Pius XII, Encyclical Letter *Mediator Dei* (20 November 1947): AAS 39 (1947), 548.
18. John Paul II, Encyclical Letter *Redemptor Hominis* (15 March 1979), 20: AAS 71 (1979), 310.
19. Dogmatic Constitution on the Church *Lumen Gentium,* 11.
20. *De Sacramentis,* V, 4, 26: CSEL 73, 70.
21. *In Ioannis Evangelium,* XII, 20: PG 74, 726.
22. Encyclical Letter *Mysterium Fidei* (3 September 1965): AAS 57 (1965), 764.
23. Session XIII, *Decretum de ss. Eucharistia,* Chapter 4: DS 1642.
24. *Mystagogical Catecheses,* IV, 6: SCh 126, 138.
25. Second Vatican Ecumenical Council, Dogmatic Constitution

on Divine Revelation *Dei Verbum,* 8.

26. *Solemn Profession of Faith,* 30 June 1968, 25: AAS 60 (1968), 442–443.

27. *Sermo IV in Hebdomadam Sanctam:* CSCO 413/Syr. 182, 55.

28. Anaphora.

29. Eucharistic Prayer III.

30. Solemnity of the Body and Blood of Christ, Second Vespers, Antiphon to the *Magnificat.*

31. *Missale Romanum,* Embolism following the Lord's Prayer.

32. *Ad Ephesios,* 20: PG 5, 661.

33. Cf. Second Vatican Ecumenical Council, Pastoral Constitution on the Church in the Modern World *Gaudium et Spes,* 39.

34. "Do you wish to honor the body of Christ? Do not ignore him when he is naked. Do not pay him homage in the temple clad in silk, only then to neglect him outside where he is cold and ill-clad. He who said: 'This is my body' is the same who said: 'You saw me hungry and you gave me no food,' and 'Whatever you did to the least of my brothers you did also to me' . . . . What good is it if the Eucharistic table is overloaded with golden chalices when your brother is dying of hunger. Start by satisfying his hunger and then with what is left you may adorn the altar as well": Saint John Chrysostom, *In Evangelium S. Matthaei, hom.* 50:3–4: PG 58, 508–509; cf. John Paul II, Encyclical Letter *Sollicitudo Rei Socialis* (30 December 1987), 31: AAS 80 (1988), 553–556.

35. Dogmatic Constitution *Lumen Gentium,* 3.

36. *Ibid.*

37. Second Vatican Ecumenical Council, Decree on the Missionary Activity of the Church *Ad Gentes,* 5.

38. "Moses took the blood and threw it upon the people, and said: 'Behold the blood of the Covenant which the Lord has made with you in accordance with all these words'" (Exodus 24:8).

39. Cf. Second Vatican Ecumenical Council, Dogmatic Constitution on the Church *Lumen Gentium,* 1.

40. Cf. *ibid.,* 9.

41. Cf. Second Vatican Ecumenical Council, Decree on the Life and Ministry of Priests *Presbyterorum Ordinis,* 5. The same Decree, in No. 6, says: "No Christian community can be built up which does not grow from and hinge on the celebration of the most holy Eucharist."

42. *In Epistolam I ad Corinthios Homiliae,* 24, 2: PG 61, 200; cf. *Didache,* IX, 4: F.X. Funk, I, 22; Saint Cyprian, *Ep.* LXIII, 13: PL 4, 384.

43. PO 26, 206.

44. Second Vatican Ecumenical Council, Dogmatic Constitution on the Church *Lumen Gentium,* 1.

45. Cf. Ecumenical Council of Trent, Session XIII, *Decretum de ss. Eucharistia,* Canon 4: DS 1654.

46. Cf. *Rituale Romanum: De sacra communione et de cultu mysterii eucharistici extra Missam,* 36 (No. 80).

47. Cf. *ibid.,* 38–39 (Nos. 86–90).

48. John Paul II, Apostolic Letter *Novo Millennio Ineunte* (6 January 2001), 32: AAS 93 (2001), 288.

49. "In the course of the day the faithful should not omit visiting the Blessed Sacrament, which in accordance with liturgical law must be reserved in churches with great reverence in a prominent place. Such visits are a sign of gratitude, an expression of love and an acknowledgment of the Lord's presence": Paul VI, Encyclical Letter *Mysterium Fidei* (3 September 1965): AAS 57 (1965), 771.

50. *Visite al SS. Sacramento e a Maria Santissima,* Introduction: Opere Ascetiche, Avellino, 2000, 295.

51. No. 857.

52. *Ibid.*

53. *Ibid.*

54. Cf. Congregation for the Doctrine of the Faith, Letter *Sacerdotium Ministeriale* (6 August 1983), III.2: AAS 75 (1983), 1005.

55. Second Vatican Ecumenical Council, Dogmatic Constitution on the Church *Lumen Gentium,* 10.

56. *Ibid.*

57. Cf. *Institutio Generalis:* Editio typica tertia, No. 147.

58. Cf. Dogmatic Constitution on the Church *Lumen Gentium,* 10 and 28; Decree on the Ministry and Life of Priests *Presbyterorum Ordinis,* 2.

59. "The minister of the altar acts in the person of Christ inasmuch as he is head, making an offering in the name of all the members": Pius XII, Encyclical Letter *Mediator Dei* (20 November 1947): AAS 39 (1947), 556; cf. Pius X, Apostolic Exhortation *Haerent Animo* (4 August 1908): *Acta Pii X,* IV, 16; Pius XI, Encyclical Letter *Ad Catholici Sacerdotii* (20 December 1935): AAS 28 (1936), 20.

60. Apostolic Letter *Dominicae Cenae* (24 February 1980), 8: AAS 72 (1980), 128–129.

61. Congregation for the Doctrine of the Faith, Letter *Sacerdotium Ministeriale* (6 August 1983), III.4: AAS 75 (1983), 1006; cf. Fourth Lateran Ecumenical Council, Chapter 1, Constitution on the Catholic Faith *Firmiter Credimus:* DS 802.

62. Second Vatican Ecumenical Council, Decree on Ecumenism *Unitatis Redintegratio,* 22.

63. Apostolic Letter *Dominicae Cenae* (24 February 1980), 2: AAS 72 (1980), 115.

64. Decree on the Life and Ministry of Priests *Presbyterorum Ordinis,* 14.

65. Ibid., 13; cf. *Code of Canon Law,* Canon 904; *Code of Canons of the Eastern Churches,* Canon 378.

66. Decree on the Ministry and Life of Priests *Presbyterorum Ordinis,* 6.

67. Cf. Final Report, II.C.1: *L'Osservatore Romano,* 10 December 1985, 7.

68. Second Vatican Ecumenical Council, Dogmatic Constitution on the Church *Lumen Gentium,* 26.

69. Nicolas Cabasilas, *Life in Christ,* IV, 10: SCh 355, 270.

70. *Camino de Perfección,* Chapter 35.

71. Cf. Congregation for the Doctrine of the Faith, Letter to the Bishops of the Catholic Church on Some Aspects of the Church Understood as Communion *Communionis Notio* (28 May 1992), 4: AAS 85 (1993), 839–840.

72. Cf. Second Vatican Ecumenical Council, Dogmatic Constitution on the Church *Lumen Gentium,* 14.
73. *Homiliae in Isaiam,* 6, 3: PG 56, 139.
74. No. 1385; cf. *Code of Canon Law,* Canon 916; *Code of Canons of the Eastern Churches,* Canon 711.
75. Address to the Members of the Sacred Apostolic Penitentiary and the Penitentiaries of the Patriarchal Basilicas of Rome (30 January 1981): AAS 73 (1981), 203. Cf. Ecumenical Council of Trent, Sess. XIII, *Decretum de ss. Eucharistia,* Chapter 7 and Canon 11: DS 1647, 1661.
76. Canon 915; *Code of Canons of the Eastern Churches,* Canon 712.
77. Dogmatic Constitution on the Church *Lumen Gentium,* 14.
78. Saint Thomas Aquinas, *Summa Theologiae,* III, q. 73, a. 3c.
79. Congregation for the Doctrine of the Faith, Letter to the Bishops of the Catholic Church on Some Aspects of the Church Understood as Communion *Communionis Notio* (28 May 1992), 11: AAS 85 (1993), 844.
80. Cf. Second Vatican Ecumenical Council, Dogmatic Constitution on the Church *Lumen Gentium,* 23.
81. *Ad Smyrnaeos,* 8: PG 5, 713.
82. Second Vatican Ecumenical Council, Dogmatic Constitution on the Church *Lumen Gentium,* 23.
83. Congregation for the Doctrine of the Faith, Letter to the Bishops of the Catholic Church on Some Aspects of the Church Understood as Communion *Communionis Notio* (28 May 1992), 14: AAS 85 (1993), 847.
84. *Sermo* 272: PL 38, 1247.
85. *Ibid.,* 1248.
86. Cf. Nos. 31-51: AAS 90 (1998), 731–746.
87. Cf. *ibid.,* Nos. 48–49: AAS 90 (1998), 744.
88. No. 36: AAS 93 (2001), 291–292.
89. Cf. Decree on Ecumenism *Unitatis Redintegratio,* 1.
90. Cf. Dogmatic Constitution on the Church *Lumen Gentium,* 11.
91. "Join all of us, who share the one bread and the one cup, to one another in the communion of the one Holy Spirit": *Anaphora of the Liturgy of Saint Basil.*
92. Cf. *Code of Canon Law,* Canon 908; *Code of Canons of the Eastern Churches,* Canon 702; Pontifical Council for the Promotion of Christian Unity, *Ecumenical Directory,* 25 March 1993, 122–125, 129–131: AAS 85 (1993), 1086–1089; Congregation for the Doctrine of the Faith, Letter *Ad Exsequendam,* 18 May 2001: AAS 93 (2001), 786.
93. "Divine law forbids any common worship which would damage the unity of the Church, or involve formal acceptance of falsehood or the danger of deviation in the faith, of scandal, or of indifferentism": Decree on the Eastern Catholic Churches *Orientalium Ecclesiarum,* 26.
94. No. 45: AAS 87 (1995), 948.
95. Decree on the Eastern Catholic Churches *Orientalium Ecclesiarum,* 27.
96. Cf. *Code of Canon Law,* Canon 844 §§ 3–4; *Code of Canons of the Eastern Churches,* Canon 671 §§ 3–4.
97. No. 46: AAS 87 (1995), 948.

98. Cf. Second Vatican Ecumenical Council, Decree on Ecumenism *Unitatis Redintegratio,* 22.

99. *Code of Canon Law,* Canon 844; *Code of Canons of the Eastern Churches,* Canon 671.

100. Cf. AAS 91 (1999), 1155–1172.

101. No. 22: AAS 92 (2000), 485.

102. Cf. No. 21: AAS 95 (2003), 20.

103. No. 29: AAS 93 (2001), 285.

104. Saint Thomas Aquinas, *Summa Theologiae,* III, q. 83, a. 4c.

CARTA ENCÍCLICA
ECCLESIA DE EUCHARISTIA

DEL SUMO PONTÍFICE
JUAN PABLO II
A LOS OBISPOS
A LOS PRESBÍTEROS Y DIÁCONOS
A LAS PERSONAS CONSAGRADAS
Y A TODOS LOS FIELES LAICOS
SOBRE LA EUCARISTÍA
EN SU RELACIÓN CON LA IGLESIA

ÍNDICE

INTRODUCCIÓN

1. La Iglesia vive de la Eucaristía. Esta verdad no expresa solamente una experiencia cotidiana de fe, sino que encierra en síntesis *el núcleo del misterio de la Iglesia.* Ésta experimenta con alegría cómo se realiza continuamente, en múltiples formas, la promesa del Señor: "He aquí que yo estoy con vosotros todos los días hasta el fin del mundo" (Mateo 28,20); en la sagrada Eucaristía, por la transformación del pan y el vino en el cuerpo y en la sangre del Señor, se alegra de esta presencia con una intensidad única. Desde que, en Pentecostés, la Iglesia, Pueblo de la Nueva Alianza, ha empezado su peregrinación hacia la patria celeste, este divino Sacramento ha marcado sus días, llenándolos de confiada esperanza.

Con razón ha proclamado el Concilio Vaticano II que el Sacrificio eucarístico es "fuente y cima de toda la vida cristiana"[1]. "La sagrada Eucaristía, en efecto, contiene todo el bien espiritual de la Iglesia, es decir, Cristo mismo, nuestra Pascua y Pan de Vida, que da la vida a los hombres por medio del Espíritu Santo"[2]. Por tanto la mirada de la Iglesia se dirige continuamente a su Señor, presente en el Sacramento del altar, en el cual descubre la plena manifestación de su inmenso amor.

2. Durante el Gran Jubileo del año 2000, tuve ocasión de celebrar la Eucaristía en el Cenáculo de Jerusalén, donde, según la tradición, fue realizada la primera vez por Cristo mismo. *El Cenáculo es el lugar de la institución de este Santísimo Sacramento.* Allí Cristo tomó en sus manos el pan, lo partió y lo dio a los discípulos diciendo: "Tomad y comed todos de él, porque esto es mi Cuerpo, que será entregado por vosotros" (cf. Mateo 26,26; Lucas 22,19; 1 Corintios 11,24). Después tomó en sus manos el cáliz del vino y les dijo: "Tomad y bebed todos de él, porque éste es el cáliz

de mi sangre, sangre de la alianza nueva y eterna, que será derramada por vosotros y por todos los hombres para el perdón de los pecados" (cf. Marcos 14,24; Lucas 22,20; 1 Corintios 11,25). Estoy agradecido al Señor Jesús que me permitió repetir en aquel mismo lugar, obedeciendo su mandato "haced esto en conmemoración mía" (Lucas 22,19), las palabras pronunciadas por Él hace dos mil años.

Los Apóstoles que participaron en la Última Cena, ¿comprendieron el sentido de las palabras que salieron de los labios de Cristo? Quizás no. Aquellas palabras se habrían aclarado plenamente sólo al final del *Triduum sacrum,* es decir, el lapso que va de la tarde del jueves hasta la mañana del domingo. En esos días se enmarca el *mysterium paschale;* en ellos se inscribe también el *mysterium eucharisticum.*

3. Del misterio pascual nace la Iglesia. Precisamente por eso la Eucaristía, que es el sacramento por excelencia del misterio pascual, *está en el centro de la vida eclesial.* Se puede observar esto ya desde las primeras imágenes de la Iglesia que nos ofrecen los Hechos de los Apóstoles: "Acudían asiduamente a la enseñanza de los apóstoles, a la comunión, a la fracción del pan y a las oraciones" (2,42). La "fracción del pan" evoca la Eucaristía. Después de dos mil años seguimos reproduciendo aquella imagen primigenia de la Iglesia. Y, mientras lo hacemos en la celebración eucarística, los ojos del alma se dirigen al Triduo pascual: a lo que ocurrió la tarde del Jueves Santo, durante la Última Cena y después de ella. La institución de la Eucaristía, en efecto, anticipaba sacramentalmente los acontecimientos que tendrían lugar poco más tarde, a partir de la agonía en Getsemaní. Vemos a Jesús que sale del Cenáculo, baja con los discípulos, atraviesa el arroyo Cedrón y llega al Huerto de los Olivos. En aquel huerto quedan aún hoy algunos árboles de olivo muy antiguos. Tal vez fueron testigos de lo que ocurrió a su sombra aquella tarde, cuando Cristo en oración experimentó una angustia mortal y "su sudor se hizo como gotas espesas de sangre que caían en tierra" (Lucas 22,44). La sangre, que poco antes había entregado a la Iglesia como bebida de salvación en el Sacramento eucarístico, *comenzó a ser derramada;* su efusión se completaría después en el Gólgota, convirtiéndose en instrumento de nuestra redención: "Cristo como Sumo Sacerdote de los bienes futuros [. . .] penetró en el santuario una vez para siempre, no con sangre de machos cabríos ni de novillos, sino con su propia sangre, consiguiendo una redención eternal" (Hebreos 9,11–12).

4. *La hora de nuestra redención.* Jesús, aunque sometido a una prueba terrible, no huye ante su "hora": "¿Qué voy a decir? ¡Padre, líbrame de esta hora! Pero ¡si he llegado a esta hora para esto!" (Juan 12,27). Desea que los discípulos le acompañen y, sin embargo, debe experimentar la soledad y el abandono: "¿Conque no habéis podido velar una hora conmigo? Velad y orad, para que no caigáis en tentación" (Mateo 26,40–41). Sólo Juan permanecerá al pie de la Cruz, junto a María y a las piadosas mujeres. La agonía en Getsemaní ha sido la introducción a la agonía de la Cruz del Viernes Santo. *La hora santa,* la hora de la redención del mundo. Cuando se celebra la Eucaristía ante la tumba de Jesús, en Jerusalén, se retorna de modo casi tangible a su "hora", la hora de la cruz y de la glorificación. A aquel lugar y a aquella hora vuelve espiritualmente todo presbítero que celebra la Santa Misa, junto con la comunidad cristiana que participa en ella.

"Fue crucificado, muerto y sepultado, descendió a los infiernos, al tercer día resucitó de entre los muertos". A las palabras de la profesión de fe hacen eco las palabras de la contemplación y la proclamación: *"Ecce lignum crucis in quo salus mundi pependit. Venite adoremus".* Ésta es la invitación que la Iglesia hace a todos en la tarde del Viernes Santo. Y hará de nuevo uso del canto durante el tiempo pascual para proclamar: *"Surrexit Dominus de sepulcro qui pro nobis pependit in ligno. Aleluya".*

5. *"Mysterium fidei!—Misterio de la fe!".* Cuando el sacerdote pronuncia o canta estas palabras, los presentes aclaman: "Anunciamos tu muerte, proclamamos tu resurrección, ¡ven Señor Jesús!".

Con éstas o parecidas palabras, la Iglesia, a la vez que se refiere a Cristo en el misterio de su Pasión, *revela también su propio misterio: Ecclesia de Eucharistia.* Si con el don del Espíritu Santo en Pentecostés la Iglesia nace y se encamina por las vías del mundo, un momento decisivo de su formación es ciertamente la institución de la Eucaristía en el Cenáculo. Su fundamento y su hontanar es todo el *Triduum paschale,* pero éste está como incluido, anticipado, y "concentrado" para siempre en el don eucarístico. En este don, Jesucristo entregaba a la Iglesia la actualización perenne del misterio pascual. Con él instituyó una misteriosa "contemporaneidad" entre aquel *Triduum* y el transcurrir de todos los siglos.

Este pensamiento nos lleva a sentimientos de gran asombro y gratitud. El acontecimiento pascual y la Eucaristía que lo actualiza a lo largo de los siglos tienen una "capacidad" verdaderamente enorme, en la que entra toda la historia como destinataria de la gracia de la redención. Este asombro ha de inundar siempre a la Iglesia, reunida en la celebración eucarística. Pero, de modo especial, debe acompañar al ministro de la Eucaristía. En efecto, es él quien, gracias a la facultad concedida por el sacramento del Orden sacerdotal, realiza la consagración. Con la potestad que le viene del Cristo del Cenáculo, dice: "Esto es mi cuerpo, que será entregado por vosotros . . . Éste es el cáliz de mi sangre, que será derramada por vosotros". El sacerdote pronuncia estas palabras o, más bien, *pone su boca y su voz a disposición de Aquél que las pronunció en el Cenáculo* y quiso que fueran repetidas de generación en generación por todos los que en la Iglesia participan ministerialmente de su sacerdocio.

6. Con la presente Carta encíclica, deseo suscitar este "asombro" eucarístico, en continuidad con la herencia jubilar que he querido dejar a la Iglesia con la Carta apostólica *Novo millennio ineunte* y con su coronamiento mariano *Rosarium Virginis Mariae.* Contemplar el rostro de Cristo, y contemplarlo con María, es el "programa" que he indicado a la Iglesia en el alba del tercer milenio, invitándola a remar mar adentro en las aguas de la historia con el entusiasmo de la nueva evangelización. Contemplar a Cristo implica saber reconocerle dondequiera que Él se manifieste, en sus multiformes presencias, pero sobre todo en el Sacramento vivo de su cuerpo y de su sangre. *La Iglesia vive del Cristo eucarístico,* de Él se alimenta y por Él es iluminada. La Eucaristía es misterio de fe y, al mismo tiempo, "misterio de luz"[3]. Cada vez que la Iglesia la celebra, los fieles pueden revivir de algún modo la experiencia de los dos discípulos de Emaús: "Entonces se les abrieron los ojos y le reconocieron" (Lucas 24,31).

7. Desde que inicié mi ministerio de Sucesor de Pedro, he reservado siempre para el Jueves Santo, día de la Eucaristía y del Sacerdocio, un signo de particular atención, dirigiendo una carta a todos los sacerdotes del mundo. Este año, para mí el vigésimo quinto de Pontificado, deseo involucrar más plenamente a toda la Iglesia en esta reflexión eucarística, para dar gracias a Dios también por el don de la Eucaristía y del Sacerdocio: "Don y misterio"[4]. Puesto que, proclamando el año del Rosario, he deseado poner este mi vigésimo quinto año *bajo el signo de la contemplación de Cristo con María,* no puedo dejar pasar este Jueves Santo de 2003 sin detenerme ante el rostro eucarístico de Cristo, señalando con nueva fuerza a la Iglesia la centralidad de la Eucaristía. De ella

vive la Iglesia. De este "pan vivo" se alimenta. ¿Cómo no sentir la necesidad de exhortar a todos a que hagan de ella siempre una renovada experiencia?

8. Cuando pienso en la Eucaristía, mirando mi vida de sacerdote, de Obispo y de Sucesor de Pedro, me resulta espontáneo recordar tantos momentos y lugares en los que he tenido la gracia de celebrarla. Recuerdo la iglesia parroquial de Niegowic donde desempeñé mi primer encargo pastoral, la colegiata de San Florián en Cracovia, la catedral del Wawel, la basílica de San Pedro y muchas basílicas e iglesias de Roma y del mundo entero. He podido celebrar la Santa Misa en capillas situadas en senderos de montaña, a orillas de los lagos, en las riberas del mar; la he celebrado sobre altares construidos en estadios, en las plazas de las ciudades . . . Estos escenarios tan variados de mis celebraciones eucarísticas me hacen experimentar intensamente su carácter universal y, por así decir, cósmico.¡Sí, cósmico! Porque también cuando se celebra sobre el pequeño altar de una iglesia en el campo, la Eucaristía se celebra, en cierto sentido, *sobre el altar del mundo.* Ella une el cielo y la tierra. Abarca e impregna toda la creación. El Hijo de Dios se ha hecho hombre, para reconducir todo lo creado, en un supremo acto de alabanza, a Aquél que lo hizo de la nada. De este modo, Él, el sumo y eterno Sacerdote, entrando en el santuario eterno mediante la sangre de su Cruz, devuelve al Creador y Padre toda la creación redimida. Lo hace a través del ministerio sacerdotal de la Iglesia y para gloria de la Santísima Trinidad. Verdaderamente, éste es el *mysterium fidei* que se realiza en la Eucaristía: el mundo nacido de las manos de Dios creador retorna a Él redimido por Cristo.

9. La Eucaristía, presencia salvadora de Jesús en la comunidad de los fieles y su alimento espiritual, es de lo más precioso que la Iglesia puede tener en su caminar por la historia. Así se explica la *esmerada atención* que ha prestado siempre al Misterio eucarístico, una atención que se manifiesta autorizadamente en la acción de los Concilios y de los Sumos Pontífices. ¿Cómo no admirar la exposición doctrinal de los Decretos sobre la Santísima Eucaristía y sobre el Sacrosanto Sacrificio de la Misa promulgados por el Concilio de Trento? Aquellas páginas han guiado en los siglos sucesivos tanto la teología como la catequesis, y aún hoy son punto de referencia dogmática para la continua renovación y crecimiento del Pueblo de Dios en la fe y en el amor a la Eucaristía. En tiempos más cercanos a nosotros, se han de mencionar tres Encíclicas:

la *Mirae Caritatis* de León XIII (28 de mayo de 1902)[5], *Mediator Dei* de Pío XII (20 de noviembre de 1947)[6] y la *Mysterium Fidei* de Pablo VI (3 de septiembre de 1965)[7].

El Concilio Vaticano II, aunque no publicó un documento específico sobre el Misterio eucarístico, ha ilustrado también sus diversos aspectos a lo largo del conjunto de sus documentos, y especialmente en la Constitución dogmática sobre la Iglesia *Lumen gentium* y en la Constitución sobre la Sagrada liturgia *Sacrosanctum Concilium.*

Yo mismo, en los primeros años de mi ministerio apostólico en la Cátedra de Pedro, con la Carta apostólica *Dominicae Cenae* (24 de febrero de 1980)[8], he tratado algunos aspectos del Misterio eucarístico y su incidencia en la vida de quienes son sus ministros. Hoy reanudo el hilo de aquellas consideraciones con el corazón aún más lleno de emoción y gratitud, como haciendo eco a la palabra del Salmista: "¿Cómo pagaré al Señor todo el bien que me ha hecho? Alzaré la copa de la salvación, invocando su nombre" (Salmo 116,12–13).

10. Este deber de anuncio por parte del Magisterio se corresponde con un crecimiento en el seno de la comunidad cristiana. No hay duda de que la *reforma litúrgica del Concilio* ha tenido grandes ventajas para una participación más consciente, activa y fructuosa de los fieles en el Santo Sacrificio del altar. En muchos lugares, además, *la adoración del Santísimo Sacramento* tiene cotidianamente una importancia destacada y se convierte en fuente inagotable de santidad. La participación devota de los fieles en la procesión eucarística en la solemnidad del Cuerpo y la Sangre de Cristo es una gracia de Dios, que cada año llena de gozo a quienes toman parte en ella. Y se podrían mencionar otros signos positivos de fe y amor eucarístico.

Desgraciadamente, junto a estas luces, *no faltan sombras.* En efecto, hay sitios donde se constata un abandono casi total del culto de adoración eucarística. A esto se añaden, en diversos contextos eclesiales, ciertos abusos que contribuyen a oscurecer la recta fe y la doctrina católica sobre este admirable Sacramento. Se nota a veces una comprensión muy limitada del Misterio eucarístico. Privado de su valor sacrificial, se vive como si no tuviera otro significado y valor que el de un encuentro convival fraterno. Además, queda a veces oscurecida la necesidad del sacerdocio ministerial, que se funda en la sucesión apostólica, y la sacramentalidad de la Eucaristía se reduce únicamente a la eficacia del anuncio. También por eso, aquí y allá, surgen iniciativas ecuménicas que, aun siendo generosas en su intención, transigen con prácticas eucarísticas contrarias a la disciplina con la cual la Iglesia expresa su fe. ¿Cómo no manifestar profundo dolor por todo esto? La Eucaristía es un don demasiado grande para admitir ambigüedades y reducciones.

Confío en que esta Carta encíclica contribuya eficazmente a disipar las sombras de doctrinas y prácticas no aceptables, para que la Eucaristía siga resplandeciendo con todo el esplendor de su misterio.

CAPÍTULO I
MISTERIO DE LA FE

11. "El Señor Jesús, la noche en que fue entregado" (1 Corintios 11,23), instituyó el Sacrificio eucarístico de su cuerpo y de su sangre. Las palabras del apóstol Pablo nos llevan a las circunstancias dramáticas en que nació la Eucaristía. En ella está inscrito de forma indeleble el acontecimiento de la pasión y muerte del Señor. No sólo lo evoca sino que lo hace sacramentalmente presente. Es el sacrificio de la Cruz que se perpetúa por los siglos[9]. Esta verdad la expresan bien las palabras con las cuales, en el rito latino, el pueblo responde a la proclamación del "misterio de la fe" que hace el sacerdote: *"Anunciamos tu muerte, Señor"*.

La Iglesia ha recibido la Eucaristía de Cristo, su Señor, no sólo como un don entre otros muchos, aunque sea muy valioso, sino como *el don por excelencia,* porque es don de sí mismo, de su persona en su santa humanidad y, además, de su obra de salvación. Ésta no queda relegada al pasado, pues "todo lo que Cristo es y todo lo que hizo y padeció por los hombres participa de la eternidad divina y domina así todos los tiempos . . ."[10].

Cuando la Iglesia celebra la Eucaristía, memorial de la muerte y resurrección de su Señor, se hace realmente presente este acontecimiento central de salvación y "se realiza la obra de nuestra redención"[11]. Este sacrificio es tan decisivo para la salvación del género humano, que Jesucristo lo ha realizado y ha vuelto al Padre sólo *después de habernos dejado el medio para participar de él,* como si hubiéramos estado presentes. Así, todo fiel puede tomar parte en él, obteniendo frutos inagotablemente. Ésta es la fe de la que han vivido a lo largo de los siglos las generaciones cristianas.

Ésta es la fe que el Magisterio de la Iglesia ha reiterado continuamente con gozosa gratitud por tan inestimable don[12]. Deseo, una vez más, llamar la atención sobre esta verdad, poniéndome con vosotros, mis queridos hermanos y hermanas, en adoración delante de este Misterio: Misterio grande, Misterio de misericordia. ¿Qué más podía hacer Jesús por nosotros? Verdaderamente, en la Eucaristía nos muestra un amor que llega "hasta el extremo" (Juan 13,1), un amor que no conoce medida.

12. Este aspecto de caridad universal del Sacramento eucarístico se funda en las palabras mismas del Salvador. Al instituirlo, no se limitó a decir "Éste es mi cuerpo", "Esta copa es la Nueva Alianza en mi sangre", sino que añadió "entregado por vosotros . . . derramada por vosotros" (Lucas 22,19–20). No afirmó solamente que lo que les daba de comer y beber era su cuerpo y su sangre, sino que manifestó *su valor sacrificial,* haciendo presente de modo sacramental su sacrificio, que cumpliría después en la cruz algunas horas más tarde, para la salvación de todos. "La misa es, a la vez e inseparablemente, el memorial sacrificial en que se perpetúa el sacrificio de la cruz, y el banquete sagrado de la comunión en el Cuerpo y la Sangre del Señor"[13].

La Iglesia vive continuamente del sacrificio redentor, y accede a él no solamente a través de un recuerdo lleno de fe, sino también en un contacto actual, puesto que *este sacrificio se hace presente,* perpetuándose sacramentalmente en cada comunidad que lo ofrece por manos del ministro consagrado. De este modo, la Eucaristía aplica a los hombres de hoy la reconciliación obtenida por Cristo una vez por todas para la humanidad de todos los tiempos. En efecto, "el sacrificio de Cristo y el sacrificio de la Eucaristía son, pues, *un único sacrificio*"[14]. Ya lo decía elocuentemente san Juan Crisóstomo: "Nosotros ofrecemos siempre el mismo Cordero, y no uno hoy y otro mañana, sino siempre el mismo. Por esta razón el sacrificio es siempre uno sólo [. . .]. También nosotros ofrecemos ahora aquella víctima, que se ofreció entonces y que jamás se consumirá"[15].

La Misa hace presente el sacrificio de la Cruz, no se le añade y no lo multiplica[16]. Lo que se repite es su celebración memorial, la "manifestación memorial" (*memorialis demonstratio*)[17], por la cual el único y definitivo sacrificio redentor de Cristo se actualiza siempre en el tiempo. La naturaleza sacrificial del Misterio eucarístico no puede ser entendida, por tanto, como algo aparte, independiente de la Cruz o con una referencia solamente indirecta al sacrificio del Calvario.

13. Por su íntima relación con el sacrificio del Gólgota, la Eucaristía es *sacrificio en sentido propio* y no sólo en sentido genérico, como si se tratara del mero ofrecimiento de Cristo a los fieles como alimento espiritual. En efecto, el don de su amor y de su obediencia hasta el extremo de dar la vida (cf. Juan 10,17–18), es en primer lugar un don a su Padre. Ciertamente es un don en favor nuestro, más aún, de toda la humanidad (cf. Mateo 26,28; Marcos 14,24; Lucas 22,20; Juan 10,15), pero *don ante todo al Padre:* "sacrificio que el Padre aceptó, correspondiendo a esta donación total de su Hijo que se hizo "obediente hasta la muerte" (Filipenses 2,8) con su entrega paternal, es decir, con el don de la vida nueva e inmortal en la resurrección"[18].

Al entregar su sacrificio a la Iglesia, Cristo ha querido además hacer suyo el sacrificio espiritual de la Iglesia, llamada a ofrecerse también a sí misma unida al sacrificio de Cristo. Por lo que concierne a todos los fieles, el Concilio Vaticano II enseña que "al participar en el sacrificio eucarístico, fuente y cima de la vida cristiana, ofrecen a Dios la Víctima divina y a sí mismos con ella"[19].

14. La Pascua de Cristo incluye, con la pasión y muerte, también su resurrección. Es lo que recuerda la aclamación del pueblo después de la consagración: "Proclamamos tu resurrección". Efectivamente, el sacrificio eucarístico no sólo hace presente el misterio de la pasión y muerte del Salvador, sino también el misterio de la resurrección, que corona su sacrificio. En cuanto viviente y resucitado, Cristo se hace en la Eucaristía "pan de vida" (Juan 6,35.48), "pan vivo" (Juan 6,51). San Ambrosio lo recordaba a los neófitos, como una aplicación del acontecimiento de la resurrección a su vida: "Si hoy Cristo está en ti, Él resucita para ti cada día"[20]. San Cirilo de Alejandría, a su vez, subrayaba que la participación en los santos Misterios "es una verdadera confesión y memoria de que el Señor ha muerto y ha vuelto a la vida por nosotros y para beneficio nuestro"[21].

15. La representación sacramental en la Santa Misa del sacrificio de Cristo, coronado por su resurrección, implica una presencia muy especial que—citando las palabras de Pablo VI—"se llama 'real', no por exclusión, como si las otras no fueran 'reales', sino por antonomasia, porque es sustancial, ya que por ella ciertamente

se hace presente Cristo, Dios y hombre, entero e íntegro"[22]. Se recuerda así la doctrina siempre válida del Concilio de Trento: "Por la consagración del pan y del vino se realiza la conversión de toda la sustancia del pan en la sustancia del cuerpo de Cristo Señor nuestro, y de toda la sustancia del vino en la sustancia de su sangre. Esta conversión, propia y convenientemente, fue llamada transustanciación por la santa Iglesia Católica"[23]. Verdaderamente la Eucaristía es *"misterium fidei"*, misterio que supera nuestro pensamiento y puede ser acogido sólo en la fe, como a menudo recuerdan las catequesis patrísticas sobre este divino Sacramento. "No veas—exhorta san Cirilo de Jerusalén—en el pan y en el vino meros y naturales elementos, porque el Señor ha dicho expresamente que son su cuerpo y su sangre: la fe te lo asegura, aunque los sentidos te sugieran otra cosa"[24].

"Adoro te devote, latens Deitas", seguiremos cantando con el Doctor Angélico. Ante este misterio de amor, la razón humana experimenta toda su limitación. Se comprende cómo, a lo largo de los siglos, esta verdad haya obligado a la teología a hacer arduos esfuerzos para entenderla.

Son esfuerzos loables, tanto más útiles y penetrantes cuanto mejor consiguen conjugar el ejercicio crítico del pensamiento con la "fe vivida" de la Iglesia, percibida especialmente en el "carisma de la verdad" del Magisterio y en la "comprensión interna de los misterios", a la que llegan sobre todo los santos[25]. La línea fronteriza es la señalada por Pablo VI: "Toda explicación teológica que intente buscar alguna inteligencia de este misterio, debe mantener, para estar de acuerdo con la fe católica, que en la realidad misma, independiente de nuestro espíritu, el pan y el vino han dejado de existir después de la consagración, de suerte que el Cuerpo y la Sangre adorables de Cristo Jesús son los que están realmente delante de nosotros"[26].

16. La eficacia salvífica del sacrificio se realiza plenamente cuando se comulga recibiendo el cuerpo y la sangre del Señor. De por sí, el sacrificio eucarístico se orienta a la íntima unión de nosotros, los fieles, con Cristo mediante la comunión: le recibimos a Él mismo, que se ha ofrecido por nosotros; su cuerpo, que Él ha entregado por nosotros en la Cruz; su sangre, "derramada por muchos para perdón de los pecados" (Mateo 26,28). Recordemos sus palabras: "Lo mismo que el Padre, que vive, me ha enviado y yo vivo por el Padre, también el que me coma vivirá por mí"

(Juan 6,57). Jesús mismo nos asegura que esta unión, que Él pone en relación con la vida trinitaria, se realiza efectivamente. *La Eucaristía es verdadero banquete,* en el cual Cristo se ofrece como alimento. Cuando Jesús anuncia por primera vez esta comida, los oyentes se quedan asombrados y confusos, obligando al Maestro a recalcar la verdad objetiva de sus palabras: "En verdad, en verdad os digo: si no coméis la carne del Hijo del hombre, y no bebéis su sangre, no tendréis vida en vosotros" (Juan 6,53). No se trata de un alimento metafórico: "Mi carne es verdadera comida y mi sangre verdadera bebida" (Juan 6,55).

17. Por la comunión de su cuerpo y de su sangre, Cristo nos comunica también su Espíritu. Escribe san Efrén: "Llamó al pan su cuerpo viviente, lo llenó de sí mismo y de su Espíritu [. . .], y quien lo come con fe, come Fuego y Espíritu [. . .]. Tomad, comed todos de él, y coméis con él el Espíritu Santo. En efecto, es verdaderamente mi cuerpo y el que vivirá eternamente"[27]. La Iglesia pide este don divino, raíz de todos los otros dones, en la epíclesis eucarística. Se lee, por ejemplo, en la *Divina Liturgia* de san Juan Crisóstomo: "Te invocamos, te rogamos y te suplicamos: manda tu Santo Espíritu sobre todos nosotros y sobre estos dones [. . .] para que sean purificación del alma, remisión de los pecados y comunicación del Espíritu Santo para cuantos participan de ellos"[28]. Y, en el *Misal Romano,* el celebrante implora que: "Fortalecidos con el Cuerpo y la Sangre de tu Hijo y llenos de su Espíritu Santo, formemos en Cristo un sólo cuerpo y un sólo espíritu"[29]. Así, con el don de su cuerpo y su sangre, Cristo acrecienta en nosotros el don de su Espíritu, infundido ya en el Bautismo e impreso como "sello" en el sacramento de la Confirmación.

18. La aclamación que el pueblo pronuncia después de la consagración se concluye oportunamente manifestando la proyección escatológica que distingue la celebración eucarística (cf. 1 Corintios 11,26): *". . . hasta que vuelvas".* La Eucaristía es tensión hacia la meta, pregustar el gozo pleno prometido por Cristo (cf. Juan 15,11); es, en cierto sentido, anticipación del Paraíso y "prenda de la gloria futura"[30]. En la Eucaristía, todo expresa la confiada espera: "mientras esperamos la gloriosa venida de nuestro Salvador Jesucristo"[31]. Quien se alimenta de Cristo en la Eucaristía no tiene que esperar el más allá para recibir la vida eterna: *la posee ya en la tierra* como primicia de la plenitud futura, que abarcará al hombre en su totalidad. En efecto, en la Eucaristía recibimos también la garantía de la resurrección corporal al final del mundo: "El que

come mi carne y bebe mi sangre, tiene vida eterna, y yo le resucitaré el último día" (Juan 6,54). Esta garantía de la resurrección futura proviene de que la carne del Hijo del hombre, entregada como comida, es su cuerpo en el estado glorioso del resucitado. Con la Eucaristía se asimila, por decirlo así, el "secreto" de la resurrección. Por eso san Ignacio de Antioquía definía con acierto el Pan eucarístico "fármaco de inmortalidad, antídoto contra la muerte"[32].

19. La tensión escatológica suscitada por la Eucaristía *expresa y consolida la comunión con la Iglesia celestial.* No es casualidad que en las anáforas orientales y en las plegarias eucarísticas latinas se recuerde siempre con veneración a la gloriosa siempre Virgen María, Madre de Jesucristo, nuestro Dios y Señor, a los ángeles, a los santos apóstoles, a los gloriosos mártires y a todos los santos. Es un aspecto de la Eucaristía que merece ser resaltado: mientras nosotros celebramos el sacrificio del Cordero, nos unimos a la liturgia celestial, asociándonos con la multitud inmensa que grita: "La salvación es de nuestro Dios, que está sentado en el trono, y del Cordero" (Apocalipsis 7,10). La Eucaristía es verdaderamente un resquicio del cielo que se abre sobre la tierra. Es un rayo de gloria de la Jerusalén celestial, que penetra en las nubes de nuestra historia y proyecta luz sobre nuestro camino.

20. Una consecuencia significativa de la tensión escatológica propia de la Eucaristía es que da impulso a nuestro camino histórico, poniendo una semilla de viva esperanza en la dedicación cotidiana de cada uno a sus propias tareas. En efecto, aunque la visión cristiana fija su mirada en un "cielo Nuevo" y una "tierra nueva" (Apocalipsis 21,1), eso no debilita, sino que más bien estimula nuestro sentido de responsabilidad respecto a la tierra presente[33]. Deseo recalcarlo con fuerza al principio del nuevo milenio, para que los cristianos se sientan más que nunca comprometidos a no descuidar los deberes de su ciudadanía terrenal. Es cometido suyo contribuir con la luz del Evangelio a la edificación de un mundo habitable y plenamente conforme al designio de Dios.

Muchos son los problemas que oscurecen el horizonte de nuestro tiempo. Baste pensar en la urgencia de trabajar por la paz, de poner premisas sólidas de justicia y solidaridad en las relaciones entre los pueblos, de defender la vida humana desde su concepción hasta su término natural. Y ¿qué decir, además, de las tantas contradicciones de un mundo "globalizado", donde los más débiles, los más pequeños y los más pobres parecen tener bien poco que esperar? En este mundo es donde tiene que brillar la esperanza cristiana. También por eso el Señor ha querido quedarse con nosotros en la Eucaristía, grabando en esta presencia sacrificial y convival la promesa de una humanidad renovada por su amor. Es significativo que el Evangelio de Juan, allí donde los Sinópticos narran la institución de la Eucaristía, propone, ilustrando así su sentido profundo, el relato del "lavatorio de los pies", en el cual Jesús se hace maestro de comunión y servicio (cf. Juan 13,1–20). El apóstol Pablo, por su parte, califica como "indigno" de una comunidad cristiana que se participe en la Cena del Señor, si se hace en un contexto de división e indiferencia hacia los pobres (Cf. 1 Corintios 11,17.22.27.34)[34].

Anunciar la muerte del Señor "hasta que venga" (1 Corintios 11,26), comporta para los que participan en la Eucaristía el compromiso de transformar su vida, para que toda ella llegue a ser en cierto modo "eucarística". Precisamente este fruto de transfiguración de la existencia y el compromiso de transformar el mundo según el Evangelio, hacen resplandecer la tensión escatológica de la celebración eucarística y de toda la vida cristiana: "¡Ven, Señor Jesús!" (Apocalipsis 22,20).

CAPÍTULO II
LA EUCARISTÍA EDIFICA LA IGLESIA

21. El Concilio Vaticano II ha recordado que la celebración eucarística es el centro del proceso de crecimiento de la Iglesia. En efecto, después de haber dicho que "la Iglesia, o el reino de Cristo presente ya en misterio, crece visiblemente en el mundo por el poder de Dios"[35], como queriendo responder a la pregunta: ¿Cómo crece?, añade: "Cuantas veces se celebra en el altar el sacrificio de la cruz, en el que Cristo, nuestra Pascua, fue inmolado (1 Corintios 5,7), se realiza la obra de nuestra redención. El sacramento del pan eucarístico significa y al mismo tiempo realiza la unidad de los creyentes, que forman un sólo cuerpo en Cristo (cf. 1 Corintios 10,17)"[36].

Hay un *influjo causal de la Eucaristía* en los orígenes mismos de la Iglesia. Los evangelistas precisan que fueron los Doce, los Apóstoles, quienes se reunieron con Jesús en la Última Cena (cf. Mateo 26,20; Marcos 14,17; Lucas 22,14). Es un detalle de notable importancia, porque los Apóstoles "fueron la semilla del nuevo Israel, a la vez que el origen de la jerarquía sagrada"[37]. Al ofrecerles como alimento su cuerpo y su sangre, Cristo los implicó misteriosamente en el sacrificio que habría de consumarse pocas horas después en el Calvario. Análogamente a la alianza del Sinaí, sellada con el sacrificio y la aspersión con la sangre[38], los gestos y las palabras de Jesús en la Última Cena fundaron la nueva comunidad mesiánica, el Pueblo de la nueva Alianza.

Los Apóstoles, aceptando la invitación de Jesús en el Cenáculo: "Tomad, comed . . . Bebed de ella todos . . ." (Mateo 26,26.27), entraron por vez primera en comunión sacramental con Él. Desde aquel momento, y hasta al final de los siglos, la Iglesia se edifica a través de la comunión sacramental con el Hijo de Dios inmolado por nosotros: "Haced esto en recuerdo mío . . . Cuantas veces la bebiereis, hacedlo en recuerdo mío" (1 Corintios 11,24–25; cf. Lucas 22,19).

22. La incorporación a Cristo, que tiene lugar por el Bautismo, se renueva y se consolida continuamente con la participación en el Sacrificio eucarístico, sobre todo cuando ésta es plena mediante la comunión sacramental. Podemos decir que no solamente *cada uno de nosotros recibe a Cristo, sino que también Cristo nos recibe a cada uno de nosotros.* Él estrecha su amistad con nosotros: "Vosotros sois mis amigos" (Juan 15,14). Más aún, nosotros vivimos gracias a Él: "el que me coma vivirá por mí" (Juan 6,57). En la comunión eucarística se realiza de manera sublime que Cristo y el discípulo "estén" el uno en el otro: "Permaneced en mí, como yo en vosotros" (Juan 15,4).

Al unirse a Cristo, en vez de encerrarse en sí mismo, el Pueblo de la nueva Alianza se convierte en "sacramento" para la humanidad[39], signo e instrumento de la salvación, en obra de Cristo, en luz del mundo y sal de la tierra (cf. Mateo 5,13–16), para la redención de todos[40]. La misión de la Iglesia continúa la de Cristo: "Como el Padre me envió, también yo os envoi" (Juan 20,21). Por tanto, la Iglesia recibe la fuerza espiritual necesaria para cumplir su misión perpetuando en la Eucaristía el sacrificio de la Cruz y comulgando el cuerpo y la sangre de Cristo. Así, la Eucaristía es la *fuente* y, al mismo tiempo, la *cumbre* de toda la evangelización, puesto que su objetivo es la comunión de los hombres con Cristo y, en Él, con el Padre y con el Espíritu Santo[41].

23. Con la comunión eucarística la Iglesia consolida también su unidad como cuerpo de Cristo. San Pablo se refiere a esta *eficacia unificadora* de la participación en el banquete eucarístico cuando escribe a los Corintios: "Y el pan que partimos ¿no es comunión

con el cuerpo de Cristo? Porque aun siendo muchos, un solo pan y un solo cuerpo somos, pues todos participamos de un solo pan" (1 Corintios 10,16–17). El comentario de san Juan Crisóstomo es detallado y profundo: "¿Qué es, en efecto, el pan? Es el cuerpo de Cristo. ¿En qué se transforman los que lo reciben? En cuerpo de Cristo; pero no muchos cuerpos sino un sólo cuerpo. En efecto, como el pan es sólo uno, por más que esté compuesto de muchos granos de trigo y éstos se encuentren en él, aunque no se vean, de tal modo que su diversidad desaparece en virtud de su perfecta fusión; de la misma manera, también nosotros estamos unidos recíprocamente unos a otros y, todos juntos, con Cristo"[42]. La argumentación es terminante: nuestra unión con Cristo, que es don y gracia para cada uno, hace que en Él estemos asociados también a la unidad de su cuerpo que es la Iglesia. La Eucaristía consolida la incorporación a Cristo, establecida en el Bautismo mediante el don del Espíritu (cf. 1 Corintios 12,13.27).

La acción conjunta e inseparable del Hijo y del Espíritu Santo, que está en el origen de la Iglesia, de su constitución y de su permanencia, continúa en la Eucaristía. Bien consciente de ello es el autor de la *Liturgia de Santiago:* en la epíclesis de la anáfora se ruega a Dios Padre que envíe el Espíritu Santo sobre los fieles y sobre los dones, para que el cuerpo y la sangre de Cristo "sirvan a todos los que participan en ellos [. . .] a la santificación de las almas y los cuerpos"[43]. La Iglesia es reforzada por el divino Paráclito a través la santificación eucarística de los fieles.

24. El don de Cristo y de su Espíritu que recibimos en la comunión eucarística colma con sobrada plenitud los anhelos de unidad fraterna que alberga el corazón humano y, al mismo tiempo, eleva la experiencia de fraternidad, propia de la participación común en la misma mesa eucarística, a niveles que están muy por encima de la simple experiencia convival humana. Mediante la comunión del cuerpo de Cristo, la Iglesia alcanza cada vez más profundamente su ser "en Cristo como sacramento o signo e instrumento de la unión íntima con Dios y de la unidad de todo el género humano"[44].

A los gérmenes de disgregación entre los hombres, que la experiencia cotidiana muestra tan arraigada en la humanidad a causa del pecado, se contrapone *la fuerza generadora de unidad* del cuerpo de Cristo. La Eucaristía, construyendo la Iglesia, crea precisamente por ello comunidad entre los hombres.

25. El *culto que se da a la Eucaristía fuera de la Misa* es de un valor inestimable en la vida de la Iglesia. Dicho culto está estrechamente unido a la celebración del Sacrificio eucarístico. La presencia de Cristo bajo las sagradas especies que se conservan después de la Misa—presencia que dura mientras subsistan las especies del pan y del vino[45]—deriva de la celebración del Sacrificio y tiende a la comunión sacramental y espiritual[46]. Corresponde a los Pastores animar, incluso con el testimonio personal, el culto eucarístico, particularmente la exposición del Santísimo Sacramento y la adoración de Cristo presente bajo las especies eucarísticas[47].

Es hermoso estar con Él y, reclinados sobre su pecho como el discípulo predilecto (cf. Juan 13,25), palpar el amor infinito de su corazón. Si el cristianismo ha de distinguirse en nuestro tiempo sobre todo por el "arte de la oración"[48], ¿cómo no sentir una renovada necesidad de estar largos ratos en conversación espiritual, en adoración silenciosa, en actitud de amor, ante Cristo presente en el Santísimo Sacramento? ¡Cuántas veces, mis queridos hermanos y hermanas, he hecho esta experiencia y en ella he encontrado fuerza, consuelo y apoyo!

Numerosos Santos nos han dado ejemplo de esta práctica, alabada y recomendada repetidamente por el Magisterio[49]. De manera particular se distinguió por ella San Alfonso María de Ligorio, que escribió: "Entre todas las devociones, ésta de adorar a Jesús sacramentado es la primera, después de los sacramentos, la más apreciada por Dios y la más útil para nosotros"[50]. La Eucaristía es un tesoro inestimable; no sólo su celebración, sino también estar ante ella fuera de la Misa, nos da la posibilidad de llegar al manantial mismo de la gracia. Una comunidad cristiana que quiera ser más capaz de contemplar el rostro de Cristo, en el espíritu que he sugerido en las Cartas apostólicas *Novo millennio ineunte* y *Rosarium Virginis Mariae,* ha de desarrollar también este aspecto del culto eucarístico, en el que se prolongan y multiplican los frutos de la comunión del cuerpo y sangre del Señor.

CAPÍTULO III
APOSTOLICIDAD DE LA EUCARISTÍA Y DE LA IGLESIA

26. Como he recordado antes, si la Eucaristía edifica la Iglesia y la Iglesia hace la Eucaristía, se deduce que hay una relación sumamente estrecha entre una y otra. Tan verdad es esto, que nos

permite aplicar al Misterio eucarístico lo que decimos de la Iglesia cuando, en el Símbolo niceno-constantinopolitano, la confesamos "una, santa, católica y apostólica". También la Eucaristía es una y católica. Es también santa, más aún, es el Santísimo Sacramento. Pero ahora queremos dirigir nuestra atención principalmente a su apostolicidad.

27. El *Catecismo de la Iglesia Católica,* al explicar cómo la Iglesia es apostólica, o sea, basada en los Apóstoles, se refiere a un *triple sentido* de la expresión. Por una parte, "fue y permanece edificada sobre 'el fundamento de los apóstoles' (Efesios 2,20), testigos escogidos y enviados en misión por el propio Cristo"[51]. También los Apóstoles están en el fundamento de la Eucaristía, no porque el Sacramento no se remonte a Cristo mismo, sino porque ha sido confiado a los Apóstoles por Jesús y transmitido por ellos y sus sucesores hasta nosotros. La Iglesia celebra la Eucaristía a lo largo de los siglos precisamente en continuidad con la acción de los Apóstoles, obedientes al mandato del Señor.

El segundo sentido de la apostolicidad de la Iglesia indicado por el Catecismo es que "guarda y transmite, con la ayuda del Espíritu Santo que habita en ella, la enseñanza, el buen depósito, las sanas palabras oídas a los apóstoles"[52]. También en este segundo sentido la Eucaristía es apostólica, porque se celebra en conformidad con la fe de los Apóstoles. En la historia bimilenaria del Pueblo de la nueva Alianza, el Magisterio eclesiástico ha precisado en muchas ocasiones la doctrina eucarística, incluso en lo que atañe a la exacta terminología, precisamente para salvaguardar la fe apostólica en este Misterio excelso. Esta fe permanece inalterada y es esencial para la Iglesia que perdure así.

28. En fin, la Iglesia es apostólica en el sentido de que "sigue siendo enseñada, santificada y dirigida por los Apóstoles hasta la vuelta de Cristo gracias a aquellos que les suceden en su ministerio pastoral: el colegio de los Obispos, a los que asisten los presbíteros, juntamente con el sucesor de Pedro y Sumo Pastor de la Iglesia"[53]. La sucesión de los Apóstoles en la misión pastoral conlleva necesariamente el sacramento del Orden, es decir, la serie ininterrumpida que se remonta hasta los orígenes, de ordenaciones episcopales válidas[54]. Esta sucesión es esencial para que haya Iglesia en sentido propio y pleno.

La Eucaristía expresa también este sentido de la apostolicidad. En efecto, como enseña el Concilio Vaticano II, los fieles "participan en la celebración de la Eucaristía en virtud de su sacerdocio real"[55], pero es el sacerdote ordenado quien "realiza como representante de Cristo el sacrificio eucarístico y lo ofrece a Dios en nombre de todo el pueblo"[56]. Por eso se prescribe en el *Misal Romano* que es únicamente el sacerdote quien pronuncia la plegaria eucarística, mientras el pueblo de Dios se asocia a ella con fe y en silencio[57].

29. La expresión, usada repetidamente por el Concilio Vaticano II, según la cual el sacerdote ordenado "realiza como representante de Cristo el Sacrificio eucarístico"[58], estaba ya bien arraigada en la enseñanza pontificia[59]. Como he tenido ocasión de aclarar en otra ocasión, *in persona Christi* "quiere decir más que "en nombre", o también, "en vez" de Cristo. In "persona": es decir, en la identificación específica, sacramental con el "sumo y eterno Sacerdote", que es el autor y el sujeto principal de su propio sacrificio, en el que, en verdad, no puede ser sustituido por nadie"[60]. El ministerio de los sacerdotes, en virtud del sacramento del Orden, en la economía de salvación querida por Cristo, manifiesta que la Eucaristía celebrada por ellos *es un don que supera radicalmente la potestad de la asamblea* y es insustituible en cualquier caso para unir válidamente la consagración eucarística al sacrificio de la Cruz y a la Última Cena.

La asamblea que se reúne para celebrar la Eucaristía necesita absolutamente, para que sea realmente asamblea eucarística, un sacerdote ordenado que la presida. Por otra parte, la comunidad no está capacitada para darse por sí sola el ministro ordenado. Éste es un don que *recibe a través de la sucesión episcopal que se remonta a los Apóstoles.* Es el Obispo quien establece un nuevo presbítero, mediante el sacramento del Orden, otorgándole el poder de consagrar la Eucaristía. Pues "el Misterio eucarístico no puede ser celebrado en ninguna comunidad si no es por un sacerdote ordenado, como ha enseñado expresamente el Concilio Lateranense IV"[61].

30. Tanto esta doctrina de la Iglesia católica sobre el ministerio sacerdotal en relación con la Eucaristía, como la referente al Sacrificio eucarístico, han sido objeto en las últimas décadas de un provechoso diálogo *en el ámbito de la actividad ecuménica.* Hemos de dar gracias a la Santísima Trinidad porque, a este respecto, se han obtenido significativos progresos y acercamientos, que nos hacen esperar en un futuro en que se comparta plenamente la fe.

Aún sigue siendo del todo válida la observación del Concilio sobre las Comunidades eclesiales surgidas en Occidente desde el siglo XVI en adelante y separadas de la Iglesia católica: "Las Comunidades eclesiales separadas, aunque les falte la unidad plena con nosotros que dimana del bautismo, y aunque creamos que, sobre todo por defecto del sacramento del Orden, no han conservado la sustancia genuina e íntegra del Misterio eucarístico, sin embargo, al conmemorar en la santa Cena la muerte y resurrección del Señor, profesan que en la comunión de Cristo se significa la vida, y esperan su venida gloriosa"[62].

Los fieles católicos, por tanto, aun respetando las convicciones religiosas de estos hermanos separados, deben abstenerse de participar en la comunión distribuida en sus celebraciones, para no avalar una ambigüedad sobre la naturaleza de la Eucaristía y, por consiguiente, faltar al deber de dar un testimonio claro de la verdad. Eso retardaría el camino hacia la plena unidad visible. De manera parecida, no se puede pensar en reemplazar la santa Misa dominical con celebraciones ecuménicas de la Palabra o con encuentros de oración en común con cristianos miembros de dichas Comunidades eclesiales, o bien con la participación en su servicio litúrgico. Estas celebraciones y encuentros, en sí mismos loables en circunstancias oportunas, preparan a la deseada comunión total, incluso eucarística, pero no pueden reemplazarla.

El hecho de que el poder de consagrar la Eucaristía haya sido confiado sólo a los Obispos y a los presbíteros no significa menoscabo alguno para el resto del Pueblo de Dios, puesto que la comunión del único cuerpo de Cristo que es la Iglesia es un don que redunda en beneficio de todos.

31. Si la Eucaristía es centro y cumbre de la vida de la Iglesia, también lo es del ministerio sacerdotal. Por eso, con ánimo agradecido a Jesucristo, nuestro Señor, reitero que la Eucaristía "es la principal y central razón de ser del sacramento del sacerdocio, nacido efectivamente en el momento de la institución de la Eucaristía y a la vez que ella"[63].

Las actividades pastorales del presbítero son múltiples. Si se piensa además en las condiciones sociales y culturales del mundo actual, es fácil entender lo sometido que está *al peligro de la dispersión* por el gran número de tareas diferentes. El Concilio Vaticano II ha identificado en la caridad pastoral el vínculo que da unidad a su vida y a sus actividades. Ésta—añade el Concilio—"brota, sobre todo, del sacrificio eucarístico que, por eso, es el centro y raíz de toda la vida del presbítero"[64]. Se entiende, pues, lo importante que es para la vida espiritual del sacerdote, como para el bien de la Iglesia y del mundo, que ponga en práctica la recomendación conciliar de celebrar cotidianamente la Eucaristía, "la cual, aunque no puedan estar presentes los fieles, es ciertamente una acción de Cristo y de la Iglesia"[65]. De este modo, el sacerdote será capaz de sobreponerse cada día a toda tensión dispersiva, encontrando en el Sacrificio eucarístico, verdadero centro de su vida y de su ministerio, la energía espiritual necesaria para afrontar los diversos quehaceres pastorales. Cada jornada será así verdaderamente eucarística.

Del carácter central de la Eucaristía en la vida y en el ministerio de los sacerdotes se deriva también su puesto central en la *pastoral de las vocaciones sacerdotales.* Ante todo, porque la plegaria por las vocaciones encuentra en ella la máxima unión con la oración de Cristo sumo y eterno Sacerdote; pero también porque la diligencia y esmero de los sacerdotes en el ministerio eucarístico, unido a la promoción de la participación consciente, activa y fructuosa de los fieles en la Eucaristía, es un ejemplo eficaz y un incentivo a la respuesta generosa de los jóvenes a la llamada de Dios. Él se sirve a menudo del ejemplo de la caridad pastoral ferviente de un sacerdote para sembrar y desarrollar en el corazón del joven el germen de la llamada al sacerdocio.

32. Toda esto demuestra lo doloroso y fuera de lo normal que resulta la situación de una comunidad cristiana que, aún pudiendo ser, por número y variedad de fieles, una parroquia, carece sin embargo de un sacerdote que la guíe. En efecto, la parroquia es una comunidad de bautizados que expresan y confirman su identidad principalmente por la celebración del Sacrificio eucarístico. Pero esto requiere la presencia de un presbítero, el único a quien compete ofrecer la Eucaristía *in persona Christi.* Cuando la comunidad no tiene sacerdote, ciertamente se ha de paliar de alguna manera, con el fin de que continúen las celebraciones dominicales y, así, los religiosos y los laicos que animan la oración de sus hermanos y hermanas ejercen de modo loable el sacerdocio común de todos los fieles, basado en la gracia del Bautismo. Pero dichas soluciones han de ser consideradas únicamente provisionales, mientras la comunidad está a la espera de un sacerdote.

El hecho de que estas celebraciones sean incompletas desde el punto de vista sacramental ha de impulsar ante todo a toda la comunidad a pedir con mayor fervor que el Señor "envíe obreros a su mies"(Mateo 9,38); y debe estimularla también a llevar a cabo una adecuada pastoral vocacional, sin ceder a la tentación de buscar soluciones que comporten una reducción de las cualidades morales y formativas requeridas para los candidatos al sacerdocio.

33. Cuando, por escasez de sacerdotes, se confía a fieles no ordenados una participación en el cuidado pastoral de una parroquia, éstos han de tener presente que, como enseña el Concilio Vaticano II, "no se construye ninguna comunidad cristiana si ésta no tiene como raíz y centro la celebración de la sagrada Eucaristía"[66]. Por tanto, considerarán como cometido suyo el mantener viva en la comunidad una verdadera "hambre" de la Eucaristía, que lleve a no perder ocasión alguna de tener la celebración de la Misa, incluso aprovechando la presencia ocasional de un sacerdote que no esté impedido por el derecho de la Iglesia para celebrarla.

CAPÍTULO IV
EUCARISTÍA Y COMUNIÓN ECLESIAL

34. En 1985, la Asamblea extraordinaria del Sínodo de los Obispos reconoció en la "eclesiología de communion" la idea central y fundamental de los documentos del Concilio Vaticano II[67]. La Iglesia, mientras peregrina aquí en la tierra, está llamada a mantener y promover tanto la comunión con Dios trinitario como la comunión entre los fieles. Para ello, cuenta con la Palabra y los Sacramentos, sobre todo la Eucaristía, de la cual "vive y se desarrolla sin cesar"[68], y en la cual, al mismo tiempo, se expresa a sí misma. No es casualidad que el término *comunión* se haya convertido en uno de los nombres específicos de este sublime Sacramento.

La Eucaristía se manifiesta, pues, como culminación de todos los Sacramentos, en cuanto lleva a perfección la comunión con Dios Padre, mediante la identificación con el Hijo Unigénito, por obra del Espíritu Santo. Un insigne escritor de la tradición bizantina expresó esta verdad con agudeza de fe: en la Eucaristía, "con preferencia respecto a los otros sacramentos, el misterio [de la comunión] es tan perfecto que conduce a la cúspide de todos los bienes: en ella culmina todo deseo humano, porque aquí llegamos a Dios y Dios se une a nosotros con la unión más perfecta"[69]. Precisamente por eso, es *conveniente cultivar en el ánimo el deseo constante del Sacramento eucarístico.* De aquí ha nacido la práctica de la "comunión espiritual", felizmente difundida desde hace siglos en la Iglesia y recomendada por Santos maestros de vida espiritual. Santa Teresa de Jesús escribió: "Cuando [. . .] no comulgáredes y oyéredes misa, podéis comulgar espiritualmente, que es de grandísimo provecho [. . .], que es mucho lo que se imprime el amor ansí deste Señor"[70].

35. La celebración de la Eucaristía, no obstante, no puede ser el punto de partida de la comunión, que la presupone previamente, para consolidarla y llevarla a perfección. El Sacramento expresa este vínculo de comunión, sea en la dimensión *invisible* que, en Cristo y por la acción del Espíritu Santo, nos une al Padre y entre nosotros, sea en la dimensión *visible,* que implica la comunión en la doctrina de los Apóstoles, en los Sacramentos y en el orden jerárquico. La íntima relación entre los elementos invisibles y visibles de la comunión eclesial, es constitutiva de la Iglesia como sacramento de salvación[71]. Sólo en este contexto tiene lugar la celebración legítima de la Eucaristía y la verdadera participación en la misma. Por tanto, resulta una exigencia intrínseca a la Eucaristía que se celebre en la comunión y, concretamente, en la integridad de todos sus vínculos.

36. La comunión invisible, aun siendo por naturaleza un crecimiento, supone la vida de gracia, por medio de la cual se nos hace "partícipes de la naturaleza divina" (2 Pedro 1,4), así como la práctica de las virtudes de la fe, de la esperanza y de la caridad. En efecto, sólo de este modo se obtiene verdadera comunión con el Padre, el Hijo y el Espíritu Santo. No basta la fe, sino que es preciso perseverar en la gracia santificante y en la caridad, permaneciendo en el seno de la Iglesia con el "cuerpo" y con el "corazón"[72]; es decir, hace falta, por decirlo con palabras de san Pablo, "la fe que actúa por la caridad"(Gálatas 5,6).

La integridad de los vínculos invisibles es un deber moral bien preciso del cristiano que quiera participar plenamente en la Eucaristía comulgando el cuerpo y la sangre de Cristo. El mismo Apóstol llama la atención sobre este deber con la advertencia: "Examínese, pues, cada cual, y coma así el pan y beba de la copa" (1 Corintios 11,28). San Juan Crisóstomo, con la fuerza de su elocuencia, exhortaba a los fieles: "También yo alzo la voz, suplico, ruego y exhorto encarecidamente a no sentarse a esta sagrada Mesa con una conciencia manchada y corrompida. Hacer esto, en efecto, nunca jamás podrá llamarse comunión, por más que toquemos mil veces el cuerpo del Señor, sino condena, tormento y mayor castigo"[73].

Precisamente en este sentido, el *Catecismo de la Iglesia Católica* establece: "Quien tiene conciencia de estar en pecado grave debe recibir el sacramento de la Reconciliación antes de acercarse a comulgar"[74]. Deseo, por tanto, reiterar que está vigente, y lo estará siempre en la Iglesia, la norma con la cual el Concilio de Trento ha concretado la severa exhortación del apóstol Pablo, al afirmar que, para recibir dignamente la Eucaristía, "debe preceder la confesión de los pecados, cuando uno es consciente de pecado mortal"[75].

37. La Eucaristía y la Penitencia son dos sacramentos estrechamente vinculados entre sí. La Eucaristía, al hacer presente el Sacrificio redentor de la Cruz, perpetuándolo sacramentalmente, significa que de ella se deriva una exigencia continua de conversión, de respuesta personal a la exhortación que san Pablo dirigía a los cristianos de Corinto: "En nombre de Cristo os suplicamos: ¡reconciliaos con Dios!" (2 Corintios 5,20). Así pues, si el cristiano tiene conciencia de un pecado grave está obligado a seguir el itinerario penitencial, mediante el sacramento de la Reconciliación para acercarse a la plena participación en el Sacrificio eucarístico.

El juicio sobre el estado de gracia, obviamente, corresponde solamente al interesado, tratándose de una valoración de conciencia. No obstante, en los casos de un comportamiento externo grave, abierta y establemente contrario a la norma moral, la Iglesia, en su cuidado pastoral por el buen orden comunitario y por respeto al Sacramento, no puede mostrarse indiferente. A esta situación de manifiesta indisposición moral se refiere la norma del Código de Derecho Canónico que no permite la admisión a la comunión eucarística a los que "obstinadamente persistanen un manifiesto pecado grave"[76].

38. La comunión eclesial, como antes he recordado, es también *visible* y se manifiesta en los lazos vinculantes enumerados por el Concilio mismo cuando enseña: "Están plenamente incorporados a la sociedad que es la Iglesia aquellos que, teniendo el Espíritu de Cristo, aceptan íntegramente su constitución y todos los medios de salvación establecidos en ella y están unidos, dentro de su estructura visible, a Cristo, que la rige por medio del Sumo Pontífice y de los Obispos, mediante los lazos de la profesión de fe, de los sacramentos, del gobierno eclesiástico y de la communion"[77].

La Eucaristía, siendo la suprema manifestación sacramental de la comunión en la Iglesia, exige que se celebre en *un contexto de integridad de los vínculos, incluso externos, de comunión.* De modo especial, por ser "como la consumación de la vida espiritual y la finalidad de todos los sacramentos"[78], requiere que los lazos de la comunión en los sacramentos sean reales, particularmente en el Bautismo y en el Orden sacerdotal. No se puede dar la comunión a una persona no bautizada o que rechace la verdad íntegra de fe sobre el Misterio eucarístico. Cristo es la verdad y da testimonio de la verdad (cf. Juan 14,6; 18,37); el Sacramento de su cuerpo y su sangre no permite ficciones.

39. Además, por el carácter mismo de la comunión eclesial y de la relación que tiene con ella el sacramento de la Eucaristía, se debe recordar que "el Sacrificio eucarístico, aun celebrándose siempre en una comunidad particular, no es nunca celebración de esa sola comunidad: ésta, en efecto, recibiendo la presencia eucarística del Señor, recibe el don completo de la salvación, y se manifiesta así, a pesar de su permanente particularidad visible, como imagen y verdadera presencia de la Iglesia una, santa, católica y apostólica"[79]. De esto se deriva que una comunidad realmente eucarística no puede encerrarse en sí misma, como si fuera autosuficiente, sino que ha de mantenerse en sintonía con todas las demás comunidades católicas.

La comunión eclesial de la asamblea eucarística es comunión con el propio *Obispo* y con el *Romano Pontífice.* En efecto, el Obispo es el principio visible y el fundamento de la unidad en su Iglesia particular[80]. Sería, por tanto, una gran incongruencia que el Sacramento por excelencia de la unidad de la Iglesia fuera celebrado sin una verdadera comunión con el Obispo. San Ignacio de Antioquía escribía: "se considere segura la Eucaristía que se realiza bajo el Obispo o quien él haya encargado"[81]. Asimismo, puesto que "el Romano Pontífice, como sucesor de Pedro, es el principio y fundamento perpetuo y visible de la unidad, tanto de los obispos como de la muchedumbre de los fieles"[82], la comunión con él es una exigencia intrínseca de la celebración del Sacrificio eucarístico. De aquí la gran verdad expresada de varios modos en la Liturgia: "Toda celebración de la Eucaristía se realiza en unión no sólo con el propio obispo sino también con el Papa, con el orden episcopal, con todo el clero y con el pueblo entero. Toda válida celebración de la Eucaristía expresa esta comunión universal con Pedro y con la Iglesia entera, o la reclama objetivamente, como en el caso de las Iglesias cristianas separadas de Roma"[83].

40. La Eucaristía *crea comunión y educa a la comunión.* San Pablo escribía a los fieles de Corinto manifestando el gran contraste de sus divisiones en las asambleas eucarísticas con lo que estaban celebrando, la Cena del Señor. Consecuentemente, el Apóstol les invitaba a reflexionar sobre la verdadera realidad de la Eucaristía con el fin de hacerlos volver al espíritu de comunión fraterna (cf. 1 Corintios 11,17–34). San Agustín se hizo eco de esta exigencia de manera elocuente cuando, al recordar las palabras del Apóstol: "vosotros sois el cuerpo de Cristo, y sus miembros cada uno por su parte" (1 Corintios 12,27), observaba: "Si vosotros sois el cuerpo y los miembros de Cristo, sobre la mesa del Señor está el misterio que sois vosotros mismos y recibís el misterio que sois vosotros"[84]. Y, de esta constatación, concluía: "Cristo el Señor [. . .] consagró en su mesa el misterio de nuestra paz y unidad. El que recibe el misterio de la unidad y no posee el vínculo de la paz, no recibe un misterio para provecho propio, sino un testimonio contra sí"[85].

41. Esta peculiar eficacia para promover la comunión, propia de la Eucaristía, es uno de los motivos de la importancia de la Misa dominical. Sobre ella y sobre las razones por las que es fundamental para la vida de la Iglesia y de cada uno de los fieles, me he ocupado en la Carta apostólica sobre la santificación del domingo *Dies Domini*[86], recordando, además, que participar en la Misa es una obligación para los fieles, a menos que tengan un impedimento grave, lo que impone a los Pastores el correspondiente deber de ofrecer a todos la posibilidad efectiva de cumplir este precepto[87]. Más recientemente, en la Carta apostólica *Novo millennio ineunte,* al trazar el camino pastoral de la Iglesia a comienzos del tercer milenio, he querido dar un relieve particular a la Eucaristía dominical, subrayando su eficacia creadora de comunión: Ella—decía—"es el lugar privilegiado donde la comunión es anunciada y cultivada constantemente. Precisamente a través de la participación eucarística, el *día del Señor* se convierte también en el *día de la Iglesia,* que puede desempeñar así de manera eficaz su papel de sacramento de unidad"[88].

42. La salvaguardia y promoción de la comunión eclesial es una tarea de todos los fieles, que encuentran en la Eucaristía, como sacramento de la unidad de la Iglesia, un campo de especial aplicación. Más en concreto, este cometido atañe con particular responsabilidad a los Pastores de la Iglesia, cada uno en el propio grado y según el propio oficio eclesiástico. Por tanto, la Iglesia ha dado

normas que se orientan a favorecer la participación frecuente y fructuosa de los fieles en la Mesa eucarística y, al mismo tiempo, a determinar las condiciones objetivas en las que no debe administrar la comunión. El esmero en procurar una fiel observancia de dichas normas se convierte en expresión efectiva de amor hacia la Eucaristía y hacia la Iglesia.

43. Al considerar la Eucaristía como Sacramento de la comunión eclesial, hay un argumento que, por su importancia, no puede omitirse: me refiero a *su relación con el compromiso ecuménico.* Todos nosotros hemos de agradecer a la Santísima Trinidad que, en estas últimas décadas, muchos fieles en todas las partes del mundo se hayan sentido atraídos por el deseo ardiente de la unidad entre todos los cristianos. El Concilio Vaticano II, al comienzo del Decreto sobre el ecumenismo, reconoce en ello un don especial de Dios[89]. Ha sido una gracia eficaz, que ha hecho emprender el camino del ecumenismo tanto a los hijos de la Iglesia católica como a nuestros hermanos de las otras Iglesias y Comunidades eclesiales.

La aspiración a la meta de la unidad nos impulsa a dirigir la mirada a la Eucaristía, que es el supremo Sacramento de la unidad del Pueblo de Dios, al ser su expresión apropiada y su fuente insuperable[90]. En la celebración del Sacrificio eucarístico la Iglesia eleva su plegaria a Dios, Padre de misericordia, para que conceda a sus hijos la plenitud del Espíritu Santo, de modo que lleguen a ser en Cristo un sólo un cuerpo y un sólo espíritu[91]. Presentando esta súplica al Padre de la luz, de quien proviene "toda dádiva buena y todo don perfecto" (Santiago 1,17), la Iglesia cree en su eficacia, pues ora en unión con Cristo, su cabeza y esposo, que hace suya la súplica de la esposa uniéndola a la de su sacrificio redentor.

44. Precisamente porque la unidad de la Iglesia, que la Eucaristía realiza mediante el sacrificio y la comunión en el cuerpo y la sangre del Señor, exige inderogablemente la completa comunión en los vínculos de la profesión de fe, de los sacramentos y del gobierno eclesiástico, no es posible concelebrar la misma liturgia eucarística hasta que no se restablezca la integridad de dichos vínculos. Una concelebración sin estas condiciones no sería un medio válido, y podría revelarse más bien un *obstáculo a la consecución de la plena comunión,* encubriendo el sentido de la distancia que queda hasta llegar a la meta e introduciendo o respaldando ambigüedades sobre una u otra verdad de fe. El camino hacia la plena

unidad no puede hacerse si no es en la verdad. En este punto, la prohibición contenida en la ley de la Iglesia no deja espacio a incertidumbres[92], en obediencia a la norma moral proclamada por el Concilio Vaticano II[93].

De todos modos, quisiera reiterar lo que añadía en la Carta encíclica *Ut unum sint,* tras haber afirmado la imposibilidad de compartir la Eucaristía: "Sin embargo, tenemos el ardiente deseo de celebrar juntos la única Eucaristía del Señor, y este deseo es ya una alabanza común, una misma imploración. Juntos nos dirigimos al Padre y lo hacemos cada vez más "con un mismo corazón"[94].

45. Si en ningún caso es legítima la concelebración si falta la plena comunión, no ocurre lo mismo con respecto a la administración de la Eucaristía, *en circunstancias especiales, a personas* pertenecientes a Iglesias o a Comunidades eclesiales que no están en plena comunión con la Iglesia católica. En efecto, en este caso el objetivo es satisfacer una grave necesidad espiritual para la salvación eterna de los fieles, singularmente considerados, pero no realizar una *intercomunión,* que no es posible mientras no se hayan restablecido del todo los vínculos visibles de la comunión eclesial.

En este sentido se orientó el Concilio Vaticano II, fijando el comportamiento que se ha de tener con los Orientales que, encontrándose de buena fe separados de la Iglesia católica, están bien dispuestos y piden espontáneamente recibir la eucaristía del ministro católico[95]. Este modo de actuar ha sido ratificado después por ambos Códigos, en los que también se contempla, con las oportunas adaptaciones, el caso de los otros cristianos no orientales que no están en plena comunión con la Iglesia católica[96].

46. En la Encíclica *Ut unum sint,* yo mismo he manifestado aprecio por esta normativa, que permite atender a la salvación de las almas con el discernimiento oportuno: "Es motivo de alegría recordar que los ministros católicos pueden, en determinados casos particulares, administrar los sacramentos de la Eucaristía, de la Penitencia, de la Unción de enfermos a otros cristianos que no están en comunión plena con la Iglesia católica, pero que desean vivamente recibirlos, los piden libremente, y manifiestan la fe que la Iglesia católica confiesa en estos Sacramentos. Recíprocamente, en determinados casos y por circunstancias particulares, también los católicos pueden solicitar los mismos Sacramentos a los ministros de aquellas Iglesias en que sean válidos"[97].

Es necesario fijarse bien en estas condiciones, que son inderogables, aún tratándose de casos particulares y determinados, puesto que el rechazo de una o más verdades de fe sobre estos sacramentos y, entre ellas, lo referente a la necesidad del sacerdocio ministerial para que sean válidos, hace que el solicitante no esté debidamente dispuesto para que le sean legítimamente administrados. Y también a la inversa, un fiel católico no puede comulgar en una comunidad que carece del válido sacramento del Orden[98].

La fiel observancia del conjunto de las normas establecidas en esta materia[99] es manifestación y, al mismo tiempo, garantía de amor, sea a Jesucristo en el Santísimo Sacramento, sea a los hermanos de otra confesión cristiana, a los que se les debe el testimonio de la verdad, como también a la causa misma de la promoción de la unidad.

CAPÍTULO V
DECORO DE LA CELEBRACIÓN EUCARÍSTICA

47. Quien lee el relato de la institución eucarística en los Evangelios sinópticos queda impresionado por la sencillez y, al mismo tiempo, la "gravedad", con la cual Jesús, la tarde de la Última Cena, instituye el gran Sacramento. Hay un episodio que, en cierto sentido, hace de preludio: la *unción de Betania.* Una mujer, que Juan identifica con María, hermana de Lázaro, derrama sobre la cabeza de Jesús un frasco de *perfume precioso,* provocando en los discípulos—en particular en Judas (cf. Mateo 26,8; Marcos 14,4; Juan 12,4)—una reacción de protesta, como si este gesto fuera un "derroche" intolerable, considerando las exigencias de los pobres. Pero la valoración de Jesús es muy diferente. Sin quitar nada al deber de la caridad hacia los necesitados, a los que se han de dedicar siempre los discípulos—"pobres tendréis siempre con vosotros" (Mateo 26,11; Marcos 14,7; cf. Juan 12,8)—Él se fija en el acontecimiento inminente de su muerte y sepultura, y aprecia la unción que se le hace como anticipación del honor que su cuerpo merece también después de la muerte, por estar indisolublemente unido al misterio de su persona.

En los Evangelios sinópticos, el relato continúa con el encargo que Jesús da a los discípulos de *preparar cuidadosamente la "sala grande",* necesaria para celebrar la cena pascual (cf. Marcos 14,15; Lucas 22,12), y con la narración de la institución de la Eucaristía.

Dejando entrever, al menos en parte, el esquema de los *ritos hebreos* de la cena pascual hasta el canto del Hallel (cf. Mateo 26,30; Marcos 14,26), el relato, aún con las variantes de las diversas tradiciones, muestra de manera tan concisa como solemne las palabras pronunciadas por Cristo sobre el pan y sobre el vino, asumidos por Él como expresión concreta de su cuerpo entregado y su sangre derramada. Todos estos detalles son recordados por los evangelistas a la luz de una praxis de la "fracción del pan" bien consolidada ya en la Iglesia primitiva. Pero el acontecimiento del Jueves Santo, desde la historia misma que Jesús vivió, deja ver los rasgos de una "sensibilidad" litúrgica, articulada sobre la tradición veterotestamentaria y preparada para remodelarse en la celebración cristiana, en sintonía con el nuevo contenido de la Pascua.

48. Como la mujer de la unción en Betania, *la Iglesia no ha tenido miedo de "derrochar"*, dedicando sus mejores recursos para expresar su reverente asombro *ante el don inconmensurable de la Eucaristía.* No menos que aquellos primeros discípulos encargados de preparar la "sala grande", la Iglesia se ha sentido impulsada a lo largo de los siglos y en las diversas culturas a celebrar la Eucaristía en un contexto digno de tan gran Misterio. *La liturgia* cristiana ha nacido en continuidad con las palabras y gestos de Jesús y desarrollando la herencia ritual del judaísmo. Y, en efecto, nada será bastante para expresar de modo adecuado la acogida del don de sí mismo que el Esposo divino hace continuamente a la Iglesia Esposa, poniendo al alcance de todas las generaciones de creyentes el Sacrificio ofrecido una vez por todas sobre la Cruz, y haciéndose alimento para todos los fieles. Aunque la lógica del "convite" inspire familiaridad, la Iglesia no ha cedido nunca a la tentación de banalizar esta "cordialidad" con su Esposo, olvidando que Él es también su Dios y que el "banquete" sigue siendo siempre, después de todo, un banquete sacrificial, marcado por la sangre derramada en el Gólgota. *El banquete eucarístico es verdaderamente un banquete "sagrado"*, en el que la sencillez de los signos contiene el abismo de la santidad de Dios: *"O Sacrum convivium, in quo Christus sumitur!"*. El pan que se parte en nuestros altares, ofrecido a nuestra condición de peregrinos en camino por las sendas del mundo, es *"panis angelorum"*, pan de los ángeles, al cual no es posible acercarse si no es con la humildad del centurión del Evangelio: "Señor, no soy digno de que entres bajo mi techo" (Mateo 8,8; Lucas 7,6).

49. En el contexto de este elevado sentido del misterio, se entiende cómo la fe de la Iglesia en el Misterio eucarístico se haya expresado en la historia no sólo mediante la exigencia de una actitud interior de devoción, sino también *a través de una serie de expresiones externas,* orientadas a evocar y subrayar la magnitud del acontecimiento que se celebra. De aquí nace el proceso que ha llevado progresivamente a establecer *una especial reglamentación de la liturgia eucarística,* en el respeto de las diversas tradiciones eclesiales legítimamente constituidas. También sobre esta base se ha ido creando un rico patrimonio de arte. La arquitectura, la escultura, la pintura, la música, dejándose guiar por el misterio cristiano, han encontrado en la Eucaristía, directa o indirectamente, un motivo de gran inspiración.

Así ha ocurrido, por ejemplo, con la arquitectura, que, de las primeras sedes eucarísticas en las *"domus"* de las familias cristianas, ha dado paso, en cuanto el contexto histórico lo ha permitido, a las solemnes *basílicas* de los primeros siglos, a las imponentes *catedrales* de la Edad Media, hasta las *iglesias,* pequeñas o grandes, que han constelado poco a poco las tierras donde ha llegado el cristianismo. Las formas de los altares y tabernáculos se han desarrollado dentro de los espacios de las sedes litúrgicas siguiendo en cada caso, no sólo motivos de inspiración estética, sino también las exigencias de una apropiada comprensión del Misterio. Igualmente se puede decir de la *música sacra,* y basta pensar para ello en las inspiradas melodías gregorianas y en los numerosos, y a menudo insignes, autores que se han afirmado con los textos litúrgicos de la Santa Misa. Y, ¿acaso no se observa una enorme cantidad de *producciones artísticas,* desde el fruto de una buena artesanía hasta verdaderas obras de arte, en el sector de los objetos y ornamentos utilizados para la celebración eucarística?

Se puede decir así que la Eucaristía, a la vez que ha plasmado la Iglesia y la espiritualidad, ha tenido una fuerte incidencia en la "cultura", especialmente en el ámbito estético.

50. En este esfuerzo de adoración del Misterio, desde el punto de vista ritual y estético, los cristianos de Occidente y de Oriente, en cierto sentido, se han hecho mutuamente la "competencia". ¿Cómo no dar gracias al Señor, en particular, por la contribución que al arte cristiano han dado las grandes obras arquitectónicas y pictóricas de la tradición greco-bizantina y de todo el ámbito geográfico y cultural eslavo? En Oriente, el arte sagrado ha conservado un sentido especialmente intenso del misterio, impulsando

a los artistas a concebir su afán de producir belleza, no sólo como manifestación de su propio genio, sino también como *auténtico servicio a la fe.* Yendo mucho más allá de la mera habilidad técnica, han sabido abrirse con docilidad al soplo del Espíritu de Dios.

El esplendor de la arquitectura y de los mosaicos en el Oriente y Occidente cristianos son un patrimonio universal de los creyentes, y llevan en sí mismos una esperanza y una prenda, diría, de la deseada plenitud de comunión en la fe y en la celebración. Eso supone y exige, como en la célebre pintura de la Trinidad de Rublëv, *una Iglesia profundamente "eucarística"* en la cual, la acción de compartir el misterio de Cristo en el pan partido está como inmersa en la inefable unidad de las tres Personas divinas, haciendo de la Iglesia misma un "icono" de la Trinidad.

En esta perspectiva de un arte orientado a expresar en todos sus elementos el sentido de la Eucaristía según la enseñanza de la Iglesia, es preciso prestar suma atención a las normas que regulan *la construcción y decoración de los edificios sagrados.* La Iglesia ha dejado siempre a los artistas un amplio margen creativo, como demuestra la historia y yo mismo he subrayado en la *Carta a los artistas*[100]. Pero el arte sagrado ha de distinguirse por su capacidad de expresar adecuadamente el Misterio, tomado en la plenitud de la fe de la Iglesia y según las indicaciones pastorales oportunamente expresadas por la autoridad competente. Ésta es una consideración que vale tanto para las artes figurativas como para la música sacra.

51. A propósito del arte sagrado y la disciplina litúrgica, lo que se ha producido en tierras de antigua cristianización está ocurriendo también *en los continentes donde el cristianismo es más joven.* Este fenómeno ha sido objeto de atención por parte del Concilio Vaticano II al tratar sobre la exigencia de una sana y, al mismo tiempo, obligada "inculturación". En mis numerosos viajes pastorales he tenido oportunidad de observar en todas las partes del mundo cuánta vitalidad puede despertar la celebración eucarística en contacto con las formas, los estilos y las sensibilidades de las diversas culturas. Adaptándose a las mudables condiciones de tiempo y espacio, la Eucaristía ofrece alimento, no solamente a las personas, sino a los pueblos mismos, plasmando culturas cristianamente inspiradas.

No obstante, es necesario que este importante trabajo de adaptación se lleve a cabo siendo conscientes siempre del inefable

Misterio, con el cual cada generación está llamada confrontarse. El "tesoro" es demasiado grande y precioso como para arriesgarse a que se empobrezca o hipoteque por experimentos o prácticas llevadas a cabo sin una atenta comprobación por parte de las autoridades eclesiásticas competentes. Además, la centralidad del Misterio eucarístico es de una magnitud tal que requiere una verificación realizada en estrecha relación con la Santa Sede. Como escribí en la Exhortación apostólica postsinodal *Ecclesia in Asia,* "esa colaboración es esencial, porque la sagrada liturgia expresa y celebra la única fe profesada por todos y, dado que constituye la herencia de toda la Iglesia, no puede ser determinada por las Iglesias locales aisladas de la Iglesia universal"[101].

52. De todo lo dicho se comprende la gran responsabilidad que en la celebración eucarística tienen principalmente los sacerdotes, a quienes compete presidirla *in persona Christi,* dando un testimonio y un servicio de comunión, no sólo a la comunidad que participa directamente en la celebración, sino también a la Iglesia universal, a la cual la Eucaristía hace siempre referencia. Por desgracia, es de lamentar que, sobre todo a partir de los años de la reforma litúrgica postconciliar, por un malentendido sentido de creatividad y de adaptación, *no hayan faltado abusos,* que para muchos han sido causa de malestar. Una cierta reacción al "formalismo" ha llevado a algunos, especialmente en ciertas regiones, a considerar como no obligatorias las "formas" adoptadas por la gran tradición litúrgica de la Iglesia y su Magisterio, y a introducir innovaciones no autorizadas y con frecuencia del todo inconvenientes.

Por tanto, siento el deber de hacer una acuciante llamada de atención para que se observen con gran fidelidad las normas litúrgicas en la celebración eucarística. Son una expresión concreta de la auténtica eclesialidad de la Eucaristía; éste es su sentido más profundo. La liturgia nunca es propiedad privada de alguien, ni del celebrante ni de la comunidad en que se celebran los Misterios. El apóstol Pablo tuvo que dirigir duras palabras a la comunidad de Corinto a causa de faltas graves en su celebración eucarística, que llevaron a divisiones (*skísmata*) y a la formación de facciones (*airéseis*) (cf. 1 Corintios 11,17–34). También en nuestros tiempos, la obediencia a las normas litúrgicas debería ser redescubierta y valorada como reflejo y testimonio de la Iglesia una y universal, que se hace presente en cada celebración de la Eucaristía. El sacerdote que celebra fielmente la Misa según las normas litúrgicas y la comunidad que se adecua a ellas, demuestran de manera silenciosa pero elocuente su amor por la Iglesia. Precisamente para reforzar este sentido profundo de las normas litúrgicas, he solicitado a los Dicasterios competentes de la Curia Romana que preparen un documento más específico, incluso con rasgos de carácter jurídico, sobre este tema de gran importancia. A nadie le está permitido infravalorar el Misterio confiado a nuestras manos: éste es demasiado grande para que alguien pueda permitirse tratarlo a su arbitrio personal, lo que no respetaría ni su carácter sagrado ni su dimensión universal.

CAPÍTULO VI
EN LA ESCUELA DE MARÍA, MUJER "EUCARÍSTICA"

53. Si queremos descubrir en toda su riqueza la relación íntima que une Iglesia y Eucaristía, no podemos olvidar a María, Madre y modelo de la Iglesia. En la Carta apostólica *Rosarium Virginis Mariae,* presentando a la Santísima Virgen como Maestra en la contemplación del rostro de Cristo, he incluido entre los misterios de la luz también la *institución de la Eucaristía*[102]. Efectivamente, María puede guiarnos hacia este Santísimo Sacramento porque tiene una relación profunda con él.

A primera vista, el Evangelio no habla de este tema. En el relato de la institución, la tarde del Jueves Santo, no se menciona a María. Se sabe, sin embargo, que estaba junto con los Apóstoles, "concordes en la oración" (cf. Hechos 1,14), *en la primera comunidad reunida después de la Ascensión en espera de Pentecostés.* Esta presencia suya no pudo faltar ciertamente en las celebraciones eucarísticas de los fieles de la primera generación cristiana, asiduos "en la fracción del pan" (Hechos 2,42).

Pero, más allá de su participación en el Banquete eucarístico, la relación de María con la Eucaristía se puede delinear indirectamente a partir de su actitud interior. *María es mujer "eucarística" con toda su vida.* La Iglesia, tomando a María como modelo, ha de imitarla también en su relación con este santísimo Misterio.

54. *Mysterium fidei!* Puesto que la Eucaristía es misterio de fe, que supera de tal manera nuestro entendimiento que nos obliga al más puro abandono a la palabra de Dios, nadie como María puede ser apoyo y guía en una actitud como ésta. Repetir el gesto

de Cristo en la Última Cena, en cumplimiento de su mandato: "¡Haced esto en conmemoración mía!", se convierte al mismo tiempo en aceptación de la invitación de María a obedecerle sin titubeos: "Haced lo que él os diga" (Juan 2,5). Con la solicitud materna que muestra en las bodas de Caná, María parece decirnos: "no dudéis, fiaros de la Palabra de mi Hijo. Él, que fue capaz de transformar el agua en vino, es igualmente capaz de hacer del pan y del vino su cuerpo y su sangre, entregando a los creyentes en este misterio la memoria viva de su Pascua, para hacerse así 'pan de vida'".

55. En cierto sentido, María ha practicado su *fe eucarística* antes incluso de que ésta fuera instituida, por el hecho mismo de *haber ofrecido su seno virginal para la encarnación del Verbo de Dios.* La Eucaristía, mientras remite a la pasión y la resurrección, está al mismo tiempo en continuidad con la Encarnación. María concibió en la anunciación al Hijo divino, incluso en la realidad física de su cuerpo y su sangre, anticipando en sí lo que en cierta medida se realiza sacramentalmente en todo creyente que recibe, en las especies del pan y del vino, el cuerpo y la sangre del Señor.

Hay, pues, una *analogía profunda* entre el *fiat* pronunciado por María a las palabras del Ángel y el *amén* que cada fiel pronuncia cuando recibe el cuerpo del Señor. A María se le pidió creer que quien concibió "por obra del Espíritu Santo" era el "Hijo de Dios" (cf. Lucas 1,30.35). En continuidad con la fe de la Virgen, en el Misterio eucarístico se nos pide creer que el mismo Jesús, Hijo de Dios e Hijo de María, se hace presente con todo su ser humano-divino en las especies del pan y del vino.

"Feliz la que ha creído" (Lucas 1,45): María ha anticipado también en el misterio de la Encarnación la fe eucarística de la Iglesia. Cuando, en la Visitación, lleva en su seno el Verbo hecho carne, se convierte de algún modo en "tabernáculo"—el primer "tabernáculo" de la historia—donde el Hijo de Dios, todavía invisible a los ojos de los hombres, se ofrece a la adoración de Isabel, como "irradiando" su luz a través de los ojos y la voz de María. Y la mirada embelesada de María al contemplar el rostro de Cristo recién nacido y al estrecharlo en sus brazos, ¿no es acaso el inigualable modelo de amor en el que ha de inspirarse cada comunión eucarística?

56. María, con toda su vida junto a Cristo y no solamente en el Calvario, hizo suya la *dimensión sacrificial de la Eucaristía.*

Cuando llevó al niño Jesús al templo de Jerusalén "para presentarle al Señor" (Lucas 2,22), oyó anunciar al anciano Simeón que aquel niño sería "señal de contradicción" y también que una "espada" traspasaría su propia alma (cf. Lucas 2,34.35). Se preanunciaba así el drama del Hijo crucificado y, en cierto modo, se prefiguraba el "stabat Mater" de la Virgen al pie de la Cruz. Preparándose día a día para el Calvario, María vive una especie de "Eucaristía anticipada" se podría decir, una "comunión espiritual" de deseo y ofrecimiento, que culminará en la unión con el Hijo en la pasión y se manifestará después, en el período postpascual, en su participación en la celebración eucarística, presidida por los Apóstoles, como "memorial" de la pasión.

¿Cómo imaginar los sentimientos de María al escuchar de la boca de Pedro, Juan, Santiago y los otros Apóstoles, las palabras de la Última Cena: "Éste es mi cuerpo que es entregado por vosotros" (Lucas 22,19)? Aquel cuerpo entregado como sacrificio y presente en los signos sacramentales, ¡era el mismo cuerpo concebido en su seno! Recibir la Eucaristía debía significar para María como si acogiera de nuevo en su seno el corazón que había latido al unísono con el suyo y revivir lo que había experimentado en primera persona al pie de la Cruz.

57. "Haced esto en recuerdo mío" (Lucas 22,19). En el "memorial" del Calvario está presente todo lo que Cristo ha llevado a cabo en su pasión y muerte. Por tanto, no falta *lo que Cristo ha realizado también con su Madre* para beneficio nuestro. En efecto, le confía al discípulo predilecto y, en él, le entrega a cada uno de nosotros: "¡He aquí a tu hijo!". Igualmente dice también a todos nosotros: "¡He aquí a tu madre!" (cf. Juan 19,26.27).

Vivir en la Eucaristía el memorial de la muerte de Cristo implica también recibir continuamente este don. Significa tomar con nosotros—a ejemplo de Juan—a quien una vez nos fue entregada como Madre. Significa asumir, al mismo tiempo, el compromiso de conformarnos a Cristo, aprendiendo de su Madre y dejándonos acompañar por ella. María está presente con la Iglesia, y como Madre de la Iglesia, en todas nuestras celebraciones eucarísticas. Así como Iglesia y Eucaristía son un binomio inseparable, lo mismo se puede decir del binomio María y Eucaristía. Por eso, el recuerdo de María en el celebración eucarística es unánime, ya desde la antigüedad, en las Iglesias de Oriente y Occidente.

58. En la Eucaristía, la Iglesia se une plenamente a Cristo y a su sacrificio, haciendo suyo el espíritu de María. Es una verdad que se puede profundizar releyendo el *Magnificat en perspectiva eucarística.* La Eucaristía, en efecto, como el canto de María, es ante todo alabanza y acción de gracias. Cuando María exclama "mi alma engrandece al Señor, mi espíritu exulta en Dios, mi Salvador", lleva a Jesús en su seno. Alaba al Padre "por" Jesús, pero también lo alaba "en" Jesús y "con" Jesús. Esto es precisamente la verdadera "actitud eucarística".

Al mismo tiempo, María rememora las maravillas que Dios ha hecho en la historia de la salvación, según la promesa hecha a nuestros padres (cf. Lucas 1,55), anunciando la que supera a todas ellas, la encarnación redentora. En el *Magnificat,* en fin, está presente la tensión escatológica de la Eucaristía. Cada vez que el Hijo de Dios se presenta bajo la "pobreza" de las especies sacramentales, pan y vino, se pone en el mundo el germen de la nueva historia, en la que se "derriba del trono a los poderosos" y se "enaltece a los humildes" (cf. Lucas 1,52). María canta el "cielo Nuevo" y la "tierra nueva" que se anticipan en la Eucaristía y, en cierto sentido, deja entrever su 'diseño' programático. Puesto que el *Magnificat* expresa la espiritualidad de María, nada nos ayuda a vivir mejor el Misterio eucarístico que esta espiritualidad. ¡La Eucaristía se nos ha dado para que nuestra vida sea, como la de María, toda ella un *magnificat*!

CONCLUSIÓN

59. *"Ave, verum corpus natum de Maria Virgine!".* Hace pocos años he celebrado el cincuentenario de mi sacerdocio. Hoy experimento la gracia de ofrecer a la Iglesia esta Encíclica sobre la Eucaristía, en el Jueves Santo de *mi vigésimo quinto año de ministerio petrino.* Lo hago con el corazón henchido de gratitud. Desde hace más de medio siglo, cada día, a partir de aquel 2 de noviembre de 1946 en que celebré mi primera Misa en la cripta de San Leonardo de la catedral del Wawel en Cracovia, mis ojos se han fijado en la hostia y el cáliz en los que, en cierto modo, el tiempo y el espacio se han "concentrado" y se ha representado de manera viviente el drama del Gólgota, desvelando su misteriosa "contemporaneidad". Cada día, mi fe ha podido reconocer en el pan y en el vino consagrados al divino Caminante que un día se puso al lado de los dos discípulos de Emaús para abrirles los ojos a la luz y el corazón a la esperanza (cf. Lucas 24,3.35).

Dejadme, mis queridos hermanos y hermanas que, con íntima emoción, en vuestra compañía y para confortar vuestra fe, os dé testimonio de fe en la Santísima Eucaristía. *"Ave, verum corpus natum de Maria Virgine, / vere passum, immolatum, in cruce pro homine!"*. Aquí está el tesoro de la Iglesia, el corazón del mundo, la prenda del fin al que todo hombre, aunque sea inconscientemente, aspira. Misterio grande, que ciertamente nos supera y pone a dura prueba la capacidad de nuestra mente de ir más allá de las apariencias. Aquí fallan nuestros sentidos— *"visus, tactus, gustus in te fallitur"*, se dice en el himno *Adoro te devote*—pero nos basta sólo la fe, enraizada en las palabras de Cristo y que los Apóstoles nos han transmitido. Dejadme que, como Pedro al final del discurso eucarístico en el Evangelio de Juan, yo le repita a Cristo, en nombre de toda la Iglesia y en nombre de todos vosotros: "Señor, ¿donde quién vamos a ir? Tú tienes palabras de vida eternal" (Juan 6,68).

60. En el alba de este tercer milenio todos nosotros, hijos de la Iglesia, estamos llamados a caminar en la vida cristiana con un renovado impulso. Como he escrito en la Carta apostólica *Novo millennio ineunte,* no se trata de "inventar un nuevo programa. El programa ya existe. Es el de siempre, recogido por el Evangelio y la Tradición viva. Se centra, en definitiva, en Cristo mismo, al que hay que conocer, amar e imitar, para vivir en él la vida trinitaria y transformar con él la historia hasta su perfeccionamiento en la Jerusalén celeste"[103]. La realización de este programa de un nuevo vigor de la vida cristiana pasa por la Eucaristía.

Todo compromiso de santidad, toda acción orientada a realizar la misión de la Iglesia, toda puesta en práctica de planes pastorales, ha de sacar del Misterio eucarístico la fuerza necesaria y se ha de ordenar a él como a su culmen. En la Eucaristía tenemos a Jesús, tenemos su sacrificio redentor, tenemos su resurrección, tenemos el don del Espíritu Santo, tenemos la adoración, la obediencia y el amor al Padre. Si descuidáramos la Eucaristía, ¿cómo podríamos remediar nuestra indigencia?

61. El Misterio eucarístico—sacrificio, presencia, banquete—*no consiente reducciones ni instrumentalizaciones;* debe ser vivido en su integridad, sea durante la celebración, sea en el íntimo coloquio con Jesús apenas recibido en la comunión, sea durante la adoración eucarística fuera de la Misa. Entonces es cuando se construye firmemente la Iglesia y se expresa realmente lo que es:

una, santa, católica y apostólica; pueblo, templo y familia de Dios; cuerpo y esposa de Cristo, animada por el Espíritu Santo; sacramento universal de salvación y comunión jerárquicamente estructurada.

La vía que la Iglesia recorre en estos primeros años del tercer milenio es también la de *un renovado compromiso ecuménico.* Los últimos decenios del segundo milenio, culminados en el Gran Jubileo, nos han llevado en esa dirección, llamando a todos los bautizados a corresponder a la oración de Jesús *"ut unum sint"* (Juan 17,11). Es un camino largo, plagado de obstáculos que superan la capacidad humana; pero tenemos la Eucaristía y, ante ella, podemos sentir en lo profundo del corazón, como dirigidas a nosotros, las mismas palabras que oyó el profeta Elías: "Levántate y come, porque el camino es demasiado largo para ti" (1 Reyes 19,7). El tesoro eucarístico que el Señor ha puesto a nuestra disposición nos alienta hacia la meta de compartirlo plenamente con todos los hermanos con quienes nos une el mismo Bautismo. Sin embargo, para no desperdiciar dicho tesoro se han de respetar las exigencias que se derivan de ser Sacramento de comunión en la fe y en la sucesión apostólica.

Al dar a la Eucaristía todo el relieve que merece, y poniendo todo esmero en no infravalorar ninguna de sus dimensiones o exigencias, somos realmente conscientes de la magnitud de este don. A ello nos invita una tradición incesante que, desde los primeros siglos, ha sido testigo de una comunidad cristiana celosa en custodiar este "tesoro." Impulsada por el amor, la Iglesia se preocupa de transmitir a las siguientes generaciones cristianas, sin perder ni un solo detalle, la fe y la doctrina sobre el Misterio eucarístico. No hay peligro de exagerar en la consideración de este Misterio, porque "en este Sacramento se resume todo el misterio de nuestra salvación"[104].

62. Sigamos, queridos hermanos y hermanas, *la enseñanza de los Santos,* grandes intérpretes de la verdadera piedad eucarística. Con ellos la teología de la Eucaristía adquiere todo el esplendor de la experiencia vivida, nos "contagia" y, por así decir, nos "enciende". Pongámonos, sobre todo, *a la escucha de María Santísima,* en quien el Misterio eucarístico se muestra, más que en ningún otro, como *misterio de luz.* Mirándola a ella conocemos la *fuerza trasformadora que tiene la Eucaristía.* En ella vemos el mundo renovado por el amor. Al contemplarla asunta al cielo en

alma y cuerpo vemos un resquicio del "cielo nuevo" y de la "tierra nueva" que se abrirán ante nuestros ojos con la segunda venida de Cristo. La Eucaristía es ya aquí, en la tierra, su prenda y, en cierto modo, su anticipación: "*Veni, Domine Iesu!*" (Apocalipsis 22,20).

En el humilde signo del pan y el vino, transformados en su cuerpo y en su sangre, Cristo camina con nosotros como nuestra fuerza y nuestro viático y nos convierte en testigos de esperanza para todos. Si ante este Misterio la razón experimenta sus propios límites, el corazón, iluminado por la gracia del Espíritu Santo, intuye bien cómo ha de comportarse, sumiéndose en la adoración y en un amor sin límites.

Hagamos nuestros los sentimientos de santo Tomás de Aquino, teólogo eximio y, al mismo tiempo, cantor apasionado de Cristo eucarístico, y dejemos que nuestro ánimo se abra también en esperanza a la contemplación de la meta, a la cual aspira el corazón, sediento como está de alegría y de paz:

Bone pastor, panis vere,
Iesu, nostri miserere . . .

Buen pastor, pan verdadero,
o Jesús, piedad de nosotros:
nútrenos y defiéndenos,
llévanos a los bienes eternos
en la tierra de los vivos.

Tú que todo lo sabes y puedes,
que nos alimentas en la tierra,
conduce a tus hermanos
a la mesa del cielo
a la alegría de tus santos.

Roma, junto a San Pedro, 17 de abril, Jueves Santo, del año 2003, vigésimo quinto de mi Pontificado y Año del Rosario.

Ioannes Paulus II

CITAS

1. Const. dogm. *Lumen gentium,* sobre la Iglesia, 11.
2. Conc. Ecum. Vat. II, Decr. *Presbyterorum Ordinis,* sobre el ministerio y vida de los presbíteros, 5.
3. Cf. Carta ap. *Rosarium Virginis Mariae* (16 octubre 2002), 21: AAS 95 (2003), 19.
4. Éste es el título que he querido dar a un testimonio autobiográfico con ocasión del quincuagésimo aniversario de mi sacerdocio.
5. *Leonis XXIII Acta* (1903), 115–136.
6. AAS 39 (1947), 521–595.
7. AAS 57 (1965), 753–774.
8. AAS 72 (1980), 113–148.
9. Cf. Conc. Ecum. Vat. II, Const. *Sacrosanctum Concilium,* sobre la sagrada liturgia, 47: "*Salvator noster* [. . .] *Sacrificium Eucharisticum Corporis et Sanguinis sui instituit, quo Sacrificium Crucis in saecula, donec veniret, perpetuaret*".
10. *Catecismo de la Iglesia Católica,* 1085.
11. Conc. Ecum. Vat. II, Const. dogm. *Lumen gentium,* sobre la Iglesia, 3.
12. Cf. Pablo VI, *El "credo" del Pueblo de Dios* (30 junio 1968), 24: AAS 60 (1968), 442; Juan Pablo II, Carta ap. *Dominicae Cenae* (24 febrero 1980), 9: AAS 72 (1980).
13. *Catecismo de la Iglesia Católica,* 1382.
14. *Catecismo de la Iglesia Católica,* 1367.
15. *Homilías sobre la carta a los Hebreos,* 17, 3: PG 63, 131.
16. Cf. Conc. Ecum. Tridentino, Ses. XXII, *Doctrina de ss. Missae sacrificio,* cap. 2: DS 1743: "En efecto, se trata de una sola e idéntica víctima y el mismo Jesús la ofrece ahora por el ministerio de los sacerdotes, Él que un día se ofreció a sí mismo en la cruz: sólo es diverso el modo de ofrecerse".
17. Cf. Pío XII, Carta enc. *Mediator Dei* (20 noviembre 1947): AAS 39 (1947), 548.
18. Carta enc. *Redemptor hominis* (15 marzo 1979), 20: AAS 71 (1979), 310.
19. Const. dogm. *Lumen gentium,* sobre la Iglesia, 11.
20. *De sacramentis,* V, 4, 26: CSEL 73, 70.
21. *Sobre el Evangelio de Juan,* XII, 20: PG 74, 726.
22. Carta. enc. *Mysterium fidei* (3 septiembre 1965): AAS 57 (1965), 764.
23. Ses. XIII, *Decr. de ss. Eucharistia,* cap. 4: DS 1642.
24. *Catequesis mistagógicas,* IV, 6: SCh 126, 138.
25. Cf.Conc. Ecum. Vat. II, Const. dogm. *Dei Verbum,* sobre la divina revelación, 8.
26. El "credo" del Pueblo de Dios (30 junio 1968), 25: AAS 60 (1968), 442–443.

27. *Homilía IV para la Semana Santa:* CSCO 413 / Syr. 182, 55.

28. *Anáfora.*

29. *Plegaria Eucarística III.*

30. Solemnidad del Santísimo Cuerpo y Sangre de Cristo, antífona al *Magnificat* de las II Vísperas.

31. *Misal Romano,* Embolismo después del Padre nuestro.

32. *Carta a los Efesios,* 20: PG 5, 661.

33. Cf. Conc. Ecum. Vat. II, Const. past. *Gaudium et spes,* sobre la Iglesia en el mundo actual, 39.

34. "¿Deseas honrar el cuerpo de Cristo? No lo desprecies, pues, cuando lo encuentres desnudo en los pobres, ni lo honres aquí en el templo con lienzos de seda, si al salir lo abandonas en su frío y desnudez. Porque el mismo que dijo: "esto es mi cuerpo", y con su palabra llevó a realidad lo que decía, afirmó también: "Tuve hambre y no me disteis de comer", y más adelante: "Siempre que dejasteis de hacerlo a uno de estos pequeñuelos, a mí en persona lo dejasteis de hacer" [. . .]. ¿De qué serviría adornar la mesa de Cristo con vasos de oro, si el mismo Cristo muere de hambre? Da primero de comer al hambriento, y luego, con lo que te sobre, adornarás la mesa de Cristo": San Juan Crisóstomo, *Homilías sobre el Evangelio de Mateo,* 50, 3–4: PG 58, 508–509; cf. Juan Pablo II, Carta enc. *Sollicitudo rei socialis* (30 diciembre 1987): AAS 80 (1988), 553–556.

35. Const. dogm. *Lumen gentium,* sobre la Iglesia, 3.

36. Ibíd.

37. Conc. Ecum. Vat. II, Decr. *Ad gentes,* sobre la actividad misionera de la Iglesia, 5.

38. "Entonces tomó Moisés la sangre, roció con ella al pueblo y dijo: "Ésta es la sangre de la Alianza que Yahveh ha hecho con vosotros, según todas estas palabras" (Éxodo 24,8).

39. Cf. Conc. Ecum. Vat. II, Const. dogm. *Lumen gentium,* sobre la Iglesia, 1.

40. Cf. ibíd., n. 9.

41. Cf. Conc. Ecum. Vat. II, Decr. *Presbyterorum Ordinis,* sobre el ministerio y vida de los presbíteros, 5. El mismo Decreto dice en el n. 6: "No se construye ninguna comunidad cristiana si ésta no tiene su raíz y centro en la celebración de la sagrada Eucaristía".

42. Homilías sobre la 1 Carta a los Corintios, 24,2: PG 61, 200; cf. *Didaché,* IX, 5: F.X. Funk, I, 22; San Cipriano, *Ep.* LXIII, 13: PL 4, 384.

43. PO 26, 206.

44. Conc. Ecum. Vat. II, Const. dogm. *Lumen gentium,* sobre la Iglesia, 1.

45. Cf. Conc. Ecum. Tridentino, Ses. XIII, *Decretum de ss. Eucharistia,* can. 4: DS 1654.

46. Cf. *Rituale Romanum: De sacra communione et de cultu mysterii eucharistici extra Missam,* 36 (n. 80).

47. Cf. ibíd., 38-39 (nn. 86–90).

48. Carta ap. *Novo millennio ineunte* (6 enero 2001), 32: AAS 93 (2001), 288.

49. "Durante el día, los fieles no omitan el hacer la visita al Santísimo Sacramento, que debe estar reservado en un sitio dignísimo con el máximo honor en las iglesias, conforme a las leyes litúrgicas, puesto que la visita es prueba de gratitud, signo de amor y deber

de adoración a Cristo Nuestro Señor, allí presente": Pablo VI, Carta enc. *Mysterium fidei* (3 septiembre 1965): AAS 57 (1965), 771.

50. *Visite al SS. Sacramento ed a Maria Santissima*, Introduzione: *Opere ascetiche*, IV, Avelino 2000, 295.

51. N. 857.

52. Ibíd.

53. Ibíd.

54. Cf. Congregación para la Doctrina de la Fe, Carta *Sacerdotium ministeriale* (6 agosto 1983), III.2: AAS 75 (1983), 1005.

55. Conc. Ecum. Vat. II, Const. dogm. *Lumen gentium*, sobre la Iglesia, 10.

56. Ibíd.

57. Cf. *Institutio generalis:* Editio typica tertia, n. 147.

58. Cf. Const. dogm. *Lumen gentium*, sobre la Iglesia, 10 y 28; Decr. *Presbyterorum Ordinis*, sobre el ministerio y vida de los presbíteros, 2.

59. "El ministro del altar actúa en la persona de Cristo en cuanto cabeza, que ofrece en nombre de todos los miembros": Pío XII, Carta enc. *Mediator Dei* 20 noviembre 1947: AAS 39 (1947), 556; cf. Pío X, Exhort. ap. *Haerent animo* (4 agosto 1908): *Pii X Acta*, IV, 16; Carta enc. *Ad catholici sacerdotii* (20 diciembre 1935): AAS 28 (1936), 20.

60. Carta ap. *Dominicae Cenae*, 24 febrero 1980, 8: AAS 72 (1980), 128–129.

61. Congregación para la Doctrina de la Fe, Carta *Sacerdotium ministeriale* (6 agosto 1983), III. 4: AAS 75 (1983), 1006; cf. Conc. Ecum. Lateranense IV, cap. 1. Const. sobre la fe católica *Firmiter credimus:* DS 802.

62. Conc. Ecum. Vat. II, Decr. *Unitatis redintegratio*, sobre el ecumenismo, 22.

63. Carta ap. *Dominicae Cenae* (24 febrero 1980), 2: AAS 72 (1980), 115.

64. Decr. *Presbyterorum Ordinis*, sobre el ministerio y vida de los presbíteros 14.

65. Ibíd., 13; cf. *Código de Derecho Canónico*, can. 904; *Código de los Cánones de las Iglesias Orientales*, can. 378.

66. Decr. *Presbyterorum Ordinis*, sobre el ministerio y vida de los presbíteros, 6.

67. Cf. Relación final, II. C.1: *L'Osservatore Romano* (10 diciembre 1985), 7.

68. Conc. Ecum. Vat. II, Const. dogm. *Lumen gentium*, sobre la Iglesia, 26.

69. Nicolás Cabasilas, *La vida en Cristo*, IV, 10: Sch 355, 270.

70. *Camino de perfección*, c. 35, 1.

71. Cf. Congregación para la Doctrina de la Fe, Carta *Communionis notio* (28 mayo 1992), 4: AAS 85 (1993), 839–840.

72. Cf. Conc. Ecum. Vat. II, Const. dogm. *Lumen gentium*, sobre la Iglesia, 14.

73. *Homilías sobre Isaías* 6, 3 PG: 56, 139.

74. N. 1385; cf. *Código de Derecho Canónico*, can. 916; *Código de los Cánones de las Iglesias Orientales*, can. 711.

75. Discurso a la Sacra Penitenciaría Apostólica y a los penitenciarios de las Basílicas Patriarcales romanas (30 enero 1981): AAS 73 (1981), 203. Cf. Conc. Ecum. Tridentino, Ses. XIII, *Decretum de*

ss. *Eucharistia,* cap. 7 et can. 11: DS 1647, 1661.

76. Can.915; cf. *Código de los Cánones de las Iglesias Orientales,* can. 712.

77. Conc. Ecum. Vat. II, Const. dogm. *Lumen gentium,* sobre la Iglesia, 14.

78. Santo Tomás de Aquino, *Summa theologiae,* III, q. 73, a. 3c.

79. Congregación para la Doctrina de la Fe, Carta *Communionis notio* (28 mayo 1992), 11: AAS 85 (1993), 844.

80. Cf. Conc. Ecum. Vat. II, Const. dogm. *Lumen gentium,* sobre la Iglesia, 23.

81. *Carta a los Esmirniotas,* 8: PG 5, 713.

82. Conc. Ecum. Vat. II, Const. dogm. *Lumen gentium,* sobre la Iglesia, 23.

83. Congregación para la Doctrina de la Fe, Carta *Communionis notio* (28 mayo 1992), 14: AAS 85 (1993), 847.

84. Sermón 272: PL 38, 1247.

85. Ibíd., 1248.

86. Cf. nn. 31-51: AAS 90 (1998), 731–746.

87. Cf. ibíd., nn. 48-49: AAS 90 (1998), 744.

88. N. 36: AAS 93 (2001), 291–292.

89. Cf. Decr. *Unitatis redintegratio,* sobre el ecumenismo, 1.

90. Cf. Conc. Ecum. Vat. II, Const. dogm. *Lumen gentium,* sobre la Iglesia, 11.

91. "Haz que nosotros, que participamos al único pan y al único cáliz, estemos unidos con los otros en la comunión del único Espíritu Santo": *Anáfora de la Liturgia de san Basilio.*

92. Cf. *Código de Derecho Canónico,* can. 908; *Código de los Cánones de las Iglesias Orientales,* can. 702; Consejo Pontificio para la Promoción de la Unidad de los Cristianos, *Directorio para el ecumenismo* (25 marzo 1993), 122–125, 129–131: AAS 85 (1993), 1086-1089; Congregación para la Doctrina de la Fe, Carta *Ad exsequendam* (18 mayo 2001): AAS 93 (2001), 786.

93. "La comunicación en las cosas sagradas que daña a la unidad de la Iglesia o lleva consigo adhesión formal al error o peligro de desviación en la fe, de escándalo o indiferentismo, está prohibido por la ley divina": Decr. *Orientalium Ecclesiarum,* sobre las Iglesias orientales católicas, 26.

94. N. 45: AAS 87 (1995), 948.

95. Cf. Decr. *Orientalium Ecclesiarum,* sobre las Iglesias orientales católicas, 27.

96. Cf. *Código de Derecho Canónico,* can. 844 §§ 3–4; *Código de los Cánones de las Iglesias Orientales,* can. 671 §§ 3–4.

97. N. 46: AAS 87 (1995), 948.

98. Cf.Conc. Ecum. Vat. II, *Unitatis redintegratio, sobre el ecumenismo,* 22.

99. Cf. *Código de Derecho Canónico,* can. 844; *Código de los Cánones de las Iglesias Orientales,* can. 671.

100. Cf. AAS 91 (1999), 1155–1172.

101. N. 22: AAS 92 (2000), 485.

102. Cf. n. 21: AAS 95 (2003), 20.

103. N. 29: AAS 93 (2001), 285.

104. Santo Tomás de Aquino, *Summa theologiae,* III, q. 83, a.4 c.

INSTRUCTION
REDEMPTIONIS SACRAMENTUM

ON CERTAIN MATTERS TO BE OBSERVED OR TO BE AVOIDED REGARDING THE MOST HOLY EUCHARIST

OUTLINE

PREAMBLE

1. In the Most Holy Eucharist, Mother Church with steadfast faith acknowledges the *Sacrament of redemption,*[1] joyfully takes it to herself, celebrates it and reveres it in adoration, proclaiming the death of Christ Jesus and confessing his Resurrection until he comes in glory[2] to hand over, as unconquered Lord and Ruler, eternal Priest and King of the Universe, a kingdom of truth and life to the immense majesty of the Almighty Father.[3]

2. The Church's doctrine regarding the Most Holy Eucharist, in which the whole spiritual wealth of the Church is contained—namely Christ, our Paschal Lamb[4]—the Eucharist which is the source and summit of the whole of Christian life,[5] and which lies as a causative force behind the very origins of the Church,[6] has been expounded with thoughtful care and with great authority over the course of the centuries in the writings of the Councils and the Supreme Pontiffs. Most recently, in fact, the Supreme Pontiff John Paul II, in the Encyclical Letter *Ecclesia de Eucharistia,* set forth afresh certain elements of great importance on this subject in view of the ecclesial circumstances of our times.[7]

In order that especially in the celebration of the Sacred Liturgy the Church might duly safeguard so great a mystery in our own time as well, the Supreme Pontiff has mandated that this Congregation for Divine Worship and the Discipline of the Sacraments,[8] in collaboration with the Congregation for the Doctrine of the Faith, should prepare this Instruction treating of certain matters pertaining to the discipline of the Sacrament of the Eucharist. Those things found in this Instruction are therefore to be read in the continuity with the above-mentioned Encyclical Letter, *Ecclesia de Eucharistia.*

It is not at all the intention here to prepare a compendium of the norms regarding the Most Holy Eucharist, but rather, to take up within this Instruction some elements of liturgical norms that have been previously expounded or laid down and even today remain in force in order to assure a deeper appreciation of the liturgical norms;[9] to establish certain norms by which those earlier ones are explained and complemented; and also to set forth for Bishops, as well as for Priests, Deacons and all the lay Christian faithful, how each should carry them out in accordance with his own responsibilities and the means at his disposal.

3. The norms contained in the present Instruction are to be understood as pertaining to liturgical matters in the Roman Rite, and, *mutatis mutandis,* in the other Rites of the Latin Church that are duly acknowledged by law.

4. "Certainly the liturgical reform inaugurated by the Council has greatly contributed to a more conscious, active and fruitful participation in the Holy Sacrifice of the Altar on the part of the faithful."[10] Even so, "shadows are not lacking."[11] In this regard it is not possible to be silent about the abuses, even quite grave ones, against the nature of the Liturgy and the Sacraments as well as the tradition and the authority of the Church, which in our day not infrequently plague liturgical celebrations in one ecclesial environment or another. In some places the perpetration of liturgical abuses has become almost habitual, a fact which obviously cannot be allowed and must cease.

5. The observance of the norms published by the authority of the Church requires conformity of thought and of word, of external action and of the application of the heart. A merely external observation of norms would obviously be contrary to the nature of the Sacred Liturgy, in which Christ himself wishes to gather his Church, so that together with himself she will be "one body and one spirit."[12] For this reason, external action must be illuminated by faith and charity, which unite us with Christ and with one another and engender love for the poor and the abandoned. The liturgical words and rites, moreover, are a faithful expression, matured over the centuries, of the understanding of Christ, and they teach us to think as he himself does;[13] by conforming our minds to these words, we raise our hearts to the Lord. All that is said in this Instruction is directed toward such a conformity of

our own understanding with that of Christ, as expressed in the words and the rites of the Liturgy.

6. For abuses "contribute to the obscuring of the Catholic faith and doctrine concerning this wonderful sacrament."[14] Thus, they also hinder the faithful from "re-living in a certain way the experience of the two disciples of Emmaus: 'and their eyes were opened, and they recognized him.'"[15] For in the presence of God's power and divinity[16] and the splendour of his goodness, made manifest especially in the Sacrament of the Eucharist, it is fitting that all the faithful should have and put into practice that power of acknowledging God's majesty that they have received through the saving Passion of the Only-Begotten Son.[17]

7. Not infrequently, abuses are rooted in a false understanding of liberty. Yet God has not granted us in Christ an illusory liberty by which we may do what we wish, but a liberty by which we may do that which is fitting and right.[18] This is true not only of precepts coming directly from God, but also of laws promulgated by the Church, with appropriate regard for the nature of each norm. For this reason, all should conform to the ordinances set forth by legitimate ecclesiastical authority.

8. It is therefore to be noted with great sadness that "ecumenical initiatives which are well-intentioned, nevertheless indulge at times in Eucharistic practices contrary to the discipline by which the Church expresses her faith." Yet the Eucharist "is too great a gift to tolerate ambiguity or depreciation." It is therefore necessary that some things be corrected or more clearly delineated so that in this respect as well "the Eucharist will continue to shine forth in all its radiant mystery."[19]

9. Finally, abuses are often based on ignorance, in that they involve a rejection of those elements whose deeper meaning is not understood and whose antiquity is not recognized. For "the liturgical prayers, orations and songs are pervaded by the inspiration and impulse" of the Sacred Scriptures themselves, "and it is from these that the actions and signs receive their meaning."[20] As for the visible signs "which the Sacred Liturgy uses in order to signify the invisible divine realities, they have been chosen by Christ or by the Church."[21] Finally, the structures and forms of the sacred celebrations according to each of the Rites of both East and West are in harmony with the practice of the universal Church

also as regards practices received universally from apostolic and unbroken tradition,[22] which it is the Church's task to transmit faithfully and carefully to future generations. All these things are wisely safeguarded and protected by the liturgical norms.

10. The Church herself has no power over those things which were established by Christ himself and which constitute an unchangeable part of the Liturgy.[23] Indeed, if the bond were to be broken which the Sacraments have with Christ himself who instituted them, and with the events of the Church's founding,[24] it would not be beneficial to the faithful but rather would do them grave harm. For the Sacred Liturgy is quite intimately connected with principles of doctrine,[25] so that the use of unapproved texts and rites necessarily leads either to the attenuation or to the disappearance of that necessary link between the *lex orandi* and the *lex credendi*.[26]

11. The Mystery of the Eucharist "is too great for anyone to permit himself to treat it according to his own whim, so that its sacredness and its universal ordering would be obscured."[27] On the contrary, anyone who acts thus by giving free reign to his own inclinations, even if he is a Priest, injures the substantial unity of the Roman Rite, which ought to be vigorously preserved,[28] and becomes responsible for actions that are in no way consistent with the hunger and thirst for the living God that is experienced by the people today. Nor do such actions serve authentic pastoral care or proper liturgical renewal; instead, they deprive Christ's faithful of their patrimony and their heritage. For arbitrary actions are not conducive to true renewal,[29] but are detrimental to the right of Christ's faithful to a liturgical celebration that is an expression of the Church's life in accordance with her tradition and discipline. In the end, they introduce elements of distortion and disharmony into the very celebration of the Eucharist, which is oriented in its own lofty way and by its very nature to signifying and wondrously bringing about the communion of divine life and the unity of the People of God.[30] The result is uncertainty in matters of doctrine, perplexity and scandal on the part of the People of God, and, almost as a necessary consequence, vigorous opposition, all of which greatly confuse and sadden many of Christ's faithful in this age of ours when Christian life is often particularly difficult on account of the inroads of "secularization" as well.[31]

12. On the contrary, it is the right of all of Christ's faithful that the Liturgy, and in particular the celebration of Holy Mass, should truly be as the Church wishes, according to her stipulations as prescribed in the liturgical books and in the other laws and norms. Likewise, the Catholic people have the right that the Sacrifice of the Holy Mass should be celebrated for them in an integral manner, according to the entire doctrine of the Church's Magisterium. Finally, it is the Catholic community's right that the celebration of the Most Holy Eucharist should be carried out for it in such a manner that it truly stands out as a sacrament of unity, to the exclusion of all blemishes and actions that might engender divisions and factions in the Church.[32]

13. All of the norms and exhortations set forth in this Instruction are connected, albeit in various ways, with the mission of the Church, whose task it is to be vigilant concerning the correct and worthy celebration of so great a mystery. The last chapter of the present Instruction will treat of the varying degrees to which the individual norms are bound up with the supreme norm of all ecclesiastical law, namely concern for the salvation of souls.[33]

CHAPTER I
THE REGULATION OF THE SACRED LITURGY

14. "The regulation of the Sacred Liturgy depends solely on the authority of the Church, which rests specifically with the Apostolic See and, according to the norms of law, with the Bishop."[34]

15. The Roman Pontiff, "the Vicar of Christ and the Pastor of the universal Church on earth, by virtue of his supreme office enjoys full, immediate and universal ordinary power, which he may always freely exercise,"[35] also by means of communication with the pastors and with the members of the flock.

16. "It pertains to the Apostolic See to regulate the Sacred Liturgy of the universal Church, to publish the liturgical books and to grant the *recognitio* for their translation into vernacular languages, as well as to ensure that the liturgical regulations, especially those governing the celebration of the most exalted celebration of the Sacrifice of the Mass, are everywhere faithfully observed."[36]

17. "The Congregation for Divine Worship and the Discipline of the Sacraments attends to those matters that pertain to the Apostolic See as regards the regulation and promotion of the Sacred Liturgy, and especially the Sacraments, with due regard for the competence of the Congregation for the Doctrine of the Faith. It fosters and enforces sacramental discipline, especially as regards their validity and their licit celebration." Finally, it "carefully seeks to ensure that the liturgical regulations are observed with precision, and that abuses are prevented or eliminated whenever they are detected."[37] In this regard, according to the tradition of the universal Church, pre-eminent solicitude is accorded the celebration of Holy Mass, and also to the worship that is given to the Holy Eucharist even outside Mass.

18. Christ's faithful have the right that ecclesiastical authority should fully and efficaciously regulate the Sacred Liturgy lest it should ever seem to be "anyone's private property, whether of the celebrant or of the community in which the mysteries are celebrated."[38]

1. THE DIOCESAN BISHOP, HIGH PRIEST OF HIS FLOCK

19. The diocesan Bishop, the first steward of the mysteries of God in the particular Church entrusted to him, is the moderator, promoter and guardian of her whole liturgical life.[39] For "the Bishop, endowed with the fullness of the Sacrament of Order, is 'the steward of the grace of the high Priesthood,'[40] especially in the Eucharist which he either himself offers or causes to be offered,[41] by which the Church continually lives and grows."[42]

20. Indeed, the pre-eminent manifestation of the Church is found whenever the rites of Mass are celebrated, especially in the Cathedral Church, "with the full and active participation of the entire holy People of God, joined in one act of prayer, at one altar at which the Bishop presides," surrounded by his presbyterate with the Deacons and ministers.[43] Furthermore, "every lawful celebration of the Eucharist is directed by the Bishop, to whom is entrusted the office of presenting the worship of the Christian religion to the Divine Majesty and ordering it according to the precepts of the Lord and the laws of the Church, further specified by his own particular judgement for the Diocese."[44]

21. It pertains to the diocesan Bishop, then, "within the limits of his competence, to set forth liturgical norms in his Diocese, by which all are bound."[45] Still, the Bishop must take care not to allow the removal of that liberty foreseen by the norms of the liturgical books so that the celebration may be adapted in an intelligent manner to the Church building, or to the group of the faithful who are present, or to particular pastoral circumstances in such a way that the universal sacred rite is truly accommodated to human understanding.[46]

22. The Bishop governs the particular Church entrusted to him,[47] and it is his task to regulate, to direct, to encourage, and sometimes also to reprove;[48] this is a sacred task that he has received through episcopal Ordination,[49] which he fulfils in order to build up his flock in truth and holiness.[50] He should elucidate the inherent meaning of the rites and the liturgical texts, and nourish the spirit of the Liturgy in the Priests, Deacons and lay faithful[51] so that they are all led to the active and fruitful celebration of the Eucharist,[52] and in like manner he should take care to ensure that the whole body of the Church is able to grow in the same understanding, in the unity of charity, in the diocese, in the nation and in the world.[53]

23. The faithful "should cling to the Bishop as the Church does to Jesus Christ, and as Jesus Christ does to the Father, so that all may be in harmonious unity, and that they may abound to the glory of God."[54] All, including members of Institutes of consecrated life and Societies of apostolic life as well as those of all ecclesial associations and movements of any kind, are subject to the authority of the diocesan Bishop in all liturgical matters,[55] apart from rights that have been legitimately conceded. To the diocesan Bishop therefore falls the right and duty of overseeing and attending to Churches and oratories in his territory in regard to liturgical matters, and this is true also of those which are founded by members of the above-mentioned institutes or under their direction, provided that the faithful are accustomed to frequent them.[56]

24. It is the right of the Christian people themselves that their diocesan Bishop should take care to prevent the occurrence of abuses in ecclesiastical discipline, especially as regards the ministry of the word, the celebration of the sacraments and sacramentals, the worship of God and devotion to the Saints.[57]

25. Commissions as well as councils or committees established by the Bishop to handle "the promotion of the Liturgy, sacred music and art in his diocese" should act in accordance with the intentions and the norms of the Bishop; they must rely on his authority and his approval so that they may carry out their office in a suitable manner[58] and so that the effective governance of the Bishop in his diocese will be preserved. As regards all these sorts of bodies and other entities and all undertakings in liturgical matters, there has long been the need for the Bishops to consider whether their working has been fruitful thus far,[59] and to consider carefully which changes or improvements should be made in their composition and activity[60] so that they might find new vigour. It should be borne in mind that the experts are to be chosen from among those whose soundness in the Catholic faith and knowledge of theological and cultural matters are evident.

2. THE CONFERENCE OF BISHOPS

26. The same holds for those commissions of this kind which have been established by the Conference of Bishops in accordance with the will of the Council,[61] commissions whose members consist of Bishops who are clearly distinguished from their expert helpers. Where the number of members of a Conference of Bishops is not sufficient for the effective establishment of a liturgical commission from among their own number, then a council or group of experts should be named, always under the presidency of a Bishop, which is to fulfil the same role insofar as possible, albeit without the name of "liturgical commission."

27. As early as the year 1970, the Apostolic See announced the cessation of all experimentation as regards the celebration of Holy Mass[62] and reiterated the same in 1988.[63] Accordingly, individual Bishops and their Conferences do not have the faculty to permit experimentation with liturgical texts or the other matters that are prescribed in the liturgical books. In order to carry out experimentation of this kind in the future, the permission of the Congregation for Divine Worship and the Discipline of the Sacraments is required. It must be in writing, and it is to be requested by the Conference of Bishops. In fact, it will not be granted without serious reason. As regards projects of inculturation in liturgical matters, the particular norms that have been established are strictly and comprehensively to be observed.[64]

28. All liturgical norms that a Conference of Bishops will have established for its territory in accordance with the law are to be submitted to the Congregation for Divine Worship and the Discipline of the Sacraments for the *recognitio,* without which they lack any binding force.[65]

3. PRIESTS

29. Priests, as capable, prudent and indispensable co-workers of the order of Bishops,[66] called to the service of the People of God, constitute one presbyterate with their Bishop,[67] though charged with differing offices. "In each local congregation of the faithful, in a certain way, they make present the Bishop with whom they are associated in trust and in generosity of heart; according to their rank, they take upon themselves his duties and his solicitude, and they carry these out in their daily work." And "because of this participation in the Priesthood and mission, Priests should recognize the Bishop as truly their father and obey him reverently."[68] Furthermore, "ever intent upon the good of God's children, they should seek to contribute to the pastoral mission of the whole diocese, and indeed of the whole Church."[69]

30. The office "that belongs to Priests in particular in the celebration of the Eucharist" is a great one, "for it is their responsibility to preside at the Eucharist *in persona Christi* and to provide a witness to and a service of communion not only for the community directly taking part in the celebration, but also for the universal Church, which is always brought into play within the context of the Eucharist. It must be lamented that, especially in the years following the post-Conciliar liturgical reform, as a result of a misguided sense of creativity and adaptation, there have been a number of abuses which have been a source of suffering for many."[70]

31. In keeping with the solemn promises that they have made in the rite of Sacred Ordination and renewed each year in the Mass of the Chrism, let Priests celebrate "devoutly and faithfully the mysteries of Christ for the praise of God and the sanctification of the Christian people, according to the tradition of the Church, especially in the Eucharistic Sacrifice and in the Sacrament of Reconciliation."[71] They ought not to detract from the profound meaning of their own ministry by corrupting the liturgical celebration either through alteration or omission, or through arbitrary additions.[72] For as St. Ambrose said, "It is not in herself . . . but in

us that the Church is injured. Let us take care so that our own failure may not cause injury to the Church."[73] Let the Church of God not be injured, then, by Priests who have so solemnly dedicated themselves to the ministry. Indeed, under the Bishop's authority let them faithfully seek to prevent others as well from committing this type of distortion.

32. "Let the Parish Priest strive so that the Most Holy Eucharist will be the center of the parish congregation of the faithful; let him work to ensure that Christ's faithful are nourished through the devout celebration of the Sacraments, and in particular, that they frequently approach the Most Holy Eucharist and the Sacrament of Penance; let him strive, furthermore, to ensure that the faithful are encouraged to offer prayers in their families as well, and to participate consciously and actively in the Sacred Liturgy, which the Parish Priest, under the authority of the diocesan Bishop, is bound to regulate and supervise in his parish lest abuses occur."[74] Although it is appropriate that he should be assisted in the effective preparation of the liturgical celebrations by various members of Christ's faithful, he nevertheless must not cede to them in any way those things that are proper to his own office.

33. Finally, all "Priests should go to the trouble of properly cultivating their liturgical knowledge and ability, so that through their liturgical ministry, God the Father, Son and Holy Spirit will be praised in an ever more excellent manner by the Christian communities entrusted to them."[75] Above all, let them be filled with that wonder and amazement that the Paschal Mystery, in being celebrated, instills in the hearts of the faithful.[76]

4. DEACONS

34. Deacons "upon whom hands are imposed not for the Priesthood but for the ministry,"[77] as men of good repute,[78] must act in such a way that with the help of God they may be recognized as the true disciples[79] of him "who came not to be served but to serve,"[80] and who was among his disciples "as one who serves."[81] Strengthened by the gift of the Holy Spirit through the laying on of hands, they are in service to the People of God, in communion with the Bishop and his presbyterate.[82] They should therefore consider the Bishop as a father, and give assistance to him and to the Priests "in the ministry of the word, of the altar, and of charity."[83]

35. Let them never fail, "as the Apostle says, to hold the mystery of faith with a clear conscience,[84] and to proclaim this faith by word and deed according to the Gospel and the tradition of the Church,"[85] in wholehearted, faithful and humble service to the Sacred Liturgy as the source and summit of ecclesial life, "so that all, made children of God through faith and Baptism, may come together as one, praising God in the midst of the Church, to participate in the Sacrifice and to eat the Lord's Supper."[86] Let all Deacons, then, do their part so that the Sacred Liturgy will be celebrated according to the norms of the duly approved liturgical books.

CHAPTER II
THE PARTICIPATION OF THE LAY CHRISTIAN FAITHFUL IN THE EUCHARISTIC CELEBRATION

1. ACTIVE AND CONSCIOUS PARTICIPATION

36. The celebration of the Mass, as the action of Christ and of the Church, is the center of the whole Christian life for the universal as well as the particular Church, and also for the individual faithful,[87] who are involved "in differing ways according to the diversity of orders, ministries, and active participation.[88] In this way the Christian people, "a chosen race, a royal priesthood, a holy people, a people God has made his own,"[89] manifests its coherent and hierarchical ordering."[90] "For the common priesthood of the faithful and the ministerial or hierarchical Priesthood, though they differ in essence and not only in degree, are ordered to one another, for both partake, each in its own way, of the one Priesthood of Christ."[91]

37. All of Christ's faithful, freed from their sins and incorporated into the Church through Baptism, are deputed by means of a sacramental character for the worship of the Christian religion,[92] so that by virtue of their royal priesthood,[93] persevering in prayer and praising God,[94] they may offer themselves as a living and holy sacrifice pleasing to God and attested to others by their works,[95] giving witness to Christ throughout the earth and providing an answer to those who ask concerning their hope of eternal life that is in them.[96] Thus the participation of the lay faithful too in the Eucharist and in the other celebrations of the Church's rites

cannot be equated with mere presence, and still less with a passive one, but is rather to be regarded as a true exercise of faith and of the baptismal dignity.

38. The constant teaching of the Church on the nature of the Eucharist not only as a meal, but also and pre-eminently as a Sacrifice, is therefore rightly understood to be one of the principal keys to the full participation of all the faithful in so great a Sacrament.[97] For when "stripped of its sacrificial meaning, the mystery is understood as if its meaning and importance were simply that of a fraternal banquet."[98]

39. For promoting and elucidating active participation, the recent renewal of the liturgical books according to the mind of the Council fostered acclamations of the people, responses, psalmody, antiphons, and canticles, as well as actions or movements and gestures, and called for sacred silence to be maintained at the proper times, while providing rubrics for the parts of the faithful as well.[99] In addition, ample flexibility is given for appropriate creativity aimed at allowing each celebration to be adapted to the needs of the participants, to their comprehension, their interior preparation and their gifts, according to the established liturgical norms. In the songs, the melodies, the choice of prayers and readings, the giving of the homily, the preparation of the prayer of the faithful, the occasional explanatory remarks, and the decoration of the Church building according to the various seasons, there is ample possibility for introducing into each celebration a certain variety by which the riches of the liturgical tradition will also be more clearly evident, and so, in keeping with pastoral requirements, the celebration will be carefully imbued with those particular features that will foster the recollection of the participants. Still, it should be remembered that the power of the liturgical celebrations does not consist in frequently altering the rites, but in probing more deeply the word of God and the mystery being celebrated.[100]

40. Nevertheless, from the fact that the liturgical celebration obviously entails activity, it does not follow that everyone must necessarily have something concrete to do beyond the actions and gestures, as if a certain specific liturgical ministry must necessarily be given to the individuals to be carried out by them. Instead, catechetical instruction should strive diligently to correct those widespread superficial notions and practices often seen in recent

years in this regard, and ever to instill anew in all of Christ's faithful that sense of deep wonder before the greatness of the mystery of faith that is the Eucharist, in whose celebration the Church is forever passing from what is obsolete into newness of life: *"in novitatem a vetustate."*[101] For in the celebration of the Eucharist, as in the whole Christian life which draws its power from it and leads toward it, the Church, after the manner of Saint Thomas the Apostle, prostrates herself in adoration before the Lord who was crucified, suffered and died, was buried and arose, and perpetually exclaims to him who is clothed in the fullness of his divine splendour: "My Lord and my God!"[102]

41. For encouraging, promoting and nourishing this interior understanding of liturgical participation, the continuous and widespread celebration of the Liturgy of the Hours, the use of the sacramentals and exercises of Christian popular piety are extremely helpful. These latter exercises—which "while not belonging to the Liturgy in the strict sense, possess nonetheless a particular importance and dignity"—are to be regarded as having a certain connection with the liturgical context, especially when they have been lauded and attested by the Magisterium itself,[103] as is the case especially of the Marian Rosary.[104] Furthermore, since these practices of piety lead the Christian people both to the reception of the sacraments—especially the Eucharist—and "to meditation on the mysteries of our Redemption and the imitation of the excellent heavenly examples of the Saints, they are therefore not without salutary effects for our participation in liturgical worship."[105]

42. It must be acknowledged that the Church has not come together by human volition; rather, she has been called together by God in the Holy Spirit, and she responds through faith to his free calling (thus the word *ekklesia* is related to *klesis,* or "calling").[106] Nor is the Eucharistic Sacrifice to be considered a "concelebration," in the univocal sense, of the Priest along with the people who are present.[107] On the contrary, the Eucharist celebrated by the Priests "is a gift which radically transcends the power of the community. . . . The community that gathers for the celebration of the Eucharist absolutely requires an ordained Priest, who presides over it so that it may truly be a eucharistic convocation. On the other hand, the community is by itself incapable of providing an ordained minister."[108] There is pressing need of a concerted will to avoid all ambiguity in this matter and to remedy the difficulties

of recent years. Accordingly, terms such as "celebrating community" or "celebrating assembly" (in other languages "asamblea celebrante," "assemblée célébrante," assemblea celebrante") and similar terms should not be used injudiciously.

2. THE MINISTRIES OF THE LAY CHRISTIAN FAITHFUL IN THE CELEBRATION OF HOLY MASS

43. For the good of the community and of the whole Church of God, some of the lay faithful according to tradition have rightly and laudably exercised ministries in the celebration of the Sacred Liturgy.[109] It is appropriate that a number of persons distribute among themselves and exercise various ministries or different parts of the same ministry.[110]

44. Apart from the duly instituted ministries of acolyte and lector,[111] the most important of these ministries are those of acolyte[112] and lector[113] by temporary deputation. In addition to these are the other functions that are described in the Roman Missal,[114] as well as the functions of preparing the hosts, washing the liturgical linens, and the like. All, "whether ordained ministers or lay faithful, in exercising their own office or ministry should do exclusively and fully that which pertains to them."[115] In the liturgical celebration itself as well as in its preparation, they should do what is necessary so that the Church's Liturgy will be carried out worthily and appropriately.

45. To be avoided is the danger of obscuring the complementary relationship between the action of clerics and that of laypersons, in such a way that the ministry of laypersons undergoes what might be called a certain "clericalization," while the sacred ministers inappropriately assume those things that are proper to the life and activity of the lay faithful.[116]

46. The lay Christian faithful called to give assistance at liturgical celebrations should be well instructed and must be those whose Christian life, morals and fidelity to the Church's Magisterium recommend them. It is fitting that such a one should have received a liturgical formation in accordance with his or her age, condition, state of life, and religious culture.[117] No one should be selected whose designation could cause consternation for the faithful.[118]

47. It is altogether laudable to maintain the noble custom by which boys or youths, customarily termed servers, provide service of the altar after the manner of acolytes, and receive catechesis regarding their function in accordance with their power of comprehension.[119] Nor should it be forgotten that a great number of sacred ministers over the course of the centuries have come from among boys such as these.[120] Associations for them, including also the participation and assistance of their parents, should be established or promoted, and in such a way greater pastoral care will be provided for the ministers. Whenever such associations are international in nature, it pertains to the competence of the Congregation for Divine Worship and the Discipline of the Sacraments to establish them or to approve and revise their statutes.[121] Girls or women may also be admitted to this service of the altar, at the discretion of the diocesan Bishop and in observance of the established norms.[122]

CHAPTER III
THE PROPER CELEBRATION OF MASS

1. THE MATTER OF THE MOST HOLY EUCHARIST

48. The bread used in the celebration of the Most Holy Eucharistic Sacrifice must be unleavened, purely of wheat, and recently made so that there is no danger of decomposition.[123] It follows therefore that bread made from another substance, even if it is grain, or if it is mixed with another substance different from wheat to such an extent that it would not commonly be considered wheat bread, does not constitute valid matter for confecting the Sacrifice and the Eucharistic Sacrament.[124] It is a grave abuse to introduce other substances, such as fruit or sugar or honey, into the bread for confecting the Eucharist. Hosts should obviously be made by those who are not only distinguished by their integrity, but also skilled in making them and furnished with suitable tools.[125]

49. By reason of the sign, it is appropriate that at least some parts of the Eucharistic Bread coming from the fraction should be distributed to at least some of the faithful in Communion. "Small hosts are, however, in no way ruled out when the number of those receiving Holy Communion or other pastoral needs require it,"[126] and indeed small hosts requiring no further fraction ought customarily to be used for the most part.

50. The wine that is used in the most sacred celebration of the Eucharistic Sacrifice must be natural, from the fruit of the grape, pure and incorrupt, not mixed with other substances.[127] During the celebration itself, a small quantity of water is to be mixed with it. Great care should be taken so that the wine intended for the celebration of the Eucharist is well conserved and has not soured.[128] It is altogether forbidden to use wine of doubtful authenticity or provenance, for the Church requires certainty regarding the conditions necessary for the validity of the sacraments. Nor are other drinks of any kind to be admitted for any reason, as they do not constitute valid matter.

2. THE EUCHARISTIC PRAYER

51. Only those Eucharistic Prayers are to be used which are found in the Roman Missal or are legitimately approved by the Apostolic See, and according to the manner and the terms set forth by it. "It is not to be tolerated that some Priests take upon themselves the right to compose their own Eucharistic Prayers"[129] or to change the same texts approved by the Church, or to introduce others composed by private individuals.[130]

52. The proclamation of the Eucharistic Prayer, which by its very nature is the climax of the whole celebration, is proper to the Priest by virtue of his Ordination. It is therefore an abuse to proffer it in such a way that some parts of the Eucharistic Prayer are recited by a Deacon, a lay minister, or by an individual member of the faithful, or by all members of the faithful together. The Eucharistic Prayer, then, is to be recited by the Priest alone in full.[131]

53. While the Priest proclaims the Eucharistic Prayer "there should be no other prayers or singing, and the organ or other musical instruments should be silent,"[132] except for the people's acclamations that have been duly approved, as described below.

54. The people, however, are always involved actively and never merely passively: for they "silently join themselves with the Priest in faith, as well as in their interventions during the course of the Eucharistic Prayer as prescribed, namely in the responses in the Preface dialogue, the *Sanctus*, the acclamation after the consecration and the "*Amen*" after the final doxology, and in other acclamations approved by the Conference of Bishops with the *recognitio* of the Holy See."[133]

55. In some places there has existed an abuse by which the Priest breaks the host at the time of the consecration in the Holy Mass. This abuse is contrary to the tradition of the Church. It is reprobated and is to be corrected with haste.

56. The mention of the name of the Supreme Pontiff and the diocesan Bishop in the Eucharistic Prayer is not to be omitted, since this is a most ancient tradition to be maintained, and a manifestation of ecclesial communion. For "the coming together of the eucharistic community is at the same time a joining in union with its own Bishop and with the Roman Pontiff."[134]

3. THE OTHER PARTS OF THE MASS

57. It is the right of the community of Christ's faithful that especially in the Sunday celebration there should customarily be true and suitable sacred music, and that there should always be an altar, vestments and sacred linens that are dignified, proper, and clean, in accordance with the norms.

58. All of Christ's faithful likewise have the right to a celebration of the Eucharist that has been so carefully prepared in all its parts that the word of God is properly and efficaciously proclaimed and explained in it; that the faculty for selecting the liturgical texts and rites is carried out with care according to the norms; and that their faith is duly safeguarded and nourished by the words that are sung in the celebration of the Liturgy.

59. The reprobated practice by which Priests, Deacons or the faithful here and there alter or vary at will the texts of the Sacred Liturgy that they are charged to pronounce, must cease. For in doing thus, they render the celebration of the Sacred Liturgy unstable, and not infrequently distort the authentic meaning of the Liturgy.

60. In the celebration of Mass, the Liturgy of the Word and the Liturgy of the Eucharist are intimately connected to one another, and form one single act of worship. For this reason it is not licit to separate one of these parts from the other and celebrate them at different times or places.[135] Nor is it licit to carry out the individual parts of Holy Mass at different times of the same day.

61. In selecting the biblical readings for proclamation in the celebration of Mass, the norms found in the liturgical books are

to be followed,[136] so that indeed "a richer table of the word of God will be prepared for the faithful, and the biblical treasures opened up for them."[137]

62. It is also illicit to omit or to substitute the prescribed biblical readings on one's own initiative, and especially "to substitute other, non-biblical texts for the readings and responsorial Psalm, which contain the word of God."[138]

63. "Within the celebration of the Sacred Liturgy, the reading of the Gospel, which is "the high point of the Liturgy of the Word,"[139] is reserved by the Church's tradition to an ordained minister.[140] Thus it is not permitted for a layperson, even a religious, to proclaim the Gospel reading in the celebration of Holy Mass, nor in other cases in which the norms do not explicitly permit it.[141]

64. The homily, which is given in the course of the celebration of Holy Mass and is a part of the Liturgy itself,[142] "should ordinarily be given by the Priest celebrant himself. He may entrust it to a concelebrating Priest or occasionally, according to circumstances, to a Deacon, but never to a layperson.[143] In particular cases and for a just cause, the homily may even be given by a Bishop or a Priest who is present at the celebration but cannot concelebrate."[144]

65. It should be borne in mind that any previous norm that may have admitted non-ordained faithful to give the homily during the eucharistic celebration is to be considered abrogated by the norm of canon 767 §1.[145] This practice is reprobated, so that it cannot be permitted to attain the force of custom.

66. The prohibition of the admission of laypersons to preach within the Mass applies also to seminarians, students of theological disciplines, and those who have assumed the function of those known as "pastoral assistants"; nor is there to be any exception for any other kind of layperson, or group, or community, or association.[146]

67. Particular care is to be taken so that the homily is firmly based upon the mysteries of salvation, expounding the mysteries of the Faith and the norms of Christian life from the biblical readings and liturgical texts throughout the course of the liturgical year and providing commentary on the texts of the Ordinary or the Proper of the Mass, or of some other rite of the Church.[147] It is

clear that all interpretations of Sacred Scripture are to be referred back to Christ himself as the one upon whom the entire economy of salvation hinges, though this should be done in light of the specific context of the liturgical celebration. In the homily to be given, care is to be taken so that the light of Christ may shine upon life's events. Even so, this is to be done so as not to obscure the true and unadulterated word of God: for instance, treating only of politics or profane subjects, or drawing upon notions derived from contemporary pseudo-religious currents as a source.[148]

68. The diocesan Bishop must diligently oversee the preaching of the homily,[149] also publishing norms and distributing guidelines and auxiliary tools to the sacred ministers, and promoting meetings and other projects for this purpose so that they may have the opportunity to consider the nature of the homily more precisely and find help in its preparation.

69. In Holy Mass as well as in other celebrations of the Sacred Liturgy, no Creed or Profession of Faith is to be introduced which is not found in the duly approved liturgical books.

70. The offerings that Christ's faithful are accustomed to present for the Liturgy of the Eucharist in Holy Mass are not necessarily limited to bread and wine for the eucharistic celebration, but may also include gifts given by the faithful in the form of money or other things for the sake of charity toward the poor. Moreover, external gifts must always be a visible expression of that true gift that God expects from us: a contrite heart, the love of God and neighbour by which we are conformed to the sacrifice of Christ, who offered himself for us. For in the Eucharist, there shines forth most brilliantly that mystery of charity that Jesus brought forth at the Last Supper by washing the feet of the disciples. In order to preserve the dignity of the Sacred Liturgy, in any event, the external offerings should be brought forward in an appropriate manner. Money, therefore, just as other contributions for the poor, should be placed in an appropriate place which should be away from the eucharistic table.[150] Except for money and occasionally a minimal symbolic portion of other gifts, it is preferable that such offerings be made outside the celebration of Mass.

71. The practice of the Roman Rite is to be maintained according to which the peace is extended shortly before Holy Communion. For according to the tradition of the Roman Rite, this practice does

not have the connotation either of reconciliation or of a remission of sins, but instead signifies peace, communion and charity before the reception of the Most Holy Eucharist.[151] It is rather the Penitential Act to be carried out at the beginning of Mass (especially in its first form) which has the character of reconciliation among brothers and sisters.

72. It is appropriate "that each one give the sign of peace only to those who are nearest and in a sober manner." "The Priest may give the sign of peace to the ministers but always remains within the sanctuary, so as not to disturb the celebration. He does likewise if for a just reason he wishes to extend the sign of peace to some few of the faithful." "As regards the sign to be exchanged, the manner is to be established by the Conference of Bishops in accordance with the dispositions and customs of the people," and their acts are subject to the *recognitio* of the Apostolic See.[152]

73. In the celebration of Holy Mass the breaking of the Eucharistic Bread—done only by the Priest celebrant, if necessary with the help of a Deacon or of a concelebrant—begins after the exchange of peace, while the *Agnus Dei* is being recited. For the gesture of breaking bread "carried out by Christ at the Last Supper, which in apostolic times gave the whole eucharistic action its name, signifies that the faithful, though they are many, are made one Body in the communion of the one Bread of Life who is Christ, who died and rose for the world's salvation" (cf. 1 Corinthian 10:17).[153] For this reason the rite must be carried out with great reverence.[154] Even so, it should be brief. The abuse that has prevailed in some places, by which this rite is unnecessarily prolonged and given undue emphasis, with laypersons also helping in contradiction to the norms, should be corrected with all haste.[155]

74. If the need arises for the gathered faithful to be given instruction or testimony by a layperson in a Church concerning the Christian life, it is altogether preferable that this be done outside Mass. Nevertheless, for serious reasons it is permissible that this type of instruction or testimony be given after the Priest has proclaimed the Prayer after Communion. This should not become a regular practice, however. Furthermore, these instructions and testimony should not be of such a nature that they could be confused with the homily,[156] nor is it permissible to dispense with the homily on their account.

4. ON THE JOINING OF VARIOUS RITES WITH THE CELEBRATION OF MASS

75. On account of the theological significance inherent in a particular rite and the Eucharistic Celebration, the liturgical books sometimes prescribe or permit the celebration of Holy Mass to be joined with another rite, especially one of those pertaining to the Sacraments.[157] The Church does not permit such a conjoining in other cases, however, especially when it is a question of trivial matters.

76. Furthermore, according to a most ancient tradition of the Roman Church, it is not permissible to unite the Sacrament of Penance to the Mass in such a way that they become a single liturgical celebration. This does not exclude, however, that Priests other than those celebrating or concelebrating the Mass might hear the confessions of the faithful who so desire, even in the same place where Mass is being celebrated, in order to meet the needs of those faithful.[158] This should nevertheless be done in an appropriate manner.

77. The celebration of Holy Mass is not to be inserted in any way into the setting of a common meal, nor joined with this kind of banquet. Mass is not to be celebrated without grave necessity on a dinner table[159] nor in a dining room or banquet hall, nor in a room where food is present, nor in a place where the participants during the celebration itself are seated at tables. If out of grave necessity Mass must be celebrated in the same place where eating will later take place, there is to be a clear interval of time between the conclusion of Mass and the beginning of the meal, and ordinary food is not to be set before the faithful during the celebration of Mass.

78. It is not permissible to link the celebration of Mass to political or secular events, nor to situations that are not fully consistent with the Magisterium of the Catholic Church. Furthermore, it is altogether to be avoided that the celebration of Mass should be carried out merely out of a desire for show, or in the manner of other ceremonies including profane ones, lest the Eucharist should be emptied of its authentic meaning.

79. Finally, it is strictly to be considered an abuse to introduce into the celebration of Holy Mass elements that are contrary to the prescriptions of the liturgical books and taken from the rites of other religions.

CHAPTER IV
HOLY COMMUNION

1. DISPOSITIONS FOR THE RECEPTION OF HOLY COMMUNION

80. The Eucharist is to be offered to the faithful, among other reasons, "as an antidote, by which we are freed from daily faults and preserved from mortal sins,"[160] as is brought to light in various parts of the Mass. As for the Penitential Act placed at the beginning of Mass, it has the purpose of preparing all to be ready to celebrate the sacred mysteries;[161] even so, "it lacks the efficacy of the Sacrament of Penance,"[162] and cannot be regarded as a substitute for the Sacrament of Penance in remission of graver sins. Pastors of souls should take care to ensure diligent catechetical instruction, so that Christian doctrine is handed on to Christ's faithful in this matter.

81. The Church's custom shows that it is necessary for each person to examine himself at depth,[163] and that anyone who is conscious of grave sin should not celebrate or receive the Body of the Lord without prior sacramental confession, except for grave reason when the possibility of confession is lacking; in this case he will remember that he is bound by the obligation of making an act of perfect contrition, which includes the intention to confess as soon as possible."[164]

82. Moreover, "the Church has drawn up norms aimed at fostering the frequent and fruitful access of the faithful to the Eucharistic table and at determining the objective conditions under which Communion may not be given."[165]

83. It is certainly best that all who are participating in the celebration of Holy Mass with the necessary dispositions should receive Communion. Nevertheless, it sometimes happens that Christ's faithful approach the altar as a group indiscriminately. It pertains to the Pastors prudently and firmly to correct such an abuse.

84. Furthermore when Holy Mass is celebrated for a large crowd—for example, in large cities—care should be taken lest out of ignorance non-Catholics or even non-Christians come forward for Holy Communion, without taking into account the Church's Magisterium in matters pertaining to doctrine and discipline. It is the duty of Pastors at an opportune moment to inform those present of the authenticity and the discipline that are strictly to be observed.

85. Catholic ministers licitly administer the Sacraments only to the Catholic faithful, who likewise receive them licitly only from Catholic ministers, except for those situations for which provision is made in canon 844 §§ 2, 3, and 4, and canon 861 § 2.[166] In addition, the conditions comprising canon 844 § 4, from which no dispensation can be given,[167] cannot be separated; thus, it is necessary that all of these conditions be present together.

86. The faithful should be led insistently to the practice whereby they approach the Sacrament of Penance outside the celebration of Mass, especially at the scheduled times, so that the Sacrament may be administered in a manner that is tranquil and truly beneficial to them, so as not to be prevented from active participation at Mass. Those who are accustomed to receiving Communion often or daily should be instructed that they should approach the Sacrament of Penance at appropriate intervals, in accordance with the condition of each.[168]

87. The First Communion of children must always be preceded by sacramental confession and absolution.[169] Moreover First Communion should always be administered by a Priest and never outside the celebration of Mass. Apart from exceptional cases, it is not particularly appropriate for First Communion to be administered on Holy Thursday of the Lord's Supper. Another day should be chosen instead, such as a Sunday between the Second and the Sixth Sunday of Easter, or the Solemnity of the Body and Blood of Christ, or the Sundays of Ordinary Time, since Sunday is rightly regarded as the day of the Eucharist.[170] "Children who have not attained the age of reason, or those whom" the Parish Priest "has determined to be insufficiently prepared" should not come forward to receive the Holy Eucharist.[171] Where it happens, however, that a child who is exceptionally mature for his age is judged to be ready for receiving the Sacrament, the child must not be denied First Communion provided he has received sufficient instruction.

2. THE DISTRIBUTION OF HOLY COMMUNION

88. The faithful should normally receive sacramental Communion of the Eucharist during Mass itself, at the moment laid down by the rite of celebration, that is to say, just after the Priest celebrant's Communion.[172] It is the Priest celebrant's responsibility to minister Communion, perhaps assisted by other Priests or Deacons; and he should not resume the Mass until after the Communion of the faithful is concluded. Only when there is a necessity may extraordinary ministers assist the Priest celebrant in accordance with the norm of law.[173]

89. "So that even by means of the signs Communion may stand out more clearly as a participation in the Sacrifice being celebrated,"[174] it is preferable that the faithful be able to receive hosts consecrated in the same Mass.[175]

90. "The faithful should receive Communion kneeling or standing, as the Conference of Bishops will have determined," with its acts having received the *recognitio* of the Apostolic See. "However, if they receive Communion standing, it is recommended that they give due reverence before the reception of the Sacrament, as set forth in the same norms."[176]

91. In distributing Holy Communion it is to be remembered that "sacred ministers may not deny the sacraments to those who seek them in a reasonable manner, are rightly disposed, and are not prohibited by law from receiving them."[177] Hence any baptized Catholic who is not prevented by law must be admitted to Holy Communion. Therefore, it is not licit to deny Holy Communion to any of Christ's faithful solely on the grounds, for example, that the person wishes to receive the Eucharist kneeling or standing.

92. Although each of the faithful always has the right to receive Holy Communion on the tongue, at his choice,[178] if any communicant should wish to receive the Sacrament in the hand, in areas where the Bishops' Conference with the *recognitio* of the Apostolic See has given permission, the sacred host is to be administered to him or her. However, special care should be taken to ensure that the host is consumed by the communicant in the presence of the minister, so that no one goes away carrying the Eucharistic species in his hand. If there is a risk of profanation, then Holy Communion should not be given in the hand to the faithful.[179]

93. The Communion-plate for the Communion of the faithful should be retained, so as to avoid the danger of the sacred host or some fragment of it falling.[180]

94. It is not licit for the faithful "to take . . . by themselves . . . and, still less, to hand . . . from one to another" the sacred host or the sacred chalice.[181] Moreover, in this regard, the abuse is to be set aside whereby spouses administer Holy Communion to each other at a Nuptial Mass.

95. A lay member of Christ's faithful "who has already received the Most Holy Eucharist may receive it again on the same day only within a Eucharistic Celebration in which he or she is participating, with due regard for the prescriptions of canon 921 § 2."[182]

96. The practice is reprobated whereby either unconsecrated hosts or other edible or inedible things are distributed during the celebration of Holy Mass or beforehand after the manner of Communion, contrary to the prescriptions of the liturgical books. For such a practice in no way accords with the tradition of the Roman Rite, and carries with it the danger of causing confusion among Christ's faithful concerning the Eucharistic doctrine of the Church. Where there exists in certain places by concession a particular custom of blessing bread after Mass for distribution, proper catechesis should very carefully be given concerning this action. In fact, no other similar practices should be introduced, nor should unconsecrated hosts ever be used for this purpose.

3. THE COMMUNION OF PRIESTS

97. A Priest must communicate at the altar at the moment laid down by the Missal each time he celebrates Holy Mass, and the concelebrants must communicate before they proceed with the distribution of Holy Communion. The Priest celebrant or a concelebrant is never to wait until the people's Communion is concluded before receiving Communion himself.[183]

98. The Communion of Priest concelebrants should proceed according to the norms prescribed in the liturgical books, always using hosts consecrated at the same Mass[184] and always with Communion under both kinds being received by all of the concelebrants. It is to be noted that if the Priest or Deacon hands the sacred host or chalice to the concelebrants, he says nothing; that

is to say, he does not pronounce the words "The Body of Christ" or "The Blood of Christ."

99. Communion under both kinds is always permitted "to Priests who are not able to celebrate or concelebrate Mass."[185]

4. COMMUNION UNDER BOTH KINDS

100. So that the fullness of the sign may be made more clearly evident to the faithful in the course of the Eucharistic banquet, lay members of Christ's faithful, too, are admitted to Communion under both kinds, in the cases set forth in the liturgical books, preceded and continually accompanied by proper catechesis regarding the dogmatic principles on this matter laid down by the Ecumenical Council of Trent.[186]

101. In order for Holy Communion under both kinds to be administered to the lay members of Christ's faithful, due consideration should be given to the circumstances, as judged first of all by the diocesan Bishop. It is to be completely excluded where even a small danger exists of the sacred species being profaned.[187] With a view to wider co-ordination, the Bishops' Conferences should issue norms, once their decisions have received the *recognitio* of the Apostolic See through the Congregation for Divine Worship and the Discipline of the Sacraments, especially as regards "the manner of distributing Holy Communion to the faithful under both kinds, and the faculty for its extension."[188]

102. The chalice should not be ministered to lay members of Christ's faithful where there is such a large number of communicants[189] that it is difficult to gauge the amount of wine for the Eucharist and there is a danger that "more than a reasonable quantity of the Blood of Christ remain to be consumed at the end of the celebration."[190] The same is true wherever access to the chalice would be difficult to arrange, or where such a large amount of wine would be required that its certain provenance and quality could only be known with difficulty, or wherever there is not an adequate number of sacred ministers or extraordinary ministers of Holy Communion with proper formation, or where a notable part of the people continues to prefer not to approach the chalice for various reasons, so that the sign of unity would in some sense be negated.

103. The norms of the Roman Missal admit the principle that in cases where Communion is administered under both kinds, "the Blood of the Lord may be received either by drinking from the chalice directly, or by intinction, or by means of a tube or a spoon."[191] As regards the administering of Communion to lay members of Christ's faithful, the Bishops may exclude Communion with the tube or the spoon where this is not the local custom, though the option of administering Communion by intinction always remains. If this modality is employed, however, hosts should be used which are neither too thin nor too small, and the communicant should receive the Sacrament from the Priest only on the tongue.[192]

104. The communicant must not be permitted to intinct the host himself in the chalice, nor to receive the intincted host in the hand. As for the host to be used for the intinction, it should be made of valid matter, also consecrated; it is altogether forbidden to use non-consecrated bread or other matter.

105. If one chalice is not sufficient for Communion to be distributed under both kinds to the Priest concelebrants or Christ's faithful, there is no reason why the Priest celebrant should not use several chalices.[193] For it is to be remembered that all Priests in celebrating Holy Mass are bound to receive Communion under both kinds. It is praiseworthy, by reason of the sign value, to use a main chalice of larger dimensions, together with smaller chalices.

106. However, the pouring of the Blood of Christ after the consecration from one vessel to another is completely to be avoided, lest anything should happen that would be to the detriment of so great a mystery. Never to be used for containing the Blood of the Lord are flagons, bowls, or other vessels that are not fully in accord with the established norms.

107. In accordance with what is laid down by the canons, "one who throws away the consecrated species or takes them away or keeps them for a sacrilegious purpose, incurs a *latae sententiae* excommunication reserved to the Apostolic See; a cleric, moreover, may be punished by another penalty, not excluding dismissal from the clerical state."[194] To be regarded as pertaining to this case is any action that is voluntarily and gravely disrespectful of the sacred species. Anyone, therefore, who acts contrary to these norms, for example casting the sacred species into the

sacrarium or in an unworthy place or on the ground, incurs the penalties laid down.[195] Furthermore all will remember that once the distribution of Holy Communion during the celebration of Mass has been completed, the prescriptions of the Roman Missal are to be observed, and in particular, whatever may remain of the Blood of Christ must be entirely and immediately consumed by the Priest or by another minister, according to the norms, while the consecrated hosts that are left are to be consumed by the Priest at the altar or carried to the place for the reservation of the Eucharist.[196]

CHAPTER V
CERTAIN OTHER MATTERS CONCERNING THE EUCHARIST

1. THE PLACE FOR THE CELEBRATION OF HOLY MASS

108. "The celebration of the Eucharist is to be carried out in a sacred place, unless in a particular case necessity requires otherwise. In this case the celebration must be in a decent place."[197] The diocesan Bishop shall be the judge for his diocese concerning this necessity, on a case-by-case basis.

109. It is never lawful for a Priest to celebrate in a temple or sacred place of any non-Christian religion.

2. VARIOUS CIRCUMSTANCES RELATING TO THE MASS

110. "Remembering always that in the mystery of the Eucharistic Sacrifice the work of redemption is constantly being carried out, Priests should celebrate frequently. Indeed, daily celebration is earnestly recommended, because, even if it should not be possible to have the faithful present, the celebration is an act of Christ and of the Church, and in carrying it out, Priests fulfil their principal role."[198]

111. A Priest is to be permitted to celebrate or concelebrate the Eucharist "even if he is not known to the rector of the church, provided he presents commendatory letters" (i.e., a *celebret*) not more than a year old from the Holy See or his Ordinary or Superior "or

unless it can be prudently judged that he is not impeded from celebrating."[199] Let the Bishops take measures to put a stop to any contrary practice.

112. Mass is celebrated either in Latin or in another language, provided that liturgical texts are used which have been approved according to the norm of law. Except in the case of celebrations of the Mass that are scheduled by the ecclesiastical authorities to take place in the language of the people, Priests are always and everywhere permitted to celebrate Mass in Latin.[200]

113. When Mass is concelebrated by several Priests, a language known both to all the concelebrating Priests and to the gathered people should be used in the recitation of the Eucharist Prayer. Where it happens that some of the Priests who are present do not know the language of the celebration and therefore are not capable of pronouncing the parts of the Eucharistic Prayer proper to them, they should not concelebrate, but instead should attend the celebration in choral dress in accordance with the norms.[201]

114. "At Sunday Masses in parishes, insofar as parishes are 'Eucharistic communities,' it is customary to find different groups, movements, associations, and even the smaller religious communities present in the parish."[202] While it is permissible that Mass should be celebrated for particular groups according to the norm of law,[203] these groups are nevertheless not exempt from the faithful observance of the liturgical norms.

115. The abuse is reprobated by which the celebration of Holy Mass for the people is suspended in an arbitrary manner contrary to the norms of the Roman Missal and the healthy tradition of the Roman Rite, on the pretext of promoting a "fast from the Eucharist."

116. Masses are not to be multiplied contrary to the norm of law, and as regards Mass stipends, all those things are to be observed which are otherwise laid down by law.[204]

3. SACRED VESSELS

117. Sacred vessels for containing the Body and Blood of the Lord must be made in strict conformity with the norms of tradition and of the liturgical books.[205] The Bishops' Conferences have the

faculty to decide whether it is appropriate, once their decisions have been given the *recognitio* by the Apostolic See, for sacred vessels to be made of other solid materials as well. It is strictly required, however, that such materials be truly noble in the common estimation within a given region,[206] so that honour will be given to the Lord by their use, and all risk of diminishing the doctrine of the Real Presence of Christ in the Eucharistic species in the eyes of the faithful will be avoided. Reprobated, therefore, is any practice of using for the celebration of Mass common vessels, or others lacking in quality, or devoid of all artistic merit or which are mere containers, as also other vessels made from glass, earthenware, clay, or other materials that break easily. This norm is to be applied even as regards metals and other materials that easily rust or deteriorate.[207]

118. Before they are used, sacred vessels are to be blessed by a Priest according to the rites laid down in the liturgical books.[208] It is praiseworthy for the blessing to be given by the diocesan Bishop, who will judge whether the vessels are worthy of the use to which they are destined.

119. The Priest, once he has returned to the altar after the distribution of Communion, standing at the altar or at the credence table, purifies the paten or ciborium over the chalice, then purifies the chalice in accordance with the prescriptions of the Missal and wipes the chalice with the purificator. Where a Deacon is present, he returns with the Priest to the altar and purifies the vessels. It is permissible, however, especially if there are several vessels to be purified, to leave them, covered as may be appropriate, on a corporal on the altar or on the credence table, and for them to be purified by the Priest or Deacon immediately after Mass once the people have been dismissed. Moreover a duly instituted acolyte assists the Priest or Deacon in purifying and arranging the sacred vessels either at the altar or the credence table. In the absence of a Deacon, a duly instituted acolyte carries the sacred vessels to the credence table and there purifies, wipes and arranges them in the usual way.[209]

120. Let Pastors take care that the linens for the sacred table, especially those which will receive the sacred species, are always kept clean and that they are washed in the traditional way. It is praiseworthy for this to be done by pouring the water from the first washing, done by hand, into the church's sacrarium or into

the ground in a suitable place. After this a second washing can be done in the usual way.

4. LITURGICAL VESTURE

121. "The purpose of a variety of colour of the sacred vestments is to give effective expression even outwardly to the specific character of the mysteries of faith being celebrated and to a sense of Christian life's passage through the course of the liturgical year."[210] On the other hand, the variety "of offices in the celebration of the Eucharist is shown outwardly by the diversity of sacred vestments. In fact, these "sacred vestments should also contribute to the beauty of the sacred action itself."[211]

122. "The alb" is "to be tied at the waist with a cincture unless it is made so as to fit even without a cincture. Before the alb is put on, if it does not completely cover the ordinary clothing at the neck, an amice should be put on."[212]

123. "The vestment proper to the Priest celebrant at Mass, and in other sacred actions directly connected with Mass unless otherwise indicated, is the chasuble, worn over the alb and stole."[213] Likewise the Priest, in putting on the chasuble according to the rubrics, is not to omit the stole. All Ordinaries should be vigilant in order that all usage to the contrary be eradicated.

124. A faculty is given in the Roman Missal for the Priest concelebrants at Mass other than the principal concelebrant (who should always put on a chasuble of the prescribed colour), for a just reason such as a large number of concelebrants or a lack of vestments, to omit "the chasuble, using the stole over the alb."[214] Where a need of this kind can be foreseen, however, provision should be made for it insofar as possible. Out of necessity the concelebrants other than the principal celebrant may even put on white chasubles. For the rest, the norms of the liturgical books are to be observed.

125. The proper vestment of the Deacon is the dalmatic, to be worn over an alb and stole. In order that the beautiful tradition of the Church may be preserved, it is praiseworthy to refrain from exercising the option of omitting the dalmatic.[215]

126. The abuse is reprobated whereby the sacred ministers celebrate Holy Mass or other rites without sacred vestments or with only a stole over the monastic cowl or the common habit of religious or ordinary clothes, contrary to the prescriptions of the liturgical books, even when there is only one minister participating.[216] In order that such abuses be corrected as quickly as possible, Ordinaries should take care that in all churches and oratories subject to their jurisdiction there is present an adequate supply of liturgical vestments made in accordance with the norms.

127. A special faculty is given in the liturgical books for using sacred vestments that are festive or more noble on more solemn occasions, even if they are not of the colour of the day.[217] However, this faculty, which is specifically intended in reference to vestments made many years ago, with a view to preserving the Church's patrimony, is improperly extended to innovations by which forms and colours are adopted according to the inclination of private individuals, with disregard for traditional practice, while the real sense of this norm is lost to the detriment of the tradition. On the occasion of a feastday, sacred vestments of a gold or silver colour can be substituted as appropriate for others of various colours, but not for purple or black.

128. Holy Mass and other liturgical celebrations, which are acts of Christ and of the people of God hierarchically constituted, are ordered in such a way that the sacred ministers and the lay faithful manifestly take part in them each according to his own condition. It is preferable therefore that "Priests who are present at a Eucharistic Celebration, unless excused for a good reason, should as a rule exercise the office proper to their Order and thus take part as concelebrants, wearing the sacred vestments. Otherwise, they wear their proper choir dress or a surplice over a cassock."[218] It is not fitting, except in rare and exceptional cases and with reasonable cause, for them to participate at Mass, as regards to externals, in the manner of the lay faithful.

CHAPTER VI
THE RESERVATION OF THE MOST HOLY EUCHARIST AND EUCHARISTIC WORSHIP OUTSIDE MASS

1. THE RESERVATION OF THE MOST HOLY EUCHARIST

129. "The celebration of the Eucharist in the Sacrifice of the Mass is truly the origin and end of the worship given to the Eucharist outside the Mass. Furthermore the sacred species are reserved after Mass principally so that the faithful who cannot be present at Mass, above all the sick and those advanced in age, may be united by sacramental Communion to Christ and his Sacrifice which is offered in the Mass."[219] In addition, this reservation also permits the practice of adoring this great Sacrament and offering it the worship due to God. Accordingly, forms of adoration that are not only private but also public and communitarian in nature, as established or approved by the Church herself, must be greatly promoted.[220]

130. "According to the structure of each church building and in accordance with legitimate local customs, the Most Holy Sacrament is to be reserved in a tabernacle in a part of the church that is noble, prominent, readily visible, and adorned in a dignified manner" and furthermore "suitable for prayer" by reason of the quietness of the location, the space available in front of the tabernacle, and also the supply of benches or seats and kneelers.[221] In addition, diligent attention should be paid to all the prescriptions of the liturgical books and to the norm of law,[222] especially as regards the avoidance of the danger of profanation.[223]

131. Apart from the prescriptions of canon 934 § 1, it is forbidden to reserve the Blessed Sacrament in a place that is not subject in a secure way to the authority of the diocesan Bishop, or where there is a danger of profanation. Where such is the case, the diocesan Bishop should immediately revoke any permission for reservation of the Eucharist that may already have been granted.[224]

132. No one may carry the Most Holy Eucharist to his or her home, or to any other place contrary to the norm of law. It should also be borne in mind that removing or retaining the consecrated species for a sacrilegious purpose or casting them away are *graviora*

delicta, the absolution of which is reserved to the Congregation for the Doctrine of the Faith.[225]

133. A Priest or Deacon, or an extraordinary minister who takes the Most Holy Eucharist when an ordained minister is absent or impeded in order to administer it as Communion for a sick person, should go insofar as possible directly from the place where the Sacrament is reserved to the sick person's home, leaving aside any profane business so that any danger of profanation may be avoided and the greatest reverence for the Body of Christ may be ensured. Furthermore the Rite for the administration of Communion to the sick, as prescribed in the Roman Ritual, is always to be used.[226]

2. CERTAIN FORMS OF WORSHIP OF THE MOST HOLY EUCHARIST OUTSIDE MASS

134. "The worship of the Eucharist outside the Sacrifice of the Mass is a tribute of inestimable value in the life of the Church. Such worship is closely linked to the celebration of the Eucharistic Sacrifice."[227] Therefore both public and private devotion to the Most Holy Eucharist even outside Mass should be vigorously promoted, for by means of it the faithful give adoration to Christ, truly and really present,[228] the "High Priest of the good things to come"[229] and Redeemer of the whole world. "It is the responsibility of sacred Pastors, even by the witness of their life, to support the practice of Eucharistic worship and especially exposition of the Most Holy Sacrament, as well as prayer of adoration before Christ present under the eucharistic species."[230]

135. The faithful "should not omit making visits during the day to the Most Holy Sacrament, as a proof of gratitude, a pledge of love, and a debt of the adoration due to Christ the Lord who is present in it."[231] For the contemplation of Jesus present in the Most Holy Sacrament, as a communion of desire, powerfully joins the faithful to Christ, as is splendidly evident in the example of so many Saints.[232] "Unless there is a grave reason to the contrary, a church in which the Most Holy Eucharist is reserved should be open to the faithful for at least some hours each day, so that they can spend time in prayer before the Most Holy Sacrament."[233]

136. The Ordinary should diligently foster Eucharistic adoration, whether brief or prolonged or almost continuous, with the participation of the people. For in recent years in so many places "adoration of the Most Holy Sacrament is also an important daily practice and becomes an inexhaustible source of holiness," although there are also places "where there is evident almost a total lack of regard for worship in the form of eucharistic adoration."[234]

137. Exposition of the Most Holy Eucharist must always be carried out in accordance with the prescriptions of the liturgical books.[235] Before the Most Holy Sacrament either reserved or exposed, the praying of the Rosary, which is admirable "in its simplicity and even its profundity," is not to be excluded either.[236] Even so, especially if there is Exposition, the character of this kind of prayer as a contemplation of the mystery of the life of Christ the Redeemer and the Almighty Father's design of salvation should be emphasized, especially by making use of readings taken from Sacred Scripture.[237]

138. Still, the Most Holy Sacrament, when exposed, must never be left unattended even for the briefest space of time. It should therefore be arranged that at least some of the faithful always be present at fixed times, even if they take alternating turns.

139. Where the diocesan Bishop has sacred ministers or others whom he can assign to this purpose, the faithful have a right to visit the Most Holy Sacrament of the Eucharist frequently for adoration, and to take part in adoration before the Most Holy Eucharist exposed at least at some time in the course of any given year.

140. It is highly recommended that at least in the cities and the larger towns the diocesan Bishop should designate a church building for perpetual adoration; in it, however, Holy Mass should be celebrated frequently, even daily if possible, while the Exposition should rigorously be interrupted while Mass is being celebrated.[238] It is fitting that the host to be exposed for adoration should be consecrated in the Mass immediately preceding the time of adoration, and that it should be placed in the monstrance upon the altar after Communion.[239]

141. The diocesan Bishop should acknowledge and foster insofar as possible the right of the various groups of Christ's faithful to form guilds or associations for the carrying out of adoration, even

almost continuous adoration. Whenever such associations assume an international character, it pertains to the Congregation for Divine Worship and the Discipline of the Sacraments to erect them and to approve their statutes.[240]

3. EUCHARISTIC CONGRESSES AND EUCHARISTIC PROCESSIONS

142. "It is for the diocesan Bishop to establish regulations about processions in order to provide for participation in them and for their being carried out in a dignified way"[241] and to promote adoration by the faithful.

143. "Wherever it is possible in the judgement of the diocesan Bishop, a procession through the public streets should be held, especially on the Solemnity of the Body and Blood of Christ as a public witness of reverence for the Most Holy Sacrament,"[242] for the "devout participation of the faithful in the eucharistic procession on the Solemnity of the Body and Blood of Christ is a grace from the Lord which yearly fills with joy those who take part in it."[243]

144. Although this cannot be done in some places, the tradition of holding eucharistic processions should not be allowed to be lost. Instead, new ways should be sought of holding them in today's conditions: for example, at shrines, or in public gardens if the civil authority agrees.

145. The pastoral value of Eucharistic Congresses should be highly esteemed, and they "should be a genuine sign of faith and charity."[244] Let them be diligently prepared and carried out in accordance with what has been laid down,[245] so that Christ's faithful may have the occasion to worship the sacred mysteries of the Body and Blood of the Son of God in a worthy manner, and that they may continually experience within themselves the fruits of the Redemption.[246]

CHAPTER VII
EXTRAORDINARY FUNCTIONS OF LAY FAITHFUL

146. There can be no substitute whatsoever for the ministerial Priesthood. For if a Priest is lacking in the community, then the community lacks the exercise and sacramental function of Christ the Head and Shepherd, which belongs to the essence of its very life.[247] For "the only minister who can confect the sacrament of the Eucharist *in persona Christi* is a validly ordained Priest."[248]

147. When the Church's needs require it, however, if sacred ministers are lacking, lay members of Christ's faithful may supply for certain liturgical offices according to the norm of law.[249] Such faithful are called and appointed to carry out certain functions, whether of greater or lesser weight, sustained by the Lord's grace. Many of the lay Christian faithful have already contributed eagerly to this service and still do so, especially in missionary areas where the Church is still of small dimensions or is experiencing conditions of persecution,[250] but also in areas affected by a shortage of Priests and Deacons.

148. Particular importance is to be attached to the training of catechists, who by means of great labours have given and still give outstanding and altogether necessary help in the spreading of the faith and of the Church.[251]

149. More recently, in some dioceses long since evangelized, members of Christ's lay faithful have been appointed as "pastoral assistants," and among them many have undoubtedly served the good of the Church by providing assistance to the Bishop, Priests and Deacons in the carrying out of their pastoral activity. Let care be taken, however, lest the delineation of this function be assimilated too closely to the form of pastoral ministry that belongs to clerics. That is to say, attention should be paid to ensuring that "pastoral assistants" do not take upon themselves what is proper to the ministry of the sacred ministers.

150. The activity of a pastoral assistant should be directed to facilitating the ministry of Priests and Deacons, to ensuring that vocations to the Priesthood and Diaconate are awakened and that lay members of Christ's faithful in each community are carefully

trained for the various liturgical functions, in keeping with the variety of charisms and in accordance with the norm of law.

151. Only out of true necessity is there to be recourse to the assistance of extraordinary ministers in the celebration of the Liturgy. Such recourse is not intended for the sake of a fuller participation of the laity but rather, by its very nature, is supplementary and provisional.[252] Furthermore, when recourse is had out of necessity to the functions of extraordinary ministers, special urgent prayers of intercession should be multiplied that the Lord may soon send a Priest for the service of the community and raise up an abundance of vocations to sacred Orders.[253]

152. These purely supplementary functions must not be an occasion for disfiguring the very ministry of Priests, in such a way that the latter neglect the celebration of Holy Mass for the people for whom they are responsible, or their personal care of the sick, or the baptism of children, or assistance at weddings or the celebration of Christian funerals, matters which pertain in the first place to Priests assisted by Deacons. It must therefore never be the case that in parishes Priests alternate indiscriminately in shifts of pastoral service with Deacons or laypersons, thus confusing what is specific to each.

153. Furthermore, it is never licit for laypersons to assume the role or the vesture of a Priest or a Deacon or other clothing similar to such vesture.

1. THE EXTRAORDINARY MINISTER OF HOLY COMMUNION

154. As has already been recalled, "the only minister who can confect the Sacrament of the Eucharist *in persona Christi* is a validly ordained Priest."[254] Hence the name "minister of the Eucharist" belongs properly to the Priest alone. Moreover, also by reason of their sacred Ordination, the ordinary ministers of Holy Communion are the Bishop, the Priest and the Deacon,[255] to whom it belongs therefore to administer Holy Communion to the lay members of Christ's faithful during the celebration of Mass. In this way their ministerial office in the Church is fully and accurately brought to light, and the sign value of the Sacrament is made complete.

155. In addition to the ordinary ministers there is the formally instituted acolyte, who by virtue of his institution is an extraordinary minister of Holy Communion even outside the celebration of Mass. If, moreover, reasons of real necessity prompt it, another lay member of Christ's faithful may also be delegated by the diocesan Bishop, in accordance with the norm of law,[256] for one occasion or for a specified time, and an appropriate formula of blessing may be used for the occasion. This act of appointment, however, does not necessarily take a liturgical form, nor, if it does take a liturgical form, should it resemble sacred Ordination in any way. Finally, in special cases of an unforeseen nature, permission can be given for a single occasion by the Priest who presides at the celebration of the Eucharist.[257]

156. This function is to be understood strictly according to the name by which it is known, that is to say, that of extraordinary minister of Holy Communion, and not "special minister of Holy Communion" nor "extraordinary minister of the Eucharist" nor "special minister of the Eucharist," by which names the meaning of this function is unnecessarily and improperly broadened.

157. If there is usually present a sufficient number of sacred ministers for the distribution of Holy Communion, extraordinary ministers of Holy Communion may not be appointed. Indeed, in such circumstances, those who may have already been appointed to this ministry should not exercise it. The practice of those Priests is reprobated who, even though present at the celebration, abstain from distributing Communion and hand this function over to laypersons.[258]

158. Indeed, the extraordinary minister of Holy Communion may administer Communion only when the Priest and Deacon are lacking, when the Priest is prevented by weakness or advanced age or some other genuine reason, or when the number of faithful coming to Communion is so great that the very celebration of Mass would be unduly prolonged.[259] This, however, is to be understood in such a way that a brief prolongation, considering the circumstances and culture of the place, is not at all a sufficient reason.

159. It is never allowed for the extraordinary minister of Holy Communion to delegate anyone else to administer the Eucharist, as for example a parent or spouse or child of the sick person who is the communicant.

160. Let the diocesan Bishop give renewed consideration to the practice in recent years regarding this matter, and if circumstances call for it, let him correct it or define it more precisely. Where such extraordinary ministers are appointed in a widespread manner out of true necessity, the diocesan Bishop should issue special norms by which he determines the manner in which this function is to be carried out in accordance with the law, bearing in mind the tradition of the Church.

2. PREACHING

161. As was already noted above, the homily on account of its importance and its nature is reserved to the Priest or Deacon during Mass.[260] As regards other forms of preaching, if necessity demands it in particular circumstances, or if usefulness suggests it in special cases, lay members of Christ's faithful may be allowed to preach in a church or in an oratory outside Mass in accordance with the norm of law.[261] This may be done only on account of a scarcity of sacred ministers in certain places, in order to meet the need, and it may not be transformed from an exceptional measure into an ordinary practice, nor may it be understood as an authentic form of the advancement of the laity.[262] All must remember besides that the faculty for giving such permission belongs to the local Ordinary, and this as regards individual instances; this permission is not the competence of anyone else, even if they are Priests or Deacons.

3. PARTICULAR CELEBRATIONS CARRIED OUT IN THE ABSENCE OF A PRIEST

162. On the day known as the Lord's Day, the Church faithful gathers together to commemorate the Lord's Resurrection and the whole Paschal Mystery, especially by the celebration of Mass.[263] For "no Christian community is built up unless it is rooted in and hinges upon the celebration of the Most Holy Eucharist."[264] Hence it is the Christian people's right to have the Eucharist celebrated for them on Sunday, and whenever holydays of obligation or other major feasts occur, and even daily insofar as this is possible. Therefore when it is difficult to have the celebration of Mass on a Sunday in a parish church or in another community of Christ's faithful, the diocesan Bishop together with his Priests should consider appropriate remedies.[265] Among such solutions will be that

other Priests be called upon for this purpose, or that the faithful transfer to a church in a nearby place so as to participate in the Eucharistic mystery there.[266]

163. All Priests, to whom the Priesthood and the Eucharist are entrusted *for the sake of* others,[267] should remember that they are enjoined to provide the faithful with the opportunity to satisfy the obligation of participating at Mass on Sundays.[268] For their part, the lay faithful have the right, barring a case of real impossibility, that no Priest should ever refuse either to celebrate Mass for the people or to have it celebrated by another Priest if the people otherwise would not be able to satisfy the obligation of participating at Mass on Sunday or the other days of precept.

164. "If participation at the celebration of the Eucharist is impossible on account of the absence of a sacred minister or for some other grave cause,"[269] then it is the Christian people's right that the diocesan Bishop should provide as far as he is able for some celebration to be held on Sundays for that community under his authority and according to the Church's norms. Sunday celebrations of this specific kind, however, are to be considered altogether extraordinary. All Deacons or lay members of Christ's faithful who are assigned a part in such celebrations by the diocesan Bishop should strive "to keep alive in the community a genuine 'hunger' for the Eucharist, so that no opportunity for the celebration of Mass will ever be missed, also taking advantage of the occasional presence of a Priest who is not impeded by Church law from celebrating Mass."[270]

165. It is necessary to avoid any sort of confusion between this type of gathering and the celebration of the Eucharist.[271] The diocesan Bishops, therefore, should prudently discern whether Holy Communion ought to be distributed in these gatherings. The matter would appropriately be determined in view of a more ample co-ordination in the Bishops' Conference, to be put into effect after the *recognitio* of the acts by the Apostolic See through the Congregation for Divine Worship and the Discipline of the Sacraments. It will be preferable, moreover, when both a Priest and a Deacon are absent, that the various parts be distributed among several faithful rather than having a single lay member of the faithful direct the whole celebration alone. Nor is it ever appropriate to refer to any member of the lay faithful as "presiding" over the celebration.

166. Likewise, especially if Holy Communion is distributed during such celebrations, the diocesan Bishop, to whose exclusive competence this matter pertains, must not easily grant permission for such celebrations to be held on weekdays, especially in places where it was possible or would be possible to have the celebration of Mass on the preceding or the following Sunday. Priests are therefore earnestly requested to celebrate Mass daily for the people in one of the churches entrusted to their care.

167. "Similarly, it is unthinkable on the Lord's Day to substitute for Holy Mass either ecumenical celebrations of the word or services of common prayer with Christians from the . . . Ecclesial Communities, or even participation in these Communities' liturgical services."[272] Should the diocesan Bishop out of necessity authorize the participation of Catholics for a single occasion, let pastors take care lest confusion arise among the Catholic faithful concerning the necessity of taking part at Mass at another hour of the day even in such circumstances, on account of the obligation.[273]

4. THOSE WHO HAVE LEFT THE CLERICAL STATE

168. "A cleric who loses the clerical state in accordance with the law . . . is prohibited from exercising the power of order."[274] It is therefore not licit for him to celebrate the sacraments under any pretext whatsoever save in the exceptional case set forth by law,[275] nor is it licit for Christ's faithful to have recourse to him for the celebration, since there is no reason which would permit this according to canon 1335.[276] Moreover, these men should neither give the homily[277] nor ever undertake any office or duty in the celebration of the sacred Liturgy, lest confusion arise among Christ's faithful and the truth be obscured.

CHAPTER VIII
REMEDIES

169. Whenever an abuse is committed in the celebration of the sacred Liturgy, it is to be seen as a real falsification of Catholic Liturgy. St Thomas wrote, "the vice of falsehood is perpetrated by anyone who offers worship to God on behalf of the Church in a manner contrary to that which is established by the Church with divine authority, and to which the Church is accustomed."[278]

170. In order that a remedy may be applied to such abuses, "there is a pressing need for the biblical and liturgical formation of the people of God, both pastors and faithful,"[279] so that the Church's faith and discipline concerning the sacred Liturgy may be accurately presented and understood. Where abuses persist, however, proceedings should be undertaken for safeguarding the spiritual patrimony and rights of the Church in accordance with the law, employing all legitimate means.

171. Among the various abuses there are some which are objectively *graviora delicta* or otherwise constitute grave matters, as well as others which are nonetheless to be carefully avoided and corrected. Bearing in mind everything that is treated especially in Chapter I of this Instruction, attention should be paid to what follows.

1. GRAVIORA DELICTA

172. *Graviora delicta* against the sanctity of the Most August Sacrifice and Sacrament of the Eucharist are to be handled in accordance with the "Norms concerning *graviora delicta* reserved to the Congregation for the Doctrine of the Faith,"[280] namely:

a) taking away or retaining the consecrated species for sacrilegious ends, or the throwing them away;[281]

b) the attempted celebration of the liturgical action of the Eucharistic Sacrifice or the simulation of the same;[282]

c) the forbidden concelebration of the Eucharistic Sacrifice with ministers of Ecclesial Communities that do not have the apostolic succession nor acknowledge the sacramental dignity of priestly Ordination;[283]

d) the consecration for sacrilegious ends of one matter without the other in the celebration of the Eucharist or even of both outside the celebration of the Eucharist.[284]

2. GRAVE MATTERS

173. Although the gravity of a matter is to be judged in accordance with the common teaching of the Church and the norms established by her, objectively to be considered among grave matters is anything that puts at risk the validity and dignity of the

Most Holy Eucharist: namely, anything that contravenes what is set out above in nn. 48–52, 56, 76–77, 79, 91–92, 94, 96, 101–102, 104, 106, 109, 111, 115, 117, 126, 131–133, 138, 153 and 168. Moreover, attention should be given to the other prescriptions of the Code of Canon Law, and especially what is laid down by canons 1364, 1369, 1373, 1376, 1380, 1384, 1385, 1386, and 1398.

3. OTHER ABUSES

174. Furthermore, those actions that are brought about which are contrary to the other matters treated elsewhere in this Instruction or in the norms established by law are not to be considered of little account, but are to be numbered among the other abuses to be carefully avoided and corrected.

175. The things set forth in this Instruction obviously do not encompass all the violations against the Church and its discipline that are defined in the canons, in the liturgical laws and in other norms of the Church for the sake of the teaching of the Magisterium or sound tradition. Where something wrong has been committed, it is to be corrected according to the norm of law.

4. THE DIOCESAN BISHOP

176. The diocesan Bishop, "since he is the principal dispenser of the mysteries of God, is to strive constantly so that Christ's faithful entrusted to his care may grow in grace through the celebration of the sacraments, and that they may know and live the Paschal Mystery."[285] It is his responsibility, "within the limits of his competence, to issue norms on liturgical matters by which all are bound."[286]

177. "Since he must safeguard the unity of the universal Church, the Bishop is bound to promote the discipline common to the entire Church and therefore to insist upon the observance of all ecclesiastical laws. He is to be watchful lest abuses encroach upon ecclesiastical discipline, especially as regards the ministry of the Word, the celebration of the Sacraments and sacramentals, the worship of God and the veneration of the Saints."[287]

178. Hence whenever a local Ordinary or the Ordinary of a religious Institute or of a Society of apostolic life receives at least a plausible notice of a delict or abuse concerning the Most Holy

Eucharist, let him carefully investigate, either personally or by means of another worthy cleric, concerning the facts and the circumstances as well as the imputability.

179. Delicts against the faith as well as *graviora delicta* committed in the celebration of the Eucharist and the other Sacraments are to be referred without delay to the Congregation for the Doctrine of the Faith, which "examines [them] and, if necessary, proceeds to the declaration or imposition of canonical sanctions according to the norm of common or proper law."[288]

180. Otherwise the Ordinary should proceed according the norms of the sacred canons, imposing canonical penalties if necessary, and bearing in mind in particular that which is laid down by canon 1326. If the matter is serious, let him inform the Congregation for Divine Worship and the Discipline of the Sacraments.

5. THE APOSTOLIC SEE

181. Whenever the Congregation for Divine Worship and the Discipline of the Sacraments receives at least a plausible notice of a delict or an abuse concerning the Most Holy Eucharist, it informs the Ordinary so that he may investigate the matter. When the matter turns out to be serious, the Ordinary should send to the same Dicastery as quickly as possible a copy of the acts of the inquiry that has been undertaken, and where necessary, the penalty imposed.

182. In more difficult cases the Ordinary, for the sake of the good of the universal Church in the care for which he too has a part by virtue of his sacred Ordination, should not fail to handle the matter, having previously taken advice from the Congregation for Divine Worship and the Discipline of the Sacraments. For its part, this Congregation, on the strength of the faculties given to it by the Roman Pontiff, according to the nature of the case, will assist the Ordinary, granting him the necessary dispensations[289] or giving him instructions or prescriptions, which he is to follow diligently.

6. COMPLAINTS REGARDING ABUSES IN LITURGICAL MATTERS

183. In an altogether particular manner, let everyone do all that is in their power to ensure that the Most Holy Sacrament of the

Eucharist will be protected from any and every irreverence or distortion and that all abuses be thoroughly corrected. This is a most serious duty incumbent upon each and every one, and all are bound to carry it out without any favoritism.

184. Any Catholic, whether Priest or Deacon or lay member of Christ's faithful, has the right to lodge a complaint regarding a liturgical abuse to the diocesan Bishop or the competent Ordinary equivalent to him in law, or to the Apostolic See on account of the primacy of the Roman Pontiff.[290] It is fitting, however, insofar as possible, that the report or complaint be submitted first to the diocesan Bishop. This is naturally to be done in truth and charity.

CONCLUSION

185. "Against the seeds of discord which daily experience shows to be so deeply ingrained in human nature as a result of sin, there stands the creative power of the unity of Christ's body. For it is precisely by building up the Church that the Eucharist establishes fellowship among men."[291] It is therefore the hope of this Congregation for Divine Worship and the Discipline of the Sacraments that also, by the diligent application of those things that are recalled in this Instruction, human weakness may come to pose less of an obstacle to the action of the Most Holy Sacrament of the Eucharist, and that with all distortion set aside and every reprobated practice removed,[292] through the intercession of the Blessed Virgin Mary, "Woman of the Eucharist," the saving presence of Christ in the Sacrament of his Body and Blood may shine brightly upon all people.

186. Let all Christ's faithful participate in the Most Holy Eucharist as fully, consciously and actively as they can,[293] honouring it lovingly by their devotion and the manner of their life. Let Bishops, Priests and Deacons, in the exercise of the sacred ministry, examine their consciences as regards the authenticity and fidelity of the actions they have performed in the name of Christ and the Church in the celebration of the Sacred Liturgy. Let each one of the sacred ministers ask himself, even with severity, whether he has respected the rights of the lay members of Christ's faithful, who confidently entrust themselves and their children to him, relying on him to fulfil for the faithful those sacred functions that the Church intends to carry out in celebrating the sacred

Liturgy at Christ's command.[294] For each one should always remember that he is a servant of the Sacred Liturgy.[295]

All things to the contrary notwithstanding.

This Instruction, prepared by the Congregation for Divine Worship and the Discipline of the Sacraments by mandate of the Supreme Pontiff John Paul II in collaboration with the Congregation for the Doctrine of the Faith, was approved by the same Pontiff on the Solemnity of St. Joseph, 19 March 2004, and he ordered it to be published and to be observed immediately by all concerned.

From the offices of the Congregation for Divine Worship and the Discipline of the Sacraments, Rome, on the Solemnity of the Annunciation of the Lord, 25 March 2004.

Francis Cardinal Arinze
Prefect

Domenico Sorrentino
Archbishop Secretary

NOTES

1. Cf. *Missale Romanum,* ex decreto sacrosancti Oecumenici Concilii Vaticani II instauratum, auctoritate Pauli Pp. VI promulgatum, Ioannis Pauli Pp. II cura recognitum, editio typica tertia, diei 20 aprilis 2000, Typis Vaticanis, 2002, Missa votiva de Dei misericordia, oratio super oblata, p. 1159.
2. Cf. 1 Corinthians 11, 26; *Missale Romanum,* Prex Eucharistica, acclamatio post consecrationem, p. 576; John Paul II, Encyclical Letter, *Ecclesia de Eucharistia,* 17 April 2003, nn. 5, 11, 14, 18: AAS 95 (2003) pp. 436, 440–441, 442, 445.
3. Cf. Isaiah 10: 33; 51, 22; *Missale Romanum,* In sollemnitate Domini nostri Iesu Christi, universorum Regis, Praefatio, p. 499.
4. Cf.1 Corinthians 5: 7; Second Vatican Ecumenical Council, Decree on the Ministry and Life of Priests, *Presbyterorum ordinis,* 7 December 1965, n. 5; John Paul II, Apostolic Exhortation., *Ecclesia in Europa,* n. 75: AAS 95 (2003) pp. 649–719, here p. 693.
5. Cf. Second Vatican Ecumenical Council, Dogmatic Constitution on the Church, *Lumen gentium,* 21 November 1964, n. 11.
6. Cf. John Paul II, Encyclical Letter *Ecclesia de Eucharistia,* 17 April 2003, n. 21: AAS 95 (2003) p. 447.
7. Ibidem: AAS 95 (2003) pp. 433-475.
8. Ibidem, n. 52: AAS 95 (2003) p. 468.
9. Ibidem.
10. Ibidem, n. 10: AAS 95 (2003) p. 439.
11. Ibidem; cf. John Paul II, Apostolic Letter, *Vicesimus quintus annus,* 4 December 1988, nn. 12–13: AAS 81 (1989) pp. 909–910; cf. also Second Vatican Ecumenical Council, Constitution on the Sacred Liturgy, *Sacrosanctum Concilium,* 4 December 1963 n. 48.
12. *Missale Romanum,* Prex Eucharistica III, p. 588; cf. 1 Corinthians 12:12–13; Ephesians 4:4.
13. Cf. Philippians 2:5.
14. John Paul II, Encyclical Letter *Ecclesia de Eucharistia,* n. 10: AAS 95 (2003), p. 439.
15. Ibidem, n. 6: AAS 95 (2003) p. 437; cf. Luke 24:31.
16. Cf. Romans 1:20.
17. Cf. *Missale Romanum,* Praefatio I de Passione Domini, p. 528.
18. Cf. John Paul II, Encyclical Letter *Veritatis splendor,* 6 August 1993, n. 35: AAS 85 (1993) pp. 1161–1162; Homily given at Camden Yards, 9 October 1995, n. 7: *Insegnamenti di Giovanni Paolo II, XVII, 2 (1995),* Libreria Editrice Vaticana, 1998, p. 788.
19. Cf. John Paul II, Encyclical Letter *Ecclesia de Eucharistia,* n. 10: AAS 95 (2003) p. 439.

20. Second Vatican Ecumenical Council, Constitution on the Sacred Liturgy, *Sacrosanctum Concilium,* n. 24; cf. Congregation for Divine Worship and the Discipline of the Sacraments, Instruction *Varietates legitimae,* 25 January 1994, nn. 19 and 23: AAS 87 (1995) pp. 295–296, 297.

21. Second Vatican Ecumenical Council, Constitution on the Sacred Liturgy, *Sacrosanctum Concilium,* n. 33.

22. Cf. St Irenaeus, *Adversus Haereses,* III, 2: SCh., 211, 24 31; St Augustine, *Epistula ad Ianuarium:* 54,I: PL 33,200: "Illa autem quae non scripta, sed tradita custodimus, quae quidem toto terrarum orbe servantur, datur intellegi vel ab ipsis Apostolis, vel plenariis conciliis, quorum est Ecclesia saluberrima auctoritas, commendata atque statuta retineri"; John Paul II, Encyclical Letter *Redemptoris missio,* 7 December 1990, nn. 53–54: AAS 83 (1991) pp. 300–302; Congregation for the Doctrine of the Faith, Letter to the Bishops of the Catholic Church on Certain Aspects of the Church as Communion, *Communionis notio,* 28 May 1992, nn. 7–10: AAS 85 (1993) pp. 842–844; Congregation for Divine Worship and the Discipline of the Sacraments, Instruction *Varietates legitimae,* n. 26: AAS 87 (1995) pp. 298–299.

23. Cf. Second Vatican Ecumenical Council, Constitution on the Sacred Liturgy, *Sacrosanctum Concilium,* n. 21.

24. Cf. Pius XII, Apostolic Constitution *Sacramentum Ordinis,* 30 November 1947: AAS 40 (1948) p. 5; Congregation for the Doctrine of the Faith, Declaration *Inter insigniores,* 15 October 1976, part IV: AAS 69 (1977) pp. 107–108; Congregation for Divine Worship and the Discipline of the Sacraments, Instruction *Varietates legitimae,* n. 25: AAS 87 (1995) p. 298.

25. Cf. Pius XII, Encyclical Letter *Mediator Dei,* 20 November 1947: AAS 39 (1947) p. 540.

26. Cf. Sacred Congregation for the Sacraments and Divine Worship, Instruction *Inaestimabile donum,* 3 April 1980: AAS 72 (1980) p. 333.

27. John Paul II, Encyclical Letter *Ecclesia de Eucharistia,* n. 52: AAS 95 (2003), p. 468.

28. Second Vatican Ecumenical Council, Constitution on the Sacred Liturgy, *Sacrosanctum Concilium,* nn. 4, 38; Decree on the Catholic Eastern Churches, *Orientalium Ecclesiarum,* 21 November 1964, nn. 1,2,6; Paul VI, Apostolic Constitution *Missale Romanum:* AAS 61 (1969) pp. 217–222; *Missale Romanum,* Institutio Generalis, n. 399; Congregation for Divine Worship and the Discipline of the Sacraments, Instruction *Liturgiam authenticam,* 28 March 2001, n. 4: AAS 93 (2001) pp. 685–726, here p. 686.

29. Cf. John Paul II, Apostolic Exhortation *Ecclesia in Europa,* n. 72: AAS 95 (2003) p. 000.

30. Cf. John Paul II, Encyclical Letter *Ecclesia de Eucharistia,* n. 23: AAS 95 (2003) pp. 448–449; S. Congregation of Rites, Instruction *Eucharisticum mysterium,* 25 May 1967, n. 6: AAS 59 (1967) p. 545.

31. Sacred Congregation for the Sacraments and Divine Worship, Instruction *Inaestimabile donum:* AAS 72 (1980) pp. 332–333.

32. Cf. 1 Corinthians 11:17–34; John Paul II, Encyclical Letter, *Ecclesia de Eucharistia*, n. 52: AAS 95 (2003) pp. 467–468.

33. Cf. *Code of Canon Law*, 25 January 1983, canon 1752.

34. Second Vatican Ecumenical Council, Constitution on the Sacred Liturgy, *Sacrosanctum Concilium*, n. 22 §1; cf. *Code of Canon Law*, canon 838 §1.

35. *Code of Canon Law*, canon 331; cf. Second Vatican Ecumenical Council, Dogmatic Constitution on the Church, *Lumen gentium*, n. 22.

36. *Code of Canon Law*, canon 838 §2.

37. Cf. John Paul II, Apostolic Constitution, *Pastor bonus*, 28 June 1988: AAS 80 (1988) pp. 841–924, here articles 62, 63, and 66, pp. 876–877.

38. Cf. John Paul II, Encyclical Letter, *Ecclesia de Eucharistia*, n. 52: AAS 95 (2003) p. 468.

39. Cf. Second Vatican Ecumenical Council, Decree on the Pastoral Office of Bishops, *Christus Dominus*, 28 October 1965, n. 15; cf. also the Constitution on the Sacred Liturgy, *Sacrosanctum Concilium*, n. 41; *Code of Canon Law*, canon 387.

40. Prayer for the Consecration of a Bishop in the Byzantine Rite: *Euchologion to mega*, Rome, 1873, p. 139.

41. Cf. St. Ignatius of Antioch, *Ad Smyrn.* 8,1: ed. F. X. Funk, I, p. 282.

42. Second Vatican Ecumenical Council, Dogmatic Constitution on the Church, *Lumen gentium*, n. 26; cf. Sacred Congregation of Rites, Instruction, *Eucharisticum mysterium*, n. 7: AAS 59 (1967) p. 545; cf. also John Paul II, Apostolic Exhortation, *Pastores gregis*, 16 October 2003, nn. 32–41: *L'Osservatore Romano*, 17 October 2003, pp. 6–8.

43. Cf. Second Vatican Ecumenical Council, Constitution on the Sacred Liturgy, *Sacrosanctum Concilium*, n. 41; cf. St. Ignatius of Antioch, *Ad Magn.* 7, *Ad Philad.* 4, *Ad Smyrn.* 8: ed. F. X. Funk, I, pp. 236, 266, 281; *Missale Romanum*, Institutio Generalis, n. 22; cf. also *Code of Canon Law*, canon 389.

44. Second Vatican Ecumenical Council, Constitution on the Sacred Liturgy, *Lumen gentium*, n. 26.

45. *Code of Canon Law*, canon 838 §4.

46. Cf. Consilium for Implementing the Constitution on the Liturgy, Dubium: *Notitiae* 1 (1965) p. 254.

47. Cf. Acts 20,28; Second Vatican Ecumenical Council, Dogmatic Constitution on the Church, *Lumen gentium*, nn. 21 and 27; Decree on the Pastoral Office of Bishops in the Church, *Christus Dominus*, n. 3.

48. Cf. S. Congregation for Divine Worship, Instruction, *Liturgicae instaurationes*, 5 September 1970: AAS 62 (1970) p. 694.

49. Cf. Second Vatican Ecumenical Council, Dogmatic Constitution on the Church, *Lumen gentium*, n. 21; Decree on the Pastoral Office of Bishops in the Church, *Christus Dominus*, n. 3.

50. Cf. Caeremoniale Episcoporum ex decreto sacrosancti Oecumenici Concilii Vaticani II instauratum, auctoritate Ioannis Pauli Pp. II promulgatum, editio typica, 14 September 1984, Vatican Polyglot Press, 1985, n. 10

51. Cf. *Missale Romanum,* Institutio Generalis, n. 387.

52. Cf. ibidem, n. 22.

53. Cf. Sacred Congregation for Divine Worship, Instruction, *Liturgicae instaurationes:* AAS 62 (1970) p. 694.

54. Second Vatican Ecumenical Council, Dogmatic Constitution on the Church, *Lumen gentium,* n. 27; cf. 2 Corinthians 4:15.

55. Cf. *Code of Canon Law,* canons 397 §1; 678 §1.

56. Cf. ibidem, canon 683 §1.

57. Ibidem, canon 392.

58. Cf. John Paul II, Apostolic Letter *Vicesimus quintus annus,* n. 21: AAS 81 (1989) p. 917; Second Vatican Ecumenical Council, Constitution on the Sacred Liturgy, *Sacrosanctum Concilium,* nn. 45–46; Pius XII, Encyclical Letter *Mediator Dei:* AAS 39 (1947) p. 562.

59. Cf. John Paul II, Apostolic Letter *Vicesimus quintus annus,* n. 20: AAS 81 (1989) p. 916.

60. Cf. ibidem.

61. Cf. Second Vatican Ecumenical Council, Constitution on the Sacred Liturgy, *Sacrosanctum Concilium,* n. 44; Congregation for Bishops, Letter sent to the Presidents of the Conferences of Bishops together with the Congregation for the Evangelization of Peoples, 21 June 1999, n. 9: AAS 91 (1999) p. 999.

62. Cf. Congregation for Divine Worship, Instruction *Liturgicae instaurationis,* n. 12: AAS 62 (1970) pp. 692–704; cf., here p. 703.

63. Cf. Congregation For Divine Worship, *Declaration on Eucharistic Prayers and liturgical experimentation,* 21 March 1988: *Notitiae* 24 (1988) pp. 234–236.

64. Cf. Congregation for Divine Worship and the Discipline of the Sacraments, Instruction *Varietates legitimae:* AAS 87 (1995) pp. 288–314.

65. Cf. *Code of Canon Law,* canon 838 § 3; S. Congregation of Rites, Instruction *Inter Oecumenici,* 26 September 1964, n. 31: AAS 56 (1964) p. 883; Congregation for Divine Worship and the Discipline of the Sacraments, Instruction *Liturgiam authenticam,* nn. 79–80: AAS 93 (2001) pp. 711–713.

66. Cf. Second Vatican Ecumenical Council, Decree on the Ministry and Life of Priests, *Presbyterorum ordinis,* 7 December 1965, n. 7; Pontificale Romanum, ed. 1962: Ordo consecrationis sacerdotalis, in Praefatione; Pontificale Romanum *ex decreto sacrosancti Oecumenici Concilii Vaticani II renovatum, auctoritate Pauli Pp. VI editum, Ioannis Pauli Pp. II cura recognitum:* De Ordinatione Episcopi, presbyterorum et diaconorum, editio typica altera, 29 June 1989, Typis Polyglottis Vaticanis, 1990, cap. II: De Ordin. presbyterorum, Praenotanda, n. 101.

67. St. Ignatius of Antioch, *Ad Philad.,* 4: ed. F. X. Funk, I, p. 266; St. Cornelius I, cited by St. Cyprian, Letter 48,2: ed. G. Hartel, III,2, p. 610.

68. Second Vatican Ecumenical Council, Dogmatic Constitution on the Church, *Lumen gentium,* n. 28.

69. Cf. *ibidem.*

70. John Paul II, Encyclical Letter *Ecclesia de Eucharistia,* n. 52; cf. n. 29: AAS 95 (2003) pp. 467–468, 452–435.

71. *Pontificale Romanum, De Ordinatione Episcopi, presbyterorum et diaconorum,* editio typica altera: *De Ordinatione Presbyterorum,* n. 124; cf. *Missale Romanum,* Feria V in Hebdomada Sancta: Ad Missam chrismatis, Renovatio promissionum sacerdotalium, p. 292.

72. Cf. Ecumenical Council of Trent, Session VII, 3 March 1547, Decree on the Sacraments, canon 13, DS 1613; Second Vatican Ecumenical Council, Constitution on the Sacred Liturgy, *Sacrosanctum Concilium,* n. 22; Pius XII, Encyclical Letter *Mediator Dei:* AAS 39 (1947) pp. 544, 546–547, 562; *Codex Iuris Canonici,* canon 846, § 1; *Missale Romanum,* Institutio Generalis, n. 24.

73. St. Ambrose, *De Virginitate,* n. 48: PL 16, 278.

74. *Code of Canon Law,* canon 528 § 2.

75. Second Vatican Ecumenical Council, Decree on the Ministry and Life of Priests, *Presbyterorum Ordinis,* n. 5.

76. Cf. John Paul II, Encyclical Letter *Ecclesia de Eucharistia,* n. 5: AAS 95 (2003) p. 436.

77. Second Vatican Ecumenical Council, Dogmatic Constitution on the Church, *Lumen gentium,* n. 29; cf. *Constitutiones Ecclesiae Aegypticae,* III, 2: ed. F. X. Funk, *Didascalia,* II, p. 103; *Statuta Ecclesiae Ant.,* 37–41: ed. D. Mansi 3, 954.

78. Cf. Acts 6:3.

79. John 13:35.

80. Matthew 20:28.

81. Cf. Luke 22:27.

82. Cf. *Caeremoniale Episcoporum,* nn. 9, 23. Cf. Second Vatican Ecumenical Council, Dogmatic Constitution on the Church, *Lumen gentium,* n. 29.

83. Cf. *Pontificale Romanum, De Ordinatione Episcopi, presbyterorum et diaconorum,* editio typica altera, cap. III, *De Ordin. diaconorum,* n. 199.

84. Cf. 1 Timothy 3:9.

85. Cf. *Pontificale Romanum, De Ordinatione Episcopi, presbyterorum et diaconorum,* editio typica altera, cap. III, *De Ordin. diaconorum,* n. 200.

86. Second Vatican Ecumenical Council, Constitution on the Sacred Liturgy, *Sacrosanctum Concilium,* n. 10.

87. Cf. ibidem, n. 41; Second Vatican Ecumenical Council, Dogmatic Constitution on the Church, *Lumen gentium,* n. 11; Decree on the Ministry and Life of Priests, *Presbyterorum ordinis,* nn. 2, 5, 6; Decree on the Pastoral Office of Bishops, *Christus Dominus,* n. 30, Decree on Ecumenism, *Unitatis redintegratio,* 21 November 1964, n. 15; Sacred Congregation of Rites, Instruction *Eucharisticum mysterium,* nn. 3e, 6: AAS 59 (1967) pp. 542, 544–545; *Missale Romanum,* Institutio Generalis, n. 16.

88. Cf. Second Vatican Ecumenical Council, Constitution on the Sacred Liturgy, *Sacrosanctum Concilium,* n. 26; *Missale Romanum,* Institutio Generalis, n. 91.

89. 1 Peter 2:9; cf. 2:4–5.

90. *Missale Romanum,* Institutio Generalis, n. 91; cf. Second Vatican Ecumenical Council, Constitution on the Sacred Liturgy, *Sacrosanctum Concilium,* n. 41.

91. Second Vatican Ecumenical Council, Dogmatic Constitution on the Church, *Lumen gentium,* n. 10.

92. Cf. St. Thomas Aquinas, *Summa Theologica,* III, q. 63, a. 2.

93. Second Vatican Ecumenical Council, Dogmatic Constitution on the Church, *Lumen gentium,* n. 10; cf. John Paul II, Encyclical Letter *Ecclesia de Eucharistia,* n. 28: AAS 95 (2003) p. 452.

94. Cf. Acts 2:42–47.

95. Cf. Romans 12:1.

96. Cf. 1 Peter 3:15; 2:4–10.

97. Cf. John Paul II, Encyclical Letter *Ecclesia de Eucharistia,* nn. 12–18: AAS 95 (2003) pp. 441–445; Letter *Dominicae Cenae,* 24 February 1980, n. 9: AAS 72 (1980) pp. 129–133.

98. John Paul II, Encyclical Letter *Ecclesia de Eucharistia,* n. 10: AAS 95 (2003) p. 439.

99. Cf. Second Vatican Ecumenical Council, Constitution on the Sacred Liturgy, *Sacrosanctum Concilium,* nn. 30–31.

100. Cf. Sacred Congregation for Divine Worship, Instruction *Liturgicae instaurationes,* n. 1: AAS 62 (1970) p. 695.

101. Cf. *Missale Romanum,* Feria secunda post Dominica V in Quadragesima, Collecta, p. 258.

102. Cf. John Paul II, Apostolic Letter *Novo Millennio ineunte,* 6 January 2001, n. 21: AAS 93 (2001) p. 280; cf. John 20:28.

103. Cf. Pius XII, Encyclical Letter *Mediator Dei:* AAS 39 (1947) p. 586; cf. also Second Vatican Ecumenical Council, Dogmatic Constitution on the Church, *Lumen gentium,* n. 67; Paul VI, Apostolic Exhortation *Marialis cultus,* 11 February 1974, n. 24: AAS 66 (1974) pp. 113–168, here p. 134; Congregation for Divine Worship and the Discipline of the Sacraments, *Direttorio su pietà popolare e Liturgia,* 17 December 2001.

104. John Paul II, Apostolic Letter, *Rosarium Virginis Mariae,* 16 October 2002: AAS 95 (2003) pp. 5–36.

105. Cf. Pius XII, Encyclical Letter *Mediator Dei:* AAS 39 (1947) pp. 586–587.

106. Cf. Congregation for Divine Worship and the Discipline of the Sacraments, Instruction, *Varietates legitimae,* n. 22: AAS 87 (1995) p. 297.

107. Cf. Pius XII, Encyclical Letter, *Mediator Dei:* AAS 39 (1947) p. 553.

108. John Paul II, Encyclical Letter, *Ecclesia de Eucharistia,* n. 29: AAS 95 (2003) p. 453; cf. Fourth Lateran Ecumenical Council, 11–30 November 1215, Chapter I: DS 802; Ecumenical Council of Trent, Session XXIII, 15 July 1563, Doctrine and Canons on Sacred Order, Chapter 4: DS 1767–1770; Pius XII, Encyclical Letter, *Mediator Dei:* AAS 39 (1947) p. 553.

109. Cf. *Code of Canon Law,* canon 230 § 2; cf. also the *Missale Romanum,* Institutio Generalis, n. 97.

110. Cf. *Missale Romanum,* General Instruction, n. 109.

111. Cf. Paul VI, Apostolic Letter (Motu Proprio) *Ministeria quaedam*, 15 August 1972, nn. VI–XII; *Pontificale Romanum* ex decreto sacrosancti oecumenici Concilii Vaticani II instauratum, auctoritate Pauli Pp. VI promulgatum, *De institutione lectorum et acolythorum, de admissione inter candidatos ad diaconatum et presbyteratum, de sacro caelibatu amplectendo*, editio typica, 3 December 1972, Typis Polyglottis Vaticanis, 1973, p. 10: AAS 64 (1972) pp. 529–534, here pp. 532–533; *Code of Canon Law*, canon 230 §1; *Missale Romanum*, Institutio Generalis, nn. 98–99, 187–193.

112. Cf. *Missale Romanum*, Institutio Generalis, nn. 187–190, 193; *Code of Canon Law*, canon 230 §2–3.

113. Cf. Second Vatican Ecumenical Council, Constitution on the Sacred Liturgy, *Sacrosanctum Concilium*, n. 24; Sacred Congregation for the Sacraments and Divine Worship, Instruction, *Inaestimabile donum*, nn. 2 and 18: AAS 72 (1980) pp. 334, 338; *Missale Romanum*, Institutio Generalis, nn. 101, 194–198; *Code of Canon Law*, canon 230 §2–3.

114. Cf. *Missale Romanum*, Institutio Generalis, nn. 100–107.

115. Ibidem, n. 91; cf. Second Vatican Ecumenical Council, Constitution on the Sacred Liturgy, *Sacrosanctum Concilium*, n. 28.

116. Cf. John Paul II, Allocution to the Conference of Bishops of the Antilles, 7 May 2002, n. 2: AAS 94 (2002) pp. 575–577; Post-Synodal Apostolic Exhortation, *Christifideles laici*, 30 December 1988, n. 23: AAS 81 (1989) pp. 393-521, here pp. 429–431; Congregation for the Clergy et al., Instruction, *Ecclesiae de mysterio*, 15 August 1997, Theological Principles, n. 4: AAS 89 (1997) pp. 860–861.

117. Cf. Second Vatican Ecumenical Council, Constitution on the Sacred Liturgy, *Sacrosanctum Concilium*, n. 19.

118. Sacred Congregation for Divine Worship, Instruction, *Immensae caritatis*, 29 January 1973: AAS 65 (1973) p. 266.

119. Cf. Sacred Congregation of Rites, Instruction, *De Musica sacra*, 3 September 1958, n. 93c: AAS 50 (1958) p. 656.

120. Cf. Pontifical Council for the Interpretation of Legislative Texts, Response to dubium, 11 July 1992: AAS 86 (1994) pp. 541–542; Congregation for Divine Worship and the Discipline of the Sacraments, Letter to the Presidents of Conferences of Bishops on the liturgical service of laypersons, 15 March 1994: *Notitiae* 30 (1994) pp. 333–335, 347–348.

121. Cf. John Paul II, Apostolic Constitution, *Pastor Bonus*, article 65: AAS 80 (1988) p. 877.

122. Cf. Pontifical Council for the Interpretation of Legislative Texts, Response to dubium, 11 July 1992: AAS 86 (1994) pp. 541–542; Congregation for Divine Worship and the Discipline of the Sacraments, Letter to the Presidents of the Conferences of Bishops concerning the liturgical service of laypersons, 15 March 1994: *Notitiae* 30 (1994) pp. 333–335, 347–348; Letter to a Bishop, 27 July 2001: *Notitiae* 38 (2002) 46–54.

123. Cf. *Code of Canon Law*, can. 924 §2; *Missale Romanum*, Institutio Generalis, n. 320.

124. Cf. Sacred Congregation for the Discipline of the Sacraments, Instruction, *Dominus Salvator noster,* 26 March 1929, n. 1: AAS 21 (1929) pp. 631–642, here p. 632.

125. Cf. ibidem, n. II: AAS 21 (1929) p. 635.

126. Cf. *Missale Romanum,* Institutio Generalis, n. 321.

127. Cf. Luke 22:18; *Code of Canon Law,* canon 924 §§ 1, 3; *Missale Romanum,* Institutio Generalis, n. 322.

128. Cf. *Missale Romanum,* Institutio Generalis, n. 323.

129. John Paul II, Apostolic Letter, *Vicesimus quintus annus,* n. 13, AAS 81 (1989).

130. Sacred Congregation for the Sacraments and Divine Worship, Instruction, *Inaestimabile donum,* n. 5: AAS 72 (1980) p. 335.

131. Cf. John Paul II, Encyclical Letter, *Ecclesia de Eucharistia,* n. 28: AAS 95 (2003) p. 452; *Missale Romanum,* Institutio Generalis, n. 147; Sacred Congregation for Divine Worship, Instruction, *Liturgicae instaurationes,* n. 4: AAS 62 (1970) p. 698; Sacred Congregation for the Sacraments and Divine Worship, Instruction, *Inaestimabile donum,* n. 4: AAS 72 (1980) p. 334.

132. *Missale Romanum,* Institutio Generalis, n. 32.

133. Ibidem, n. 147; cf. John Paul II, Encyclical Letter, *Ecclesia de Eucharistia,* n. 28: AAS 95 (2003) p. 452; cf. also Congregation for the Sacraments and Divine Worship, Instruction, *Inaestimabile donum,* n. 4: AAS 72 (1980) pp. 334–335.

134. John Paul II, Encyclical Letter, *Ecclesia de Eucharistia,* n. 39: AAS 95 (2003) p. 459.

135. Cf. Sacred Congregation for Divine Worship, Instruction, *Liturgicae instaurationes,* n. 2b: AAS 62 (1970) p. 696.

136. Cf. *Missale Romanum,* Institutio Generalis, nn. 356–362.

137. Cf. Second Vatican Ecumenical Council, Constitution on the Sacred Liturgy, *Sacrosanctum Concilium,* n. 51.

138. *Missale Romanum,* Institutio Generalis, n. 57; cf. John Paul II, Apostolic Letter, *Vicesimus quintus annus,* n. 13: AAS 81 (1989) p. 910; Congregation for the Doctrine of the Faith, Declaration, *Dominus Iesus,* on the unicity and salvific universality of Jesus Christ and the Church, 6 August 2000: AAS 92 (2000) pp. 742–765.

139. *Missale Romanum,* General Instruction, n. 60.

140. Cf. ibidem, nn. 59–60.

141. Cf., e.g., *Rituale Romanum,* ex decreto sacrosancti Oecumenici Concilii Vaticani II renovatum, auctoritate Pauli Pp. VI editum Ioannis Pauli Pp. II cura recognitum: *Ordo celebrandi Matrimonium,* editio typica altera, 19 March 1990, Typis Polyglottis Vaticanis 1991, n. 125; *Roman Ritual,* renewed by decree of the Second Vatican Ecumenical Council and promulgated by authority of Pope Paul VI: Order for Anointing of the Sick and for their Pastoral Care, *editio typica,* 7 December 1972, Vatican Polyglot Press, 1972, n. 72.

142. Cf. *Code of Canon Law,* canon 767 §1.

143. Cf. *Missale Romanum,* Institutio Generalis, n. 66; cf. also the *Code of Canon Law,* canon 6, §1, 2; also canon 767 §1, regarding which other noteworthy prescriptions may be found in Congregation for the Clergy et al., Instruction, *Ecclesiae de mysterio,* Practical Provisions, article 3 § 1: AAS 89 (1997) p. 865.

144. *Missale Romanum,* Institutio Generalis, n. 66; cf. also the *Code of Canon Law,* canon 767 §1.

145. Cf. Congregation for the Clergy et al., Instruction, *Ecclesiae de mysterio,* Practical Provisions, article 3 §1: AAS 89 (1997) p. 865; cf. also the *Code of Canon Law,* canon 6 §1, 2; Pontifical Commission for the Authentic Interpretation of the Code of Canon Law, Response to dubium, 20 June 1987: AAS 79 (1987) p. 1249.

146. Cf. Congregation for the Clergy et al., Instruction, *Ecclesiae de mysterio,* Practical Provisions, article 3 § 1: AAS 89 (1997) pp. 864–865.

147. Cf. Ecumenical Council of Trent, Session XXII, 17 September 1562, on the Most Holy Sacrifice of the Mass, Chapter 8: DS 1749; *Missale Romanum,* Institutio Generalis, n. 65.

148. Cf. John Paul II, Allocution to a number of Bishops from the United States of America who had come to Rome for a visit "ad Limina Apostolorum," 28 May 1993, n. 2: AAS 86 (1994) p. 330.

149. Cf. *Code of Canon Law,* canon 386 §1.

150. Cf. *Missale Romanum,* Institutio Generalis, n. 73.

151. Cf. ibidem, n. 154.

152. Cf. ibidem, nn. 82, 154.

153. Cf. ibidem, n. 83.

154. Cf. Sacred Congregation for Divine Worship, Instruction, *Liturgicae instaurationes,* n. 5: AAS 62 (1970) p. 699.

155. Cf. *Missale Romanum,* Institutio Generalis, nn. 83, 240, 321.

156. Cf. Congregation For the Clergy et al., Instruction, *Ecclesiae de mysterio,* Practical Provisions, article 3 §2: AAS 89 (1997) p. 865.

157. Cf. especially the General Instruction of the Liturgy of the Hours, nn. 93–98; *Roman Ritual,* revised by decree of the Second Vatican Ecumenical Council and published by authority of Pope John Paul II: *Book of Blessings,* editio typica, 31 May 1984, General Introduction, n. 28; Order of Crowning an Image of the Blessed Virgin Mary, editio typica, 25 March 1981, nn. 10 and 14; S. Congregation for Divine Worship, Instruction, on Masses with Particular Groups, *Actio pastoralis,* 15 May 1969: AAS 61 (1969) pp. 806–811; Directory for Masses with Children, Pueros baptizatos, 1 November 1973: AAS 66 (1974) pp. 30–46; *Missale Romanum,* Institutio Generalis, n. 21.

158. Cf. John Paul II, Apostolic Letter (Motu Proprio), *Misericordia Dei,* 7 April 2002, n. 2: AAS 94 (2002) p. 455; Cf. Congregation for Divine Worship and the Discipline of the Sacraments, Response to Dubium: *Notitiae* 37 (2001) pp. 259–260.

159. Cf. Sacred Congregation for Divine Worship, Instruction, *Liturgicae instaurationes,* n. 9: AAS 62 (1970) p. 702.

160. Ecumenical Council of Trent, Session XIII, 11 October 1551, Decree on the Most Holy Eucharist, Chapter 2: DS 1638; cf. Session XXII, 17 September 1562, On the Most Holy Sacrifice of the Mass, Chapters 1–2: DS 1740, 1743; Sacred Congregation of Rites, Instruction, *Eucharisticum mysterium,* n. 35: AAS 59 (1967) p. 560.

161. Cf. *Missale Romanum,* Ordo Missae, n. 4, p. 505.

162. *Missale Romanum,* Institutio Generalis, n. 51.

163. Cf. 1 Corinthians 11:28.

164. Cf. *Code of Canon Law,* canon 916; cf. Ecumenical Council of Trent, Session XIII, 11 October 1551, Decree on the Most Holy Eucharist, Chapter 7: DS 1646–1647; John Paul II, Encyclical Letter, *Ecclesia de Eucharistia,* n. 36: AAS 95 (2003) pp. 457–458; Sacred Congregation of Rites, Instruction, *Eucharisticum mysterium,* n. 35: AAS 59 (1967) p. 561.

165. Cf. John Paul II, Encyclical Letter, *Ecclesia de Eucharistia,* n. 42: AAS 95 (2003) p. 461.

166. Cf. *Code of Canon Law,* n. 844 § 1; John Paul II, Encyclical Letter *Ecclesia de Eucharistia,* nn. 45–46: AAS 95 (2003) pp. 463–464; cf. also Pontifical Council for the Promotion of Christian Unity, Directory for the application of the principles and norms on ecumenism, *La recherche de l'unité,* nn. 130-131: AAS 85 (1993) 1039–1119, here p. 1089.

167. Cf. John Paul II, Encyclical Letter *Ecclesia de Eucharistia,* n. 46: AAS 95 (2003) pp. 463–464.

168. Cf. Sacred Congregation of Rites, Instruction, *Eucharisticum mysterium,* n. 35: AAS 59 (1967) p. 561.

169. Cf. *Code of Canon Law,* can. 914; Sacred Congregation for the Discipline of the Sacraments, Declaration, *Sanctus Pontifex,* diei 24 maii 1973: AAS 65 (1973) p. 410; Sacred Congregation for the Sacraments and Divine Worship and Sacred Congregation for the Clergy, Letter to the Presidents of the Bishops' Conferences. Episcoporum, *In quibusdam,* 31 March 1977: *Enchiridion Documentorum Instaurationis Liturgicae,* II, pp. 142–144; Sacred Congregation for the Sacraments and Divine Worship and S. Congregation for the Clergy, Response to dubium, 20 May 1977: AAS 69 (1977) p. 427.

170. Cf. John Paul II, Apostolic Letter, *Dies Domini,* 31 May 1998, nn. 31–34: AAS 90 (1998) pp. 713-766, here pp. 731–734.

171. Cf. *Code of Canon Law,* canon 914.

172. Cf. Second Vatican Ecumenical Council, Constitution on the Sacred Liturgy, *Sacrosanctum Concilium,* n. 55.

173. Cf. Sacred Congregation of Rites, Instruction, *Eucharisticum mysterium,* n. 31: AAS 59 (1967) p. 558; Pontifical Commission for the Authentic Interpretation of the Code of Canon Law, Response to dubium, 1 June 1988: AAS 80 (1988) p. 1373.

174. *Missale Romanum,* Institutio Generalis, n. 85.

175. Cf. Second Vatican Ecumenical Council, Constitution on the Sacred Liturgy, *Sacrosanctum Concilium,* n. 55; Sacred Congregation of Rites, Instruction, *Eucharisticum mysterium,* n. 31: AAS 59 (1967) p. 558; *Missale Romanum,* Institutio Generalis, nn. 85, 157, 243.

176. Cf. *Missale Romanum,* Institutio Generalis, n. 160.

177. *Code of Canon Law,* canon 843 § 1; cf. canon 915.

178. Cf. *Missale Romanum,* Institutio Generalis, n. 161.

179. Congregation for Divine Worship and the Discipline of the Sacraments, Dubium: *Notitiae* 35 (1999) pp. 160–161.

180. Cf. *Missale Romanum,* Institutio Generalis, n. 118.

181. Ibidem, n.160.

182. Cf. *Code of Canon Law,* can. 917; Pontifical Commission for the Authentic Interpretation of the Code of Canon Law, Response to Dubium, 11 July 1984: AAS 76 (1984) p. 746.

183. Cf. Second Vatican Ecumenical Council, Constitution on the Sacred Liturgy, *Sacrosanctum Concilium,* n. 55; *Missale Romanum,* General Instruction, nn. 158–160, 243–244, 246.

184. Cf. *Missale Romanum,* Institutio Generalis, nn. 237–249; cf. also nn. 85, 157.

185. Cf. ibidem, n. 283a.

186. Cf. Ecumenical Council of Trent, Session XXI, 16 July 1562, Decree on Eucharistic Communion, Chapters 1–3: DS 1725–1729; Second Vatican Ecumenical Council, Constitution on the Sacred Liturgy, *Sacrosanctum Concilium,* n. 55; *Missale Romanum,* Institutio Generalis, nn. 282–283.

187. Cf. *Missale Romanum,* Institutio Generalis, n. 283.

188. Cf. ibidem.

189. Cf. Sacred Congregation for Divine Worship, Instruction, *Sacramentali Communione,* 29 June 1970: AAS 62 (1970) p. 665; Instruction, *Liturgicae instaurationes,* n. 6a: AAS 62 (1970) p. 699.

190. *Missale Romanum,* Institutio Generalis, n. 285a.

191. Ibidem, n. 245.

192. Cf. ibidem, nn. 285b and 287.

193. Cf. ibidem, nn. 207 and 285a.

194. Cf. *Code of Canon Law,* canon 1367.

195. Cf. Pontifical Council for the Interpretation of Legislative Texts, Response to dubium, 3 July 1999: AAS 91 (1999) p. 918.

196. Cf. *Missale Romanum,* Institutio Generalis, nn. 163, 284.

197. *Code of Canon Law,* canon 932 § 1; Sacred Congregation for Divine Worship, Instruction, *Liturgicae instaurationes,* n. 9: AAS 62 (1970) p. 701.

198. *Code of Canon Law,* canon 904; cf. Second Vatican Ecumenical Council, Dogmatic Constitution on the Church, *Lumen gentium,* n. 3; Decree on the Ministry and Life of Priests, *Presbyterorum ordinis,* n. 13; cf. also Ecumenical Council of Trent, Session XXII, 17 September 1562, On the Most Holy Sacrifice of the Mass, Chapter 6: DS 1747; Paul Pp. VI, Encyclical Letter *Mysterium fidei,* 3 September 1965: AAS 57 (1965) pp. 753–774, here pp. 761–762; cf. John Paul II, Encyclical Letter, *Ecclesia de Eucharistia,* n. 11: AAS 95 (2003) pp. 440–441; Sacred Congregation of Rites, Instruction, *Eucharisticum mysterium,* n. 44: AAS 59 (1967) p. 564; *Missale Romanum,* Institutio Generalis, n. 19.

199. Cf. *Code of Canon Law,* canon 903; *Missale Romanum,* Institutio Generalis, n. 200.

200. Cf. Second Vatican Ecumenical Council, Constitution on the Sacred Liturgy, *Sacrosanctum Concilium*, n. 36 § 1; *Code of Canon Law*, canon 928.

201. Cf. *Missale Romanum*, Institutio Generalis, n. 114.

202. John Paul II, Apostolic Letter *Dies Domini*, n. 36: AAS 90 (1998) p. 735; cf. also Sacred Congregation of Rites, Instruction *Eucharisticum mysterium*, n. 27: AAS 59 (1967) p. 556.

203. Cf. John Paul II, Apostolic Letter *Dies Domini*, esp. n. 36: AAS 90 (1998) pp. 713–766, here pp. 735–736; Sacred Congregation for Divine Worship, Instruction *Actio pastoralis:* AAS 61 (1969) pp. 806–811.

204. Cf. *Code of Canon Law*, canon 905, 945-958; cf. Congregation for the Clergy, Decree, *Mos iugiter*, 22 February 1991: AAS 83 (1991), pp. 443–446.

205. Cf. *Missale Romanum*, Institutio Generalis, nn. 327–333.

206. Cf. ibidem, n. 332.

207. Cf. ibidem, n. 332; Congregation for Divine Worship and the Discipline of the Sacraments, Instruction, *Inaestimabile donum*, n. 16: AAS 72 (1980) p. 338.

208. Cf. *Missale Romanum*, Institutio Generalis, n. 333; Appendix IV. *Ordo benedictionis calicis et patenae intra Missam adhibendus*, pp. 1255–1257; *Pontificale Romanum* ex decreto sacrosancti Oecumenici Concilii Vaticani II instauratum, auctoritate Pauli Pp. VI promulgatum, *Ordo Dedicationis ecclesiae et altaris*, editio typica, diei 29 maii 1977, Typis Polyglottis Vaticanis, 1977, cap. VII, pp. 125–132.

209. Cf. *Missale Romanum*, Institutio Generalis, nn. 163, 183, 192.

210. Ibidem, n. 345.

211. Ibidem, n. 335.

212. Cf. ibidem, n. 336.

213. Cf. ibidem, n. 337.

214. Cf. ibidem, n. 209.

215. Cf. ibidem, n. 338.

216. Cf. Sacred Congregation for Divine Worship, Instruction, *Liturgicae Instaurationes*, n. 8c: AAS 62 (1970) p. 701.

217. Cf. *Missale Romanum*, Institutio Generalis, n. 346g.

218. *Ibidem*, n. 114 cf. nn. 16–17.

219. Sacred Congregation for Divine Worship, Decree, *Eucharistiae sacramentum*, 21 June 1973: AAS 65 (1973) 610.

220. Cf. ibidem.

221. Cf. Sacred Congregation of Rites, Instruction, *Eucharisticum mysterium*, n. 54: AAS 59 (1967) p. 568; Instruction, *Inter Oecumenici*, 26 September 1964, n. 95: AAS 56 (1964) pp. 877–900, here p. 898; *Missale Romanum*, Institutio Generalis, n. 314.

222. Cf. John Paul II, Letter, *Dominicae Cenae*, n. 3: AAS 72 (1980) pp. 117–119; Sacred Congregation of Rites, Instruction, *Eucharisticum mysterium*, n. 53: AAS 59 (1967) p. 568; *Code of Canon Law*, canon 938 § 2; *Roman Ritual, Holy Communion and Worship of the Eucharist Outside Mass*, Introduction, n. 9; *Missale Romanum*, Institutio Generalis, nn. 314–317.

223. Cf. *Code of Canon Law*, canon 938 §§ 3–5.

224. Sacred Congregation for the Discipline of the Sacraments, Instruction, Nullo unquam, diei

26 maii 1938, n. 10d: AAS 30 (1938), pp. 198–207, here p. 206.

225. Cf. John Paul II, Apostolic Letter (Motu Proprio), *Sacramentorum sanctitatis tutela,* 30 April 2001: AAS 93 (2001) pp. 737–739; Congregation for the Doctrine of the Faith, Ep. ad totius Catholicae Ecclesiae Episcopos aliosque Ordinarios et Hierarchas quorum interest: de delictis gravioribus eidem Congregationi pro Doctrina Fidei reservatis: AAS 93 (2001) p. 786.

226. Cf. *Roman Ritual, Holy Communion and Worship of the Eucharist Outside Mass,* nn. 26–78.

227. John Paul II, Encyclical Letter, *Ecclesia de Eucharistia,* n. 25: AAS 95 (2003) pp. 449–450.

228. Cf. Ecumenical Council of Trent, Session XIII, 11 October 1551, Decree on the Most Holy Eucharist, Chapter 5: DS 1643; Pius Pp. XII, Encyclical Letter *Mediator Dei:* AAS 39 (1947) p. 569; Paul Pp. VI, Encyclical Letter *Mysterium Fidei,* 3 September 1965: AAS 57 (1965) pp. 751–774, here 769–770; S. Congregation of Rites, Instruction, *Eucharisticum mysterium,* n. 3f: AAS 59 (1967) p. 543; Sacred Congregation for the Sacraments and Divine Worship, Instruction, *Inaestimabile donum,* n. 20: AAS 72 (1980) p. 339; John Paul II, Encyclical Letter, *Ecclesia de Eucharistia,* n. 25: AAS 95 (2003) pp. 449–450.

229. Cf. Hebrews 9:11; John Paul II, Encyclical Letter, *Ecclesia de Eucharistia,* n. 3: AAS 95 (2003) p. 435.

230. John Paul II, Encyclical Letter, *Ecclesia de Eucharistia,* n. 25: AAS 95 (2003) p. 450.

231. Paul. VI, Encyclical Letter *Mysterium fidei:* AAS 57 (1965) p. 771.

232. Cf. John Paul II, Encyclical Letter, *Ecclesia de Eucharistia,* n. 25: AAS 95 (2003) pp. 449–450.

233. *Code of Canon Law,* canon 937.

234. John Paul II, Encyclical Letter, *Ecclesia de Eucharistia,* n. 10: AAS 95 (2003) p. 439.

235. Cf. *Roman Ritual, Holy Communion and Worship of the Eucharist Outside Mass,* nn. 82–100; *Missale Romanum,* Institutio Generalis, n. 317; *Code of Canon Law,* canon 941 § 2.

236. John Paul II, Apostolic Letter, *Rosarium Virginis Mariae,* diei 16 octobris 2002: AAS 95 (2003) pp. 5–36; here n. 2, p. 6.

237. Cf. Congregation for Divine Worship and the Discipline of the Sacraments, Letter of the Congregation, 15 January 1997: *Notitiae* 34 (1998) pp. 506–510; Apostolic Penitentiary, Letter to a Priest, 8 March 1996: *Notitiae* 34 (1998) p. 511.

238. Cf. Sacred Congregation of Rites, Instruction, *Eucharisticum mysterium,* n. 61: AAS 59 (1967) p. 571; *Roman Ritual, Holy Communion and Worship of the Eucharist Outside Mass,* n. 83; *Missale Romanum,* Institutio Generalis, n. 317; *Code of Canon Law,* canon 941 § 2.

239. Cf. *Roman Ritual, Holy Communion and Worship of the Eucharist Outside Mass,* n. 94.

240. Cf. John Paul II, Apostolic Constitution, *Pastor bonus,* article 65: AAS 80 (1988) p. 877.

241. *Code of Canon Law,* canon 944 § 2; cf. *Roman Ritual, Holy Communion and Worship of the Eucharist Outside Mass,* Introduction, n. 102; *Missale Romanum,* Institutio Generalis, n. 317.

242. *Code of Canon Law,* canon 944 § 1; cf. *Roman Ritual, Holy Communion and Worship of the Eucharist Outside Mass,* Introduction, nn. 101–102; *Missale Romanum,* Institutio Generalis, n. 317.

243. John Paul II, Encyclical Letter, *Ecclesia de Eucharistia,* n. 10: AAS 95 (2003) p. 439

244. Cf. *Roman Ritual, Holy Communion and Worship of the Eucharist Outside Mass,* Introduction, n. 109.

245. Cf. *ibidem,* nn. 109–112.

246. Cf. *Missale Romanum,* In sollemnitate sanctissimi Corporis et Sanguinis Christi, Collecta, p. 489.

247. Cf. Congregation for the Clergy, and others, Instruction, *Ecclesiae de mysterio,* Theological Principles, n. 3: AAS 89 (1997) p. 859.

248. Cf. *Code of Canon Law,* can. 900 § 1; cf. Fourth Lateran Ecumenical Council, 11–30 November 1215, Chapter 1: DS802; Clement VI, Letter to Mekhitar, Catholicos of the Armenians, *Super quibusdam,* 29 September 1351: DS 1084; Ecumenical Council of Trent, Session XXIII, 15 July 1563, Doctrine and Canons on Sacred Orders, Chapter 4: DS 1767–1770; Pius XII, Encyclical Letter, *Mediator Dei:* AAS 39 (1947) p. 553.

249. Cf. *Code of Canon Law,* canon 230 § 3; John Paul II, Allocution during a Symposium concerning the collaboration of laypersons in the pastoral ministry of Priests, 22 April 1994, n. 2: *L'Osservatore Romano,* 23 April 1994; Congregation for the Clergy et al., Instruction, *Ecclesiae de mysterio,* Prooemium: AAS 89 (1997) pp. 852–856.

250. Cf. John Paul II, Encyclical Letter, *Redemptoris missio,* nn. 53–54: AAS 83 (1991) pp. 300–302; Congregation for the Clergy et al., Instruction, *Ecclesiae de mysterio,* Prooemium: AAS 89 (1997) pp. 852–856.

251. Cf. Second Vatican Ecumenical Council, Decree on the Missionary Activity of the Church, *Ad gentes,* 7 December 1965, n. 17; John Paul II, Encyclical Letter *Redemptoris missio,* n. 73: AAS 83 (1991) p. 321.

252. Cf. Congregation for the Clergy et al., Instruction, *Ecclesiae de mysterio,* Practical Provisions, article 8 § 2: AAS 89 (1997) p. 872.

253. Cf. John Paul II, Encyclical Letter, *Ecclesia de Eucharistia,* n. 32: AAS 95 (2003) p. 455.

254. Cf. *Code of Canon Law,* canon 900 § 1.

255. Cf. *ibidem,* canon 910 § 1; cf. also John Paul II, Letter, *Dominicae Cenae,* n. 11: AAS 72 (1980) p. 142; Congregation for the Clergy et al., Instruction, *Ecclesiae de mysterio,* Practical Provisions, article 8 § 1: AAS 89 (1997) pp. 870–871.

256. Cf. *Code of Canon Law,* canon 230 § 3.

257. Cf. Sacred Congregation for the Discipline of the Sacraments, Instruction, *Immensae caritatis,* prooemium: AAS 65 (1973) p. 264; Paul VI, Apostolic Letter (Motu Proprio), *Ministeria quaedam,* 15 August 1972: AAS 64 (1972) p. 532; *Missale Romanum,*

Appendix III: Ritus ad deputandum ministrum sacrae Communionis ad actum distribuendae, p. 1253; Congregation for the Clergy et al., Instruction, *Ecclesiae de mysterio,* Practical Provisions, article 8 § 1: AAS 89 (1997) p. 871.

258. Sacred Congregation for the Sacraments and Divine Worship, Instruction, *Inaestimabile donum,* n. 10: AAS 72 (1980) p. 336; Pontifical Commission for the Authentic Interpretation of the Code of Canon Law, Response to dubium, 11 July 1984: AAS 76 (1984) p. 746.

259. Cf. Sacred Congregation for the Discipline of the Sacraments, Instruction, *Immensae caritatis,* n. 1: AAS 65 (1973) pp. 264–271, here pp. 265–266; Pontifical Commission for the Authentic Interpretation of the Code of Canon Law, Responsio ad propositum dubium, 1 June 1988: AAS 80 (1988) p. 1373; Congregation for the Clergy et al., Instruction, *Ecclesiae de mysterio,* Practical Provisions, article 8 § 2: AAS 89 (1997) p. 871.

260. Cf. *Code of Canon Law,* canon 767 § 1.

261. Cf. ibidem, canon 766.

262. Cf. Congregation for the Clergy et al., Instruction, *Ecclesiae de mysterio,* Practical Provisions, article 2 §§ 3–4: AAS 89 (1997) p. 865.

263. Cf. John Paul II, Apostolic Letter, *Dies Domini,* esp. nn. 31–51: AAS 90 (1998) pp. 713–766, here pp. 731–746; Pope John Paul II, Apostolic Letter, *Novo Millennio ineunte,* diei 6 ianuarii 2001, nn. 35–36: AAS 93 (2001) pp. 290-292; John Paul II, Encyclical Letter, *Ecclesia de Eucharistia,* n. 41: AAS 95 (2003) pp. 460–461.

264. Second Vatican Ecumenical Council, Decree on the Ministry and Life of Priests, *Presbyterorum ordinis,* n. 6; cf. John Paul II, Encyclical Letter, *Ecclesia de Eucharistia,* nn. 22, 33: AAS 95 (2003) pp. 448, 455–456.

265. Cf. Sacred Congregation of Rites, Instruction, *Eucharisticum mysterium,* n. 26: AAS 59 (1967) pp. 555–556; Congregation for Divine Worship, Directory for Sunday Celebrations in the Absence of a Priest, *Christi Ecclesia,* 2 June 1988, nn. 5 and 25: *Notitiae* 24 (1988) pp. 366–378, here pp. 367, 372.

266. Cf. Congregation for Divine Worship, Directory for Sunday Celebrations in the Absence of a Priest, *Christi Ecclesia,* n. 18: *Notitiae* 24 (1988) p. 370.

267. Cf. John Paul II, Letter, *Dominicae Cenae,* n. 2: AAS 72 (1980) p. 116.

268. Cf. John Paul II, Apostolic Letter, *Dies Domini,* n. 49: AAS 90 (1998) p. 744; Encyclical Letter, *Ecclesia de Eucharistia,* n. 41: AAS 95 (2003) pp. 460–461; *Code of Canon Law,* canon 1246–1247.

269. Cf. *Code of Canon Law,* canon 1248 § 2; Congregation for Divine Worship, Directory for Sunday Celebrations in the Absence of a Priest, *Christi Ecclesia,* nn. 1–2: *Notitiae* 24 (1988) p. 366.

270. John Paul II, Encyclical Letter, *Ecclesia de Eucharistia,* n. 33: AAS 95 (2003) pp. 455–456.

271. Cf. Congregation for Divine Worship, Directory for Sunday Celebrations in the Absence of a Priest, *Christi Ecclesia,* n. 22: *Notitiae* 24 (1988) p. 371.

272. John Paul II, Encyclical Letter, *Ecclesia de Eucharistia,* n. 30: AAS 95 (2003) pp. 453–454; cf. also Pontifical Council for the Promotion of Christian Unity, Directory for the application of the principles and norms on ecumenism, *La recherche de l'unité,* 25 March 1993, n. 115: AAS 85 (1993) pp. 1039–1119, here p. 1085.

273. Cf. Pontifical Council for the Promotion of Christian Unity, Directory for the application of the principles and norms on ecumenism, *La recherche de l'unité,* n. 115: AAS 85 (1993) p. 1085.

274. Cf. *Code of Canon Law,* can. 292; Pontifical Council for the Interpretation of Legislative Texts, Declaration de recta interpretatione canon 1335, secundae partis, C.I.C., 15 May 1997, n. 3: AAS 90 (1998) p. 64.

275. Cf. *Code of Canon Law,* canon 976; 986 § 2.

276. Cf. Pontifical Council for the Interpretation of Legislative Texts, Declaratio de recta interpretatione can. 1335, secundae partis, C.I.C., 15 May 1997, nn. 1–2: AAS 90 (1998) pp. 63–64.

277. As regards Priests who have obtained the dispensation from celibacy, cf. Sacred Congregation for the Doctrine of the Faith, Normae de dispensatione a sacerdotali caelibatu ad instantiam partis, *Normae substantiales,* 14 October 1980, article 5; cf. also Congregation for the Clergy et al., Instruction, *Ecclesiae de mysterio,* Practical Provisions, article 3 § 5: AAS 89 (1997) p. 865.

278. St Thomas Aquinas, *Summa Theologica.,* II, 2, q. 93, a. 1.

279. Cf. John Paul II, Apostolic Letter, *Vicesimus quintus annus,* n. 15: AAS 81 (1989) p. 911; cf. also Second Vatican Ecumenical Council, Constitution on the Sacred Liturgy, *Sacrosanctum Concilium,* nn. 15–19.

280. Cf. John Paul II, Apostolic Letter (Motu Proprio), *Sacramentorum sanctitatis tutela:* AAS 93 (2001) pp. 737–739; Congregation for the Doctrine of the Faith, Ep. ad totius Catholicae Ecclesiae Episcopos aliosque Ordinarios et Hierarchas quorum interest: de delictis gravioribus eidem Congregationi pro Doctrina Fidei reservatis: AAS 93 (2001) p. 786.

281. Cf. *Code of Canon Law,* can. 1367; Pontifical Council for the Interpretation of Legislative Texts, Responsio ad propositum dubium, 3 July 1999: AAS 91 (1999) p. 918; Congregation for the Doctrine of the Faith, Ep. ad totius Catholicae Ecclesiae Episcopos aliosque Ordinarios et Hierarchas quorum interest: de delictis gravioribus eidem Congregationi pro Doctrina Fidei reservatis: AAS 93 (2001) p. 786.

282. Cf. *Code of Canon Law,* canon 1378 § 2 n. 1 et 1379; Congregation for the Doctrine of the Faith, Ep. ad totius Catholicae Ecclesiae Episcopos aliosque Ordinarios et Hierarchas quorum interest: de delictis gravioribus eidem Congregationi pro Doctrina Fidei reservatis: AAS 93 (2001) p. 786.

283. Cf. *Code of Canon Law,* canon 908 et 1365; Congregation for the Doctrine of the Faith, Ep. ad totius Catholicae Ecclesiae Episcopos aliosque Ordinarios et Hierarchas quorum interest: de delictis gravioribus eidem Congregationi pro Doctrina Fidei reservatis: AAS 93 (2001) p. 786.

284. Cf. *Code of Canon Law,* canon 927; Congregation for the Doctrine of the Faith, Ep. ad totius Catholicae Ecclesiae Episcopos aliosque Ordinarios et Hierarchas quorum interest: de delictis gravioribus eidem Congregationi pro Doctrina Fidei reservatis: AAS 93 (2001) p. 786.

285. *Code of Canon Law,* canon 387.

286. *Ibidem,* canon 838 § 4.

287. *Ibidem,* canon 392.

288. Cf. John Paul II, Apostolic Constitution, *Pastor bonus,* article 52: AAS 80 (1988) p. 874.

289. Cf. *ibidem,* n. 63: AAS 80 (1988) p. 876.

290. Cf. ibidem, canon 1417 § 1.

291. John Paul II, Encyclical Letter, *Ecclesia de Eucharistia,* n. 24: AAS 95 (2003) p. 449.

292. Cf. *ibidem,* nn. 53-58: AAS 95 (2003) pp. 469–472.

293. Cf. Second Vatican Ecumenical Council, Constitution on the Sacred Liturgy, *Sacrosanctum Concilium,* n. 14; cf. also nn. 11, 41, et 48.

294. Cf. S. Thomas Aquinas, *Summa Theologica.,* III, q. 64, a. 9 ad 1.

295. Cf. *Missale Romanum,* Institutio Generalis, n. 24.

CONGREGACIÓN PARA EL CULTO DIVINO
Y LA DISCIPLINA DE LOS SACRAMENTOS

INSTRUCCIÓN

REDEMPTIONIS SACRAMENTUM

SOBRE ALGUNAS COSAS QUE SE DEBEN OBSERVAR
O EVITAR ACERCA DE LA SANTÍSIMA EUCARISTÍA

ÍNDICE

PROEMIO

1. El Sacramento de la Redención, que la Madre Iglesia confiesa con firme fe y recibe con alegría, celebra y adora con veneración, en la santísima Eucaristía[1], anuncia la muerte de Jesucristo y proclama su resurrección, hasta que Él vuelva en gloria[2], como Señor y Dominador invencible, Sacerdote eterno y Rey del universo, y entregue al Padre omnipotente, de majestad infinita, el reino de la verdad y la vida[3].

2. La doctrina de la Iglesia sobre la santísima Eucaristía ha sido expuesta con sumo cuidado y la máxima autoridad, a lo largo de los siglos, en los escritos de los Concilios y de los Sumos Pontífices, puesto que en la Eucaristía se contiene todo el bien espiritual de la Iglesia, que es Cristo, nuestra Pascua[4], fuente y cumbre de toda la vida cristiana[5], y cuya fuerza alienta a la Iglesia desde los inicios[6]. Recientemente, en la Carta Encíclica *Ecclesia de Eucharistia,* el Sumo Pontífice Juan Pablo II ha expuesto de nuevo algunos principios sobre esta materia, de gran importancia eclesial para nuestra época[7].

Para que también en los tiempos actuales, tan gran misterio sea debidamente protegido por la Iglesia, especialmente en la celebración de la sagrada Liturgia, el Sumo Pontífice mandó a esta Congregación para el Culto Divino y la Disciplina de los Sacramentos[8] que, en colaboración con la Congregación para la Doctrina de la Fe, preparara esta Instrucción, en la que se trataran algunas cuestiones referentes a la disciplina del sacramento de la Eucaristía. Por consiguiente, lo que en esta Instrucción se expone, debe ser leído en continuidad con la mencionada Carta Encíclica *Ecclesia de Eucharistia.*

Sin embargo, la intención no es tanto preparar un compendio de normas sobre la santísima Eucaristía sino más bien retomar, con esta Instrucción, algunos elementos de la normativa litúrgica anteriormente enunciada y establecida, que continúan siendo válidos, para reforzar el sentido profundo de las normas litúrgicas[9] e indicar otras que aclaren y completen las precedentes, explicándolas a los Obispos, y también a los presbíteros, diáconos y a todos los fieles laicos, para que cada uno, conforme al propio oficio y a las propias posibilidades, las puedan poner en práctica.

3. Las normas que se contienen en esta Instrucción se refieren a cuestiones litúrgicas concernientes al Rito romano y, con las debidas salvedades, también a los otros Ritos de la Iglesia latina, aprobados por el derecho.

4. "No hay duda de que la reforma litúrgica del Concilio ha tenido grandes ventajas para una participación más consciente, activa y fructuosa de los fieles en el santo Sacrificio del altar"[10]. Sin embargo, "no faltan sombras"[11]. Así, no se puede callar ante los abusos, incluso gravísimos, contra la naturaleza de la Liturgia y de los sacramentos, también contra la tradición y autoridad de la Iglesia, que en nuestros tiempos, no raramente, dañan las celebraciones litúrgicas en diversos ámbitos eclesiales. En algunos lugares, los abusos litúrgicos se han convertido en una costumbre, lo cual no se puede admitir y debe terminarse.

5. La observancia de las normas que han sido promulgadas por la autoridad de la Iglesia exige que concuerden la mente y la voz, las acciones externas y la intención del corazón. La mera observancia externa de las normas, como resulta evidente, es contraria a la esencia de la sagrada Liturgia, con la que Cristo quiere congregar a su Iglesia, y con ella formar "un sólo cuerpo y un sólo espíritu"[12]. Por esto la acción externa debe estar iluminada por la fe y la caridad, que nos unen con Cristo y los unos a los otros, y suscitan en nosotros la caridad hacia los pobres y necesitados. Las palabras y los ritos litúrgicos son expresión fiel, madurada a lo largo de los siglos, de los sentimientos de Cristo y nos enseñan a tener los mismos sentimientos que él[13]; conformando nuestra mente con sus palabras, elevamos al Señor nuestro corazón. Cuanto se dice en esta Instrucción, intenta conducir a esta conformación de nuestros sentimientos con los sentimientos de Cristo, expresados en las palabras y ritos de la Liturgia.

6. Los abusos, sin embargo, "contribuyen a oscurecer la recta fe y la doctrina católica sobre este admirable Sacramento"[14]. De esta

forma, también se impide que puedan "los fieles revivir de algún modo la experiencia de los dos discípulos de Emaús: *Entonces se les abrieron los ojos y lo reconocieron*"[15]. Conviene que todos los fieles tengan y realicen aquellos sentimientos que han recibido por la pasión salvadora del Hijo Unigénito, que manifiesta la majestad de Dios, ya que están ante la fuerza, la divinidad y el esplendor de la bondad de Dios[16], especialmente presente en el sacramento de la Eucaristía[17].

7. No es extraño que los abusos tengan su origen en un falso concepto de libertad. Pero Dios nos ha concedido, en Cristo, no una falsa libertad para hacer lo que queramos, sino la libertad para que podamos realizar lo que es digno y justo[18]. Esto es válido no sólo para los preceptos que provienen directamente de Dios, sino también, según la valoración conveniente de cada norma, para las leyes promulgadas por la Iglesia. Por ello, todos deben ajustarse a las disposiciones establecidas por la legítima autoridad eclesiástica.

8. Además, se advierte con gran tristeza la existencia de "iniciativas ecuménicas que, aún siendo generosas en su intención, transigen con prácticas eucarísticas contrarias a la disciplina con la cual la Iglesia expresa su fe". Sin embargo, "la Eucaristía es un don demasiado grande para admitir ambigüedades y reducciones". Por lo que conviene corregir algunas cosas y definirlas con precisión, para que también en esto "la Eucaristía siga resplandeciendo con todo el esplendor de su misterio"[19].

9. Finalmente, los abusos se fundamentan con frecuencia en la ignorancia, ya que casi siempre se rechaza aquello de lo que no se comprende su sentido más profundo y su antigüedad. Por eso, con su raíz en la misma Sagrada Escritura, "las preces, oraciones e himnos litúrgicos están penetrados de su espíritu, y de ella reciben su significado las acciones y los signos"[20]. Por lo que se refiere a los signos visibles "que usa la sagrada Liturgia, han sido escogidos por Cristo o por la Iglesia para significar las realidades divinas invisibles"[21]. Justamente, la estructura y la forma de las celebraciones sagradas según cada uno de los Ritos, sea de la tradición de Oriente sea de la de Occidente, concuerdan con la Iglesia Universal y con las costumbres universalmente aceptadas por la constante tradición apostólica[22], que la Iglesia entrega, con solicitud y fidelidad, a las generaciones futuras. Todo esto es sabiamente custodiado y protegido por las normas litúrgicas.

10. La misma Iglesia no tiene ninguna potestad sobre aquello que ha sido establecido por Cristo, y que constituye la parte inmutable de la Liturgia[23]. Pero si se rompiera este vínculo que los sacramentos tienen con el mismo Cristo, que los ha instituido, y con los acontecimientos en los que la Iglesia ha sido fundada[24], nada aprovecharía a los fieles, sino que podría dañarles gravemente. De hecho, la sagrada Liturgia está estrechamente ligada con los principios doctrinales[25], por lo que el uso de textos y ritos que no han sido aprobados lleva a que disminuya o desaparezca el nexo necesario entre la *lex orandi y la lex credendi*[26].

11. El Misterio de la Eucaristía es demasiado grande "para que alguien pueda permitirse tratarlo a su arbitrio personal, lo que no respetaría ni su carácter sagrado ni su dimensión universal"[27]. Quien actúa contra esto, cediendo a sus propias inspiraciones, aunque sea sacerdote, atenta contra la unidad substancial del Rito romano, que se debe cuidar con decisión[28], y realiza acciones que de ningún modo corresponden con el hambre y la sed del Dios vivo, que el pueblo de nuestros tiempos experimenta, ni a un auténtico celo pastoral, ni sirve a la adecuada renovación litúrgica, sino que más bien defrauda el patrimonio y la herencia de los fieles. Los actos arbitrarios no benefician la verdadera renovación[29], sino que lesionan el verdadero derecho de los fieles a la acción litúrgica, que es expresión de la vida de la Iglesia, según su tradición y disciplina. Además, introducen en la misma celebración de la Eucaristía elementos de discordia y la deforman, cuando ella tiende, por su propia naturaleza y de forma eminente, a significar y realizar admirablemente la comunión con la vida divina y la unidad del pueblo de Dios[30]. De estos actos arbitrarios se deriva incertidumbre en la doctrina, duda y escándalo para el pueblo de Dios y, casi inevitablemente, una violenta repugnancia que confunde y aflige con fuerza a muchos fieles en nuestros tiempos, en que frecuentemente la vida cristiana sufre el ambiente, muy difícil, de la "secularización"[31].

12. Por otra parte, todos los fieles cristianos gozan del derecho de celebrar una liturgia verdadera, y especialmente la celebración de la santa Misa, que sea tal como la Iglesia ha querido y establecido, como está prescrito en los libros litúrgicos y en las otras leyes y normas. Además, el pueblo católico tiene derecho a que se celebre por él, de forma íntegra, el santo sacrificio de la Misa, conforme a toda la enseñanza del Magisterio de la Iglesia. Finalmente, la comunidad católica tiene derecho a que de tal modo se realice

para ella la celebración de la santísima Eucaristía, que aparezca verdaderamente como sacramento de unidad, excluyendo absolutamente todos los defectos y gestos que puedan manifestar divisiones y facciones en la Iglesia[32].

13. Todas las normas y recomendaciones expuestas en esta Instrucción, de diversas maneras, están en conexión con el oficio de la Iglesia, a quien corresponde velar por la adecuada y digna celebración de este gran misterio. De los diversos grados con que cada una de las normas se unen con la norma suprema de todo el derecho eclesiástico, que es el cuidado para la salvación de las almas, trata el último capítulo de la presente Instrucción[33].

CAPÍTULO I
LA ORDENACIÓN DE LA SAGRADA LITURGIA

14. "La ordenación de la sagrada Liturgia es de la competencia exclusiva de la autoridad eclesiástica; ésta reside en la Sede Apostólica y, en la medida que determine la ley, en el Obispo"[34].

15. El Romano Pontífice, "Vicario de Cristo y Pastor de la Iglesia universal en la tierra . . . tiene, en virtud de su función, potestad ordinaria, que es suprema, plena, inmediata y universal en la Iglesia, y que puede siempre ejercer libremente"[35], aún comunicando con los pastores y los fieles.

16. Compete a la Sede Apostólica ordenar la sagrada Liturgia de la Iglesia universal, editar los libros litúrgicos, revisar sus traducciones a lenguas vernáculas y vigilar para que las normas litúrgicas, especialmente aquellas que regulan la celebración del santo Sacrificio de la Misa, se cumplan fielmente en todas partes[36].

17. "La Congregación para el Culto Divino y la Disciplina de los Sacramentos trata lo que corresponde a la Sede Apostólica, salvo la competencia de la Congregación para la Doctrina de la Fe, respecto a la ordenación y promoción de la sagrada liturgia, en primer lugar de los sacramentos. Fomenta y tutela la disciplina de los sacramentos, especialmente en lo referente a su celebración válida y lícita". Finalmente, "vigila atentamente para que se observen con exactitud las disposiciones litúrgicas, se prevengan

sus abusos y se erradiquen donde se encuentren"[37]. En esta materia, conforme a la tradición de toda la Iglesia, destaca el cuidado de la celebración de la santa Misa y del culto que se tributa a la Eucaristía fuera de la Misa.

18. Los fieles tienen derecho a que la autoridad eclesiástica regule la sagrada Liturgia de forma plena y eficaz, para que nunca sea considerada la liturgia como "propiedad privada de alguien, ni del celebrante ni de la comunidad en que se celebran los Misterios"[38].

1. EL OBISPO DIOCESANO, GRAN SACERDOTE DE SU GREY

19. El Obispo diocesano, primer administrador de los misterios de Dios en la Iglesia particular que le ha sido encomendada, es el moderador, promotor y custodio de toda la vida litúrgica[39]. Pues "el Obispo, por estar revestido de la plenitud del sacramento del Orden, es 'el administrador de la gracia del supremo sacerdocio"[40], sobre todo en la Eucaristía, que él mismo celebra o procura que sea celebrada[41], y mediante la cual la Iglesia vive y crece continuamente"[42].

20. La principal manifestación de la Iglesia tiene lugar cada vez que se celebra la Misa, especialmente en la iglesia catedral, "con la participación plena y activa de todo el pueblo santo de Dios, [. . .] en una misma oración, junto al único altar, donde preside el Obispo" rodeado por su presbiterio, los diáconos y ministros[43]. Además, "toda legítima celebración de la Eucaristía es dirigida por el Obispo, a quien ha sido confiado el oficio de ofrecer a la Divina Majestad el culto de la religión cristiana y de reglamentarlo en conformidad con los preceptos del Señor y las leyes de la Iglesia, precisadas más concretamente para su diócesis según su criterio"[44].

21. En efecto, "al Obispo diocesano, en la Iglesia a él confiada y dentro de los límites de su competencia, le corresponde dar normas obligatorias para todos, sobre materia litúrgica"[45]. Sin embargo, el Obispo debe tener siempre presente que no se quite la libertad prevista en las normas de los libros litúrgicos, adaptando la celebración, de modo inteligente, sea a la iglesia, sea al grupo de fieles, sea a las circunstancias pastorales, para que todo el rito sagrado universal esté verdaderamente acomodado al carácter de los fieles[46].

22. El Obispo rige la Iglesia particular que le ha sido encomendada[47] y a él corresponde regular, dirigir, estimular y algunas veces también reprender[48], cumpliendo el ministerio sagrado que ha recibido por la ordenación episcopal[49], para edificar su grey en la verdad y en la santidad[50]. Explique el auténtico sentido de los ritos y de los textos litúrgicos y eduque en el espíritu de la sagrada Liturgia a los presbíteros, diáconos y fieles laicos[51], para que todos sean conducidos a una celebración activa y fructuosa de la Eucaristía[52], y cuide igualmente para que todo el cuerpo de la Iglesia, con el mismo espíritu, en la unidad de la caridad, pueda progresar en la diócesis, en la nación, en el mundo[53].

23. Los fieles "deben estar unidos a su Obispo como la Iglesia a Jesucristo, y como Jesucristo al Padre, para que todas las cosas se armonicen en la unidad y crezcan para gloria de Dios"[54]. Todos, incluso los miembros de los Institutos de Vida Consagrada y las Sociedades de Vida Apostólica, y todas las asociaciones o movimientos eclesiales de cualquier genero, están sometidos a la autoridad del Obispo diocesano en todo lo que se refiere a la liturgia[55], salvo las legítimas concesiones del derecho. Por lo tanto, compete al Obispo diocesano el derecho y el deber de visitar y vigilar la liturgia en las iglesias y oratorios situados en su territorio, también aquellos que sean fundados o dirigidos por los citados institutos religiosos, si los fieles acuden a ellos de forma habitual[56].

24. El pueblo cristiano, por su parte, tiene derecho a que el Obispo diocesano vigile para que no se introduzcan abusos en la disciplina eclesiástica, especialmente en el ministerio de la palabra, en la celebración de los sacramentos y sacramentales, en el culto a Dios y a los santos[57].

25. Las comisiones, consejos o comités, instituidos por el Obispo, para que contribuyan a "promover la acción litúrgica, la música y el arte sacro en su diócesis", deben actuar según el juicio y normas del Obispo, bajo su autoridad y contando con su confirmación; así cumplirán su tarea adecuadamente[58] y se mantendrá en la diócesis el gobierno efectivo del Obispo. De estos organismos, de otros institutos y de cualquier otra iniciativa en materia litúrgica, después de cierto tiempo, resulta urgente que los Obispos indaguen si hasta el momento ha sido fructuosa[59] su actividad, y valoren atentamente cuáles correcciones o mejoras se deben introducir en su estructura y en su actividad[60], para que encuentren nueva vitalidad. Se tenga siempre presente que los expertos deben

ser elegidos entre aquellos que sean firmes en la fe católica y verdaderamente preparados en las disciplinas teológicas y culturales.

2. LA CONFERENCIA DE OBISPOS

26. Esto vale también para las comisiones de la misma materia, que, vivamente deseadas por el Concilio[61], son instituidas por la Conferencia de Obispos y de la cual es necesario que sean miembros los Obispos, distinguiéndose con claridad de los ayudantes peritos. Cuando el número de los miembros de la Conferencia de Obispos no sea suficiente para que se elijan de entre ellos, sin dificultad, y se instituya la comisión litúrgica, nómbrese un consejo o grupo de expertos que, en cuanto sea posible y siempre bajo la presidencia de un Obispo, desempeñen estas tareas; evitando, sin embargo, el nombre de "comisión litúrgica".

27. La interrupción de todos los experimentos sobre la celebración de la santa Misa, ha sido notificada por la Santa Sede ya desde el año 1970[62] y nuevamente se repitió, para recordarlo, en el año 1988[63]. Por lo tanto, cada Obispo y la misma Conferencia no tienen ninguna facultad para permitir experimentos sobre los textos litúrgicos o sobre otras cosas que se indican en los libros litúrgicos. Para que se puedan realizar en el futuro tales experimentos, se requiere el permiso de la Congregación para el Culto Divino y la Disciplina de los Sacramentos, que lo concederá por escrito, previa petición de la Conferencia de Obispos. Pero esto no se concederá sin una causa grave. Por lo que se refiere a la enculturación en materia litúrgica, se deben observar, estricta e íntegramente, las normas especiales establecidas[64].

28. Todas las normas referentes a la liturgia, que la Conferencia de Obispos determine para su territorio, conforme a las normas del derecho, se deben someter a la *recognitio* de la Congregación para el Culto Divino y la Disciplina de los Sacramentos, sin la cual, carecen de valor legal[65].

3. LOS PRESBÍTEROS

29. Los presbíteros, como colaboradores fieles, diligentes y necesarios, del orden Episcopal[66], llamados para servir al Pueblo de Dios, constituyen un único presbiterio[67] con su Obispo, aunque

dedicados a diversas funciones. "En cada una de las congregaciones locales de fieles representan al Obispo, con el que están confiada y animosamente unidos, y toman sobre sí una parte de la carga y solicitud pastoral y la ejercen en el diario trabajo". Y, "por esta participación en el sacerdocio y en la misión, los presbíteros reconozcan verdaderamente al Obispo como a padre suyo y obedézcanle reverentemente"[68]. Además, "preocupados siempre por el bien de los hijos de Dios, procuren cooperar en el trabajo pastoral de toda la diócesis e incluso de toda la Iglesia"[69].

30. Grande es el ministerio "que en la celebración eucarística tienen principalmente los sacerdotes, a quienes compete presidirla *in persona Christi*, dando un testimonio y un servicio de comunión, no sólo a la comunidad que participa directamente en la celebración, sino también a la Iglesia universal, a la cual la Eucaristía hace siempre referencia. Por desgracia, es de lamentar que, sobre todo a partir de los años de la reforma litúrgica después del Concilio Vaticano II, por un malentendido sentido de creatividad y de adaptación, no hayan faltado abusos, que para muchos han sido causa de malestar"[70].

31. Coherentemente con lo que prometieron en el rito de la sagrada Ordenación y cada año renuevan dentro de la Misal Crismal, los presbíteros presidan "con piedad y fielmente la celebración de los misterios de Cristo, especialmente el sacrificio de la Eucaristía y el sacramento de la reconciliación"[71]. No vacíen el propio ministerio de su significado profundo, deformando de manera arbitraria la celebración litúrgica, ya sea con cambios, con mutilaciones o con añadidos[72]. En efecto, dice San Ambrosio: "No en si, [. . .] sino en nosotros es herida la Iglesia. Por lo tanto, tengamos cuidado para que nuestras caídas no hieran la Iglesia"[73]. Es decir, que no sea ofendida la Iglesia de Dios por los sacerdotes, que tan solemnemente se han ofrecido, ellos mismos, al ministerio. Al contrario, bajo la autoridad del Obispo vigilen fielmente para que no sean realizadas por otros estas deformaciones.

32. "Esfuércese el párroco para que la santísima Eucaristía sea el centro de la comunidad parroquial de fieles; trabaje para que los fieles se alimenten con la celebración piadosa de los sacramentos, de modo peculiar con la recepción frecuente de la santísima Eucaristía y de la penitencia; procure moverles a la oración, también en el seno de las familias, y a la participación consciente y activa en la sagrada liturgia, que, bajo la autoridad del Obispo diocesano,

debe moderar el párroco en su parroquia, con la obligación de vigilar para que no se introduzcan abusos"[74]. Aunque es oportuno que las celebraciones litúrgicas, especialmente la santa Misa, sean preparadas de manera eficaz, siendo ayudado por algunos fieles, sin embargo, de ningún modo debe ceder aquellas cosas que son propias de su ministerio, en esta materia.

33. Por último, todos "los presbíteros procuren cultivar convenientemente la ciencia y el arte litúrgicos, a fin de que por su ministerio litúrgico las comunidades cristianas que se les han encomendado alaben cada día con más perfección a Dios, Padre, Hijo y Espíritu Santo"[75]. Sobre todo, deben estar imbuidos de la admiración y el estupor que la celebración del misterio pascual, en la Eucaristía, produce en los corazones de los fieles[76].

4. LOS DIÁCONOS

34. Los diáconos, "que reciben la imposición de manos no en orden al sacerdocio, sino en orden al ministerio"[77], hombres de buena fama[78], deben actuar de tal manera, con la ayuda de Dios, que sean conocidos como verdaderos discípulos[79] de aquel "que no ha venido a ser servido sino a servir"[80] y estuvo en medio de sus discípulos "como el que sirve"[81] Y fortalecidos con el don del mismo Espíritu Santo, por la imposición de las manos, sirven al pueblo de Dios en comunión con el Obispo y su presbiterio[82]. Por tanto, tengan al Obispo como padre, y a él y a los presbíteros, préstenles ayuda "en el ministerio de la palabra, del altar y de la caridad"[83].

35. No dejen nunca de "vivir el misterio de la fe con alma limpia[84], como dice el Apóstol, y proclamar esta fe, de palabra y de obra, según el Evangelio y la tradición de la Iglesia"[85], sirviendo fielmente y con humildad, con todo el corazón, en la sagrada Liturgia que es fuente y cumbre de toda la vida eclesial, "para que, una vez hechos hijos de Dios por la fe y el Bautismo, todos se reúnan para alabar a Dios en medio de la Iglesia, participen en el Sacrificio y coman la cena del Señor"[86]. Por tanto, todos los diáconos, por su parte, empléense en esto, para que la sagrada Liturgia sea celebrada conforme a las normas de los libros litúrgicos debidamente aprobados.

CAPÍTULO II
LA PARTICIPACIÓN DE LOS FIELES LAICOS EN LA CELEBRACIÓN DE LA EUCARISTÍA

1. UNA PARTICIPACIÓN ACTIVA Y CONSCIENTE

36. La celebración de la Misa, como acción de Cristo y de la Iglesia, es el centro de toda la vida cristiana, en favor de la Iglesia, tanto universal como particular, y de cada uno de los fieles[87], a los que de diverso modo afecta, según la diversidad de órdenes, funciones y participación actual[88]. De este modo el pueblo cristiano, "raza elegida, sacerdocio real, nación santa, pueblo adquirido"[89], manifiesta su orden coherente y jerárquico"[90]. "El sacerdocio común de los fieles y el sacerdocio ministerial o jerárquico, aunque diferentes esencialmente y no sólo en grado, se ordenan, sin embargo, el uno al otro, pues ambos participan de forma peculiar del único sacerdocio de Cristo"[91].

37. Todos los fieles, por el bautismo, han sido liberados de sus pecados e incorporados a la Iglesia, destinados por el carácter al culto de la religión cristiana[92], para que por su sacerdocio real[93], perseverantes en la oración y en la alabanza a Dios[94], ellos mismos se ofrezcan como hostia viva, santa, agradable a Dios y todas sus obras lo confirmen[95], y testimonien a Cristo en todos los lugares de la tierra, dando razón a todo el que lo pida, de que en él está la esperanza de la vida eterna[96]. Por lo tanto, también la participación de los fieles laicos en la celebración de la Eucaristía, y en los otros ritos de la Iglesia, no puede equivaler a una mera presencia, más o menos pasiva, sino que se debe valorar como un verdadero ejercicio de la fe y la dignidad bautismal.

38. Así pues, la doctrina constante de la Iglesia sobre la naturaleza de la Eucaristía, no sólo convival sino también, y sobre todo, como sacrificio, debe ser rectamente considerada como una de las claves principales para la plena participación de todos los fieles en tan gran Sacramento[97]. "Privado de su valor sacrificial, se vive como si no tuviera otro significado y valor que el de un encuentro convival fraterno"[98].

39. Para promover y manifestar una participación activa, la reciente renovación de los libros litúrgicos, según el espíritu del Concilio, ha favorecido las aclamaciones del pueblo, las respuestas,

salmos, antífonas, cánticos, así como acciones, gestos y posturas corporales, y el sagrado silencio que cuidadosamente se debe observar en algunos momentos, como prevén las rúbricas, también de parte de los fieles[99]. Además, se ha dado un amplio espacio a una adecuada libertad de adaptación, fundamentada sobre el principio de que toda celebración responda a la necesidad, a la capacidad, a la mentalidad y a la índole de los participantes, conforme a las facultades establecidas en las normas litúrgicas. En la elección de los cantos, melodías, oraciones y lecturas bíblicas; en la realización de la homilía; en la preparación de la oración de los fieles; en las moniciones que a veces se pronuncian; y en adornar la iglesia en los diversos tiempos; existe una amplia posibilidad de que en toda celebración se pueda introducir, cómodamente, una cierta variedad para que aparezca con mayor claridad la riqueza de la tradición litúrgica y, atendiendo a las necesidades pastorales, se comunique diligentemente el sentido peculiar de la celebración, de modo que se favorezca la participación interior. También se debe recordar que la fuerza de la acción litúrgica no está en el cambio frecuente de los ritos, sino, verdaderamente, en profundizar en la palabra de Dios y en el misterio que se celebra[100].

40. Sin embargo, por más que la liturgia tiene, sin duda alguna, esta característica de la participación activa de todos los fieles, no se deduce necesariamente que todos deban realizar otras cosas, en sentido material, además de los gestos y posturas corporales, como si cada uno tuviera que asumir, necesariamente, una tarea litúrgica específica. La catequesis procure con atención que se corrijan las ideas y los comportamientos superficiales, que en los últimos años se han difundido en algunas partes, en esta materia; y despierte siempre en los fieles un renovado sentimiento de gran admiración frente a la altura del misterio de fe, que es la Eucaristía, en cuya celebración la Iglesia pasa continuamente "de lo viejo a lo Nuevo"[101]. En efecto, en la celebración de la Eucaristía, como en toda la vida cristiana, que de ella saca la fuerza y hacia ella tiende, la Iglesia, a ejemplo de Santo Tomás apóstol, se postra en adoración ante el Señor crucificado, muerto, sepultado y resucitado "en la plenitud de su esplendor divino, y perpetuamente exclama: *¡Señor mío y Dios mío!*"[102].

41. Son de gran utilidad, para suscitar, promover y alentar esta disposición interior de participación litúrgica, la asidua y difundida celebración de la Liturgia de las Horas, el uso de los sacramentales y los ejercicios de la piedad popular cristiana. Este tipo

de ejercicios "que, aunque en el rigor del derecho no pertenecen a la sagrada Liturgia, tienen, sin embargo, una especial importancia y dignidad," se deben conservar por el estrecho vínculo que existe con el ordenamiento litúrgico, especialmente cuando han sido aprobados y alabados por el mismo Magisterio[103]; esto vale sobre todo para el rezo del rosario[104]. Además, estas prácticas de piedad conducen al pueblo cristiano a frecuentar los sacramentos, especialmente la Eucaristía, "también a meditar los misterios de nuestra redención y a imitar los insignes ejemplos de los santos del cielo, que nos hacen así participar en el culto litúrgico, no sin gran provecho espiritual"[105].

42. Es necesario reconocer que la Iglesia no se reúne por voluntad humana, sino convocada por Dios en el Espíritu Santo, y responde por la fe a su llamada gratuita (en efecto, *ekklesia* tiene relación con *Klesis,* esto es, llamada)[106]. Ni el Sacrificio eucarístico se debe considerar como "concelebración", en sentido unívoco, del sacerdote al mismo tiempo que del pueblo presente[107]. Al contrario, la Eucaristía celebrada por los sacerdotes es un don "que supera radicalmente la potestad de la asamblea [. . .]. La asamblea que se reúne para celebrar la Eucaristía necesita absolutamente, para que sea realmente asamblea eucarística, un sacerdote ordenado que la presida. Por otra parte, la comunidad no está capacitada para darse por sí sola el ministro ordenado"[108]. Urge la necesidad de un interés común para que se eviten todas las ambigüedades en esta materia y se procure el remedio de las dificultades de estos últimos años. Por tanto, solamente con precaución se emplearán términos como comunidad celebrante" o "asamblea celebrante", en otras lenguas vernáculas: "celebrating assembly", "assemblée célébrante", "assemblea celebrante", y otros de este tipo.

2. TAREAS DE LOS FIELES LAICOS EN LA CELEBRACIÓN DE LA SANTA MISA

43. Algunos de entre los fieles laicos ejercen, recta y laudablemente, tareas relacionadas con la sagrada Liturgia, conforme a la tradición, para el bien de la comunidad y de toda la Iglesia de Dios[109]. Conviene que se distribuyan y realicen entre varios las tareas o las diversas partes de una misma tarea[110].

44. Además de los ministerios instituidos, de lector y de acólito[111], entre las tareas arriba mencionadas, en primer lugar están los de acólito[112] y de lector[113] con un encargo temporal, a los que

se unen otros servicios, descritos en el Misal Romano[114], y también la tarea de preparar las hostias, lavar los paños litúrgicos y similares. Todos "los ministros ordenados y los fieles laicos, al desempeñar su función u oficio, harán todo y sólo aquello que les corresponde"[115], y, ya lo hagan en la misma celebración litúrgica, ya en su preparación, sea realizado de tal forma que la liturgia de la Iglesia se desarrolle de manera digna y decorosa.

45. Se debe evitar el peligro de oscurecer la complementariedad entre la acción de los clérigos y los laicos, para que las tareas de los laicos no sufran una especie de "clericalización", como se dice, mientras los ministros sagrados asumen indebidamente lo que es propio de la vida y de las acciones de los fieles laicos[116].

46. El fiel laico que es llamado para prestar una ayuda en las celebraciones litúrgicas, debe estar debidamente preparado y ser recomendable por su vida cristiana, fe, costumbres y su fidelidad hacia el Magisterio de la Iglesia. Conviene que haya recibido la formación litúrgica correspondiente a su edad, condición, género de vida y cultura religiosa[117]. No se elija a ninguno cuya designación pueda suscitar el asombro de los fieles[118].

47. Es muy loable que se conserve la benemérita costumbre de que niños o jóvenes, denominados normalmente monaguillos, estén presentes y realicen un servicio junto al altar, como acólitos, y reciban una catequesis conveniente, adaptada a su capacidad, sobre esta tarea[119]. No se puede olvidar que del conjunto de estos niños, a lo largo de los siglos, ha surgido un número considerable de ministros sagrados[120]. Institúyanse y promuévanse asociaciones para ellos, en las que también participen y colaboren los padres, y con las cuales se proporcione a los monaguillos una atención pastoral eficaz. Cuando este tipo de asociaciones tenga carácter internacional, le corresponde a la Congregación para el Culto Divino y la Disciplina de los Sacramentos erigirlas, aprobarlas y reconocer sus estatutos[121]. A esta clase de servicio al altar pueden ser admitidas niñas o mujeres, según el juicio del Obispo diocesano y observando las normas establecidas[122].

CAPÍTULO III
LA CELEBRACIÓN CORRECTA DE LA SANTA MISA

1. LA MATERIA DE LA SANTÍSIMA EUCARISTÍA

48. El pan que se emplea en el santo Sacrificio de la Eucaristía debe ser ázimo, de sólo trigo y hecho recientemente, para que no haya ningún peligro de que se corrompa[123]. Por consiguiente, no puede constituir la materia válida, para la realización del Sacrificio y del Sacramento eucarístico, el pan elaborado con otras sustancias, aunque sean cereales, ni aquel que lleva mezcla de una sustancia diversa del trigo, en tal cantidad que, según la valoración común, no se puede llamar pan de trigo[124]. Es un abuso grave introducir, en la fabricación del pan para la Eucaristía, otras sustancias como frutas, azúcar o miel. Es claro que las hostias deben ser preparadas por personas que no sólo se distingan por su honestidad, sino que además sean expertas en la elaboración y dispongan de los instrumentos adecuados[125].

49. Conviene, en razón del signo, que algunas partes del pan eucarístico que resultan de la fracción del pan, se distribuyan al menos a algunos fieles, en la Comunión. "No obstante, de ningún modo se excluyen las hostias pequeñas, cuando lo requiere el número de los que van a recibir la sagrada Comunión, u otras razones pastorales lo exijan"[126]; más bien, según la costumbre, sean usadas sobretodo formas pequeñas, que no necesitan una fracción ulterior.

50. El vino que se utiliza en la celebración del santo Sacrificio eucarístico debe ser natural, del fruto de la vid, puro y sin corromper, sin mezcla de sustancias extrañas[127]. En la misma celebración de la Misa se le debe mezclar un poco de agua. Téngase diligente cuidado de que el vino destinado a la Eucaristía se conserve en perfecto estado y no se avinagre[128]. Está totalmente prohibido utilizar un vino del que se tiene duda en cuanto a su carácter genuino o a su procedencia, pues la Iglesia exige certeza sobre las condiciones necesarias para la validez de los sacramentos. No se debe admitir bajo ningún pretexto otras bebidas de cualquier género, que no constituyen una materia válida.

2. LA PLEGARIA EUCARÍSTICA

51. Sólo se pueden utilizar las Plegarias Eucarística que se encuentran en el Misal Romano o aquellas que han sido legítimamente aprobadas por la Sede Apostólica, en la forma y manera que se determina en la misma aprobación. "No se puede tolerar que algunos sacerdotes se arroguen el derecho de componer plegarias eucarísticas"[129], ni cambiar el texto aprobado por la Iglesia, ni utilizar otros, compuestos por personas privadas[130].

52. La proclamación de la Plegaria Eucarística, que por su misma naturaleza es como la cumbre de toda la celebración, es propia del sacerdote, en virtud de su misma ordenación. Por tanto, es un abuso hacer que algunas partes de la Plegaria Eucarística sean pronunciadas por el diácono, por un ministro laico, o bien por uno sólo o por todos los fieles juntos. La Plegaria Eucarística, por lo tanto, debe ser pronunciada en su totalidad, y solamente, por el Sacerdote[131].

53. Mientras el Sacerdote celebrante pronuncia la Plegaria Eucarística, "no se realizarán otras oraciones o cantos, y estarán en silencio el órgano y los otros instrumentos musicales"[132], salvo las aclamaciones del pueblo, como rito aprobado, de que se hablará más adelante.

54. Sin embargo, el pueblo participa siempre activamente y nunca de forma puramente pasiva: "se asocia al sacerdote en la fe y con el silencio, también con las intervenciones indicadas en el curso de la Plegaria Eucarística, que son: las respuestas en el diálogo del Prefacio, el *Santo,* la aclamación después de la consagración y la aclamación *'Amén',* después de la doxología final, así como otras aclamaciones aprobadas por la Conferencia de Obispos y *confirmadas* por la Santa Sede"[133].

55. En algunos lugares se ha difundido el abuso de que el sacerdote parte la hostia en el momento de la consagración, durante la celebración de la santa Misa. Este abuso se realiza contra la tradición de la Iglesia. Sea reprobado y corregido con urgencia.

56. En la Plegaria Eucarística no se omita la mención del Sumo Pontífice y del Obispo diocesano, conservando así una antiquísima tradición y manifestando la comunión eclesial. En efecto, "la reunión eclesial de la asamblea eucarística es comunión con el propio Obispo y con el Romano Pontífice"[134].

3. LAS OTRAS PARTES DE LA MISA

57. Es un derecho de la comunidad de fieles que, sobre todo en la celebración dominical, haya una música sacra adecuada e idónea, según costumbre, y siempre el altar, los paramentos y los paños sagrados, según las normas, resplandezcan por su dignidad, nobleza y limpieza.

58. Igualmente, todos los fieles tienen derecho a que la celebración de la Eucaristía sea preparada diligentemente en todas sus partes, para que en ella sea proclamada y explicada con dignidad y eficacia la palabra de Dios; la facultad de seleccionar los textos litúrgicos y los ritos debe ser ejercida con cuidado, según las normas, y las letras de los cantos de la celebración Litúrgica custodien y alimenten debidamente la fe de los fieles.

59. Cese la práctica reprobable de que sacerdotes, o diáconos, o bien fieles laicos, cambian y varían a su propio arbitrio, aquí o allí, los textos de la sagrada Liturgia que ellos pronuncian. Cuando hacen esto, convierten en inestable la celebración de la sagrada Liturgia y no raramente adulteran el sentido auténtico de la Liturgia.

60. En la celebración de la Misa, la liturgia de la palabra y la liturgia eucarística están íntimamente unidas entre sí y forman ambas un sólo y el mismo acto de culto. Por lo tanto, no es lícito separar una de otra, ni celebrarlas en lugares y tiempos diversos[135]. Tampoco está permitido realizar cada parte de la sagrada Misa en momentos diversos, aunque sea el mismo día.

61. Para elegir las lecturas bíblicas, que se deben proclamar en la celebración de la Misa, se deben seguir las normas que se encuentran en los libros litúrgicos[136], a fin de que verdaderamente "la mesa de la Palabra de Dios se prepare con más abundancia para los fieles y se abran a ellos los tesoros bíblicos"[137].

62. No está permitido omitir o sustituir, arbitrariamente, las lecturas bíblicas prescritas ni, sobre todo, cambiar "las lecturas y el salmo responsorial, que contienen la Palabra de Dios, con otros textos no bíblicos"[138].

63. La lectura evangélica, que "constituye el momento culminante de la liturgia de la palabra"[139], en las celebraciones de la sagrada Liturgia se reserva al ministro ordenado, conforme a la

tradición de la Iglesia[140]. Por eso no está permitido a un laico, aunque sea religioso, proclamar la lectura evangélica en la celebración de la santa Misa; ni tampoco en otros casos, en los cuales no sea explícitamente permitido por las normas[141].

64. La homilía, que se hace en el curso de la celebración de la santa Misa y es parte de la misma Liturgia[142], "la hará, normalmente, el mismo sacerdote celebrante, o él se la encomendará a un sacerdote concelebrante, o a veces, según las circunstancias, también al diácono, pero nunca a un laico[143]. En casos particulares y por justa causa, también puede hacer la homilía un obispo o un presbítero que está presente en la celebración, aunque sin poder concelebrar"[144].

65. Se recuerda que debe tenerse por abrogada, según lo prescrito en el canon 767 § 1, cualquier norma precedente que admitiera a los fieles no ordenados para poder hacer la homilía en la celebración eucarística[145]. Se reprueba esta concesión, sin que se pueda admitir ninguna fuerza de la costumbre.

66. La prohibición de admitir a los laicos para predicar, dentro de la celebración de la Misa, también es válida para los alumnos de seminarios, los estudiantes de teología, para los que han recibido la tarea de "asistentes pastorals" y para cualquier otro tipo de grupo, hermandad, comunidad o asociación, de laicos[146].

67. Sobre todo, se debe cuidar que la homilía se fundamente estrictamente en los misterios de la salvación, exponiendo a lo largo del año litúrgico, desde los textos de las lecturas bíblicas y los textos litúrgicos, los misterios de la fe y las normas de la vida cristiana, y ofreciendo un comentario de los textos del Ordinario y del Propio de la Misa, o de los otros ritos de la Iglesia[147]. Es claro que todas las interpretaciones de la sagrada Escritura deben conducir a Cristo, como eje central de la economía de la salvación, pero esto se debe realizar examinándola desde el contexto preciso de la celebración litúrgica. Al hacer la homilía, procúrese iluminar desde Cristo los acontecimientos de la vida. Hágase esto, sin embargo, de tal modo que no se vacíe el sentido auténtico y genuino de la palabra de Dios, por ejemplo, tratando sólo de política o de temas profanos, o tomando como fuente ideas que provienen de movimientos pseudo-religiosos de nuestra época[148].

68. El Obispo diocesano vigile con atención la homilía[149], difundiendo, entre los ministros sagrados, incluso normas, orientaciones y ayudas, y promoviendo a este fin reuniones y otras iniciativas; de esta manera tendrán ocasión frecuente de reflexionar con mayor atención sobre el carácter de la homilía y encontrarán también una ayuda para su preparación.

69. En la santa Misa y en otras celebraciones de la sagrada Liturgia no se admita un "Credo" o Profesión de fe que no se encuentre en los libros litúrgicos debidamente aprobados.

70. Las ofrendas que suelen presentar los fieles en la santa Misa, para la Liturgia eucarística, no se reducen necesariamente al pan y al vino para celebrar la Eucaristía, sino que también pueden comprender otros dones, que son ofrecidos por los fieles en forma de dinero o bien de otra manera útil para la caridad hacia los pobres. Sin embargo, los dones exteriores deben ser siempre expresión visible del verdadero don que el Señor espera de nosotros: un corazón contrito y el amor a Dios y al prójimo, por el cual nos configuramos con el sacrificio de Cristo, que se entregó a sí mismo por nosotros. Pues en la Eucaristía resplandece, sobre todo, el misterio de la caridad que Jesucristo reveló en la Última Cena, lavando los pies de los discípulos. Con todo, para proteger la dignidad de la sagrada Liturgia, conviene que las ofrendas exteriores sean presentadas de forma apta. Por lo tanto, el dinero, así como otras ofrendas para los pobres, se pondrán en un lugar oportuno, pero fuera de la mesa eucarística[150]. Salvo el dinero y, cuando sea el caso, una pequeña parte de los otros dones ofrecidos, por razón del signo, es preferible que estas ofrendas sean presentadas fuera de la celebración de la Misa.

71. Consérvese la costumbre del Rito romano, de dar la paz un poco antes de distribuir la sagrada Comunión, como está establecido en el Ordinario de la Misa. Además, conforme a la tradición del Rito romano, esta práctica no tiene un sentido de reconciliación ni de perdón de los pecados, sino que más bien significa la paz, la comunión y la caridad, antes de recibir la santísima Eucaristía[151]. En cambio, el sentido de reconciliación entre los hermanos se manifiesta claramente en el acto penitencial que se realiza al inicio de la Misa, sobre todo en la primera de sus formas.

72. Conviene "que cada uno dé la paz, sobriamente, sólo a los más cercanos a él". "El sacerdote puede dar la paz a los ministros,

permaneciendo siempre dentro del presbiterio, para no alterar la celebración. Hágase del mismo modo si, por una causa razonable, desea dar la paz a algunos fieles". "En cuanto al signo para darse la paz, establezca el modo la Conferencia de Obispos", con el reconocimiento de la Sede Apostólica, "según la idiosincrasia y las costumbres de los pueblos"[152].

73. En la celebración de la santa Misa, la fracción del pan eucarístico la realiza solamente el sacerdote celebrante, ayudado, si es el caso, por el diácono o por un concelebrante, pero no por un laico; se comienza después de dar la paz, mientras se dice el "Cordero de Dios". El gesto de la fracción del pan, "realizada por Cristo en la Última Cena, que en el tiempo apostólico dio nombre a toda la acción eucarística, significa que los fieles, siendo muchos, forman un solo cuerpo por la comunión de un solo pan de vida, que es Cristo muerto y resucitado para la salvación del mundo (1 Corintios 10,17)"[153]. Por esto, se debe realizar el rito con gran respeto[154]. Sin embargo, debe ser breve. El abuso, extendido en algunos lugares, de prolongar sin necesidad este rito, incluso con la ayuda de laicos, contrariamente a las normas, o de atribuirle una importancia exagerada, debe ser corregido con gran urgencia[155].

74. Si se diera la necesidad de que instrucciones o testimonios sobre la vida cristiana sean expuestos por un laico a los fieles congregados en la iglesia, siempre es preferible que esto se haga fuera de la celebración de la Misa. Por causa grave, sin embargo, está permitido dar este tipo de instrucciones o testimonios, después de que el sacerdote pronuncie la oración después de la Comunión. Pero esto no puede hacerse una costumbre. Además, estas instrucciones y testimonios de ninguna manera pueden tener un sentido que pueda ser confundido con la homilía[156], ni se permite que por ello se suprima totalmente la homilía.

4. LA UNIÓN DE VARIOS RITOS CON LA CELEBRACIÓN DE LA MISA

75. Por el sentido teológico inherente a la celebración de la eucaristía o de un rito particular, los libros litúrgicos permiten o prescriben, algunas veces, la celebración de la santa Misa unida con otro rito, especialmente de los Sacramentos[157]. En otros casos, sin embargo, la Iglesia no admite esta unión, especialmente cuando lo que se añadiría tiene un carácter superficial y sin importancia.

76. Además, según la antiquísima tradición de la Iglesia romana, no es lícito unir el Sacramento de la Penitencia con la santa Misa y hacer así una única acción litúrgica. Esto no impide que algunos sacerdotes, independientemente de los que celebran o concelebran la Misa, escuchen las confesiones de los fieles que lo deseen, incluso mientras en el mismo lugar se celebra la Misa, para atender las necesidades de los fieles[158]. Pero esto, hágase de manera adecuada.

77. La celebración de la santa Misa de ningún modo puede ser intercalada como añadido a una cena común, ni unirse con cualquier tipo de banquete. No se celebre la Misa, a no ser por grave necesidad, sobre una mesa de comedor[159], o en el comedor, o en el lugar que será utilizado para un convite, ni en cualquier sala donde haya alimentos, ni los participantes en la Misa se sentarán a la mesa, durante la celebración. Si, por una grave necesidad, se debe celebrar la Misa en el mismo lugar donde después será la cena, debe mediar un espacio suficiente de tiempo entre la conclusión de la Misa y el comienzo de la cena, sin que se muestren a los fieles, durante la celebración de la Misa, alimentos ordinarios.

78. No está permitido relacionar la celebración de la Misa con acontecimientos políticos o mundanos, o con otros elementos que no concuerden plenamente con el Magisterio de la Iglesia Católica. Además, se debe evitar totalmente la celebración de la Misa por el simple deseo de ostentación o celebrarla según el estilo de otras ceremonias, especialmente profanas, para que la Eucaristía no se vacíe de su significado auténtico.

79. Por último, el abuso de introducir ritos tomados de otras religiones en la celebración de la santa Misa, en contra de lo que se prescribe en los libros litúrgicos, se debe juzgar con gran severidad.

CAPÍTULO IV
LA SAGRADA COMUNIÓN

1. LAS DISPOSICIONES PARA RECIBIR LA SAGRADA COMUNIÓN

80. La Eucaristía sea propuesta a los fieles, también, "como antídoto por el que somos liberados de las culpas cotidianas y preservados de los pecados mortales"[160], como se muestra claramente en diversas partes de la Misa. Por lo que se refiere al acto penitencial, situado al comienzo de la Misa, este tiene la finalidad de disponer

a todos para que celebren adecuadamente los sagrados misterios[161], aunque "carece de la eficacia del sacramento de la Penitencia"[162], y no se puede pensar que sustituye, para el perdón de los pecados graves, lo que corresponde al sacramento de la Penitencia. Los pastores de almas cuiden diligentemente la catequesis, para que la doctrina cristiana sobre esta materia se transmita a los fieles.

81. La costumbre de la Iglesia manifiesta que es necesario que cada uno se examine a sí mismo en profundidad[163], para que quien sea consciente de estar en pecado grave no celebre la Misa ni comulgue el Cuerpo del Señor sin acudir antes a la confesión sacramental, a no ser que concurra un motivo grave y no haya oportunidad de confesarse; en este caso, recuerde que está obligado a hacer un acto de contrición perfecta, que incluye el propósito de confesarse cuanto antes[164].

82. Además, "la Iglesia ha dado normas que se orientan a favorecer la participación frecuente y fructuosa de los fieles en la Mesa eucarística y, al mismo tiempo, a determinar las condiciones objetivas en las que no debe administrarse la communion"[165].

83. Ciertamente, lo mejor es que todos aquellos que participan en la celebración de la santa Misa y tiene las debidas condiciones, reciban en ella la sagrada Comunión. Sin embargo, alguna vez sucede que los fieles se acercan en grupo e indiscriminadamente a la mesa sagrada. Es tarea de los pastores corregir con prudencia y firmeza tal abuso.

84. Además, donde se celebre la Misa para una gran multitud o, por ejemplo, en las grandes ciudades, debe vigilarse para que no se acerquen a la sagrada Comunión, por ignorancia, los no católicos o, incluso, los no cristianos, sin tener en cuenta el Magisterio de la Iglesia en lo que se refiere a la doctrina y la disciplina. Corresponde a los Pastores advertir en el momento oportuno a los presentes sobre la verdad y disciplina que se debe observar estrictamente.

85. Los ministros católicos administran lícitamente los sacramentos, sólo a los fieles católicos, los cuales, igualmente, los reciben lícitamente sólo de ministros católicos, salvo lo que se prescribe en los canon 844 §§ 2, 3 y 4, y en el canon 861 § 2[166]. Además, las condiciones establecidas por el canon 844 § 4, de las que nada se puede derogar[167], son inseparables entre sí; por lo que es necesario que siempre sean exigidas simultáneamente.

86. Los fieles deben ser guiados con insistencia hacia la costumbre de participar en el sacramento de la penitencia, fuera de la celebración de la Misa, especialmente en horas establecidas, para que así se pueda administrar con tranquilidad, sea para ellos de verdadera utilidad y no se impida una participación activa en la Misa. Los que frecuente o diariamente suelen comulgar, sean instruidos para que se acerquen al sacramento de la penitencia cada cierto tiempo, según la disposición de cada uno[168].

87. La primera Comunión de los niños debe estar siempre precedida de la confesión y absolución sacramental[169]. Además, la primera Comunión siempre debe ser administrada por un sacerdote y, ciertamente, nunca fuera de la celebración de la Misa. Salvo casos excepcionales, es poco adecuado que se administre el Jueves Santo, "in Cena Domini". Es mejor escoger otro día, como los domingos II–VI de Pascua, la solemnidad del Santísimo Cuerpo y Sangre de Cristo o los domingos del Tiempo Ordinario, puesto que el domingo es justamente considerado como el día de la Eucaristía[170]. No se acerquen a recibir la sagrada Eucaristía "los niños que aún no han llegado al uso de razón o los que" el párroco "no juzgue suficientemente dispuestos"[171]. Sin embargo, cuando suceda que un niño, de modo excepcional con respecto a los de su edad, sea considerado maduro para recibir el sacramento, no se le debe negar la primera Comunión, siempre que esté suficientemente instruido.

2. LA DISTRIBUCIÓN DE LA SAGRADA COMUNIÓN

88. Los fieles, habitualmente, reciban la Comunión sacramental de la Eucaristía en la misma Misa y en el momento prescrito por el mismo rito de la celebración, esto es, inmediatamente después de la Comunión del sacerdote celebrante[172]. Corresponde al sacerdote celebrante distribuir la Comunión, si es el caso, ayudado por otros sacerdotes o diáconos; y este no debe proseguir la Misa hasta que haya terminado la Comunión de los fieles. Sólo donde la necesidad lo requiera, los ministros extraordinarios pueden ayudar al sacerdote celebrante, según las normas del derecho[173].

89. Para que también "por los signos, aparezca mejor que la Comunión es participación en el Sacrificio que se está celebrando"[174], es deseable que los fieles puedan recibirla con hostias consagradas en la misma Misa[175].

90. "Los fieles comulgan de rodillas o de pie, según lo establezca la Conferencia de Obispos", con la confirmación de la Sede Apostólica. "Cuando comulgan de pie, se recomienda hacer, antes de recibir el Sacramento, la debida reverencia, que deben establecer las mismas normas"[176].

91. En la distribución de la sagrada Comunión se debe recordar que "los ministros sagrados no pueden negar los sacramentos a quienes los pidan de modo oportuno, estén bien dispuestos y no les sea prohibido por el derecho recibirlos"[177]. Por consiguiente, cualquier bautizado católico, a quien el derecho no se lo prohiba, debe ser admitido a la sagrada Comunión. Así pues, no es lícito negar la sagrada Comunión a un fiel, por ejemplo, sólo por el hecho de querer recibir la Eucaristía arrodillado o de pie.

92. Aunque todo fiel tiene siempre derecho a elegir si desea recibir la sagrada Comunión en la boca[178], si el que va a comulgar quiere recibir en la mano el Sacramento, en los lugares donde la Conferencia de Obispos lo haya permitido, con la confirmación de la Sede Apostólica, se le debe administrar la sagrada hostia. Sin embargo, póngase especial cuidado en que el comulgante consuma inmediatamente la hostia, delante del ministro, y ninguno se aleje teniendo en la mano las especies eucarísticas. Si existe peligro de profanación, no se distribuya a los fieles la Comunión en la mano[179].

93. La bandeja para la Comunión de los fieles se debe mantener, para evitar el peligro de que caiga la hostia sagrada o algún fragmento[180].

94. No está permitido que los fieles tomen la hostia consagrada ni el cáliz sagrado "por sí mismos, ni mucho menos que se lo pasen entre sí de mano en mano"[181]. En esta materia, además, debe suprimirse el abuso de que los esposos, en la Misa nupcial, se administren de modo recíproco la sagrada Comunión.

95. El fiel laico "que ya ha recibido la santísima Eucaristía, puede recibirla otra vez el mismo día solamente dentro de la celebración eucarística en la que participe, quedando a salvo lo que prescribe el c. 921 § 2"[182].

96. Se reprueba la costumbre, que es contraria a las prescripciones de los libros litúrgicos, de que sean distribuidas a manera de Comunión, durante la Misa o antes de ella, ya sean hostias no

consagradas ya sean otros comestibles o no comestibles. Puesto que estas costumbres de ningún modo concuerdan con la tradición del Rito romano y llevan consigo el peligro de inducir a confusión a los fieles, respecto a la doctrina eucarística de la Iglesia. Donde en algunos lugares exista, por concesión, la costumbre particular de bendecir y distribuir pan, después de la Misa, téngase gran cuidado de que se dé una adecuada catequesis sobre este acto. No se introduzcan otras costumbres similares, ni sean utilizadas para esto, nunca, hostias no consagradas.

3. LA COMUNIÓN DE LOS SACERDOTES

97. Cada vez que celebra la santa Misa, el sacerdote debe comulgar en el altar, cuando lo determina el Misal, pero antes de que proceda a la distribución de la Comunión, lo hacen los concelebrantes. Nunca espere para comulgar, el sacerdote celebrante o los concelebrantes, hasta que termine la comunión del pueblo[183].

98. La Comunión de los sacerdotes concelebrantes se realice según las normas prescritas en los libros litúrgicos, utilizando siempre hostias consagradas en esa misma Misa[184] y recibiendo todos los concelebrantes, siempre, la Comunión bajo las dos especies. Nótese que si un sacerdote o diácono entrega a los concelebrantes la hostia sagrada o el cáliz, no dice nada, es decir, en ningún caso pronuncia las palabras "el Cuerpo de Cristo" o "la Sangre de Cristo".

99. La Comunión bajo las dos especies está siempre permitida "a los sacerdotes que no pueden celebrar o concelebrar en la acción sagrada"[185].

4. LA COMUNIÓN BAJO LAS DOS ESPECIES

100. Para que, en el banquete eucarístico, la plenitud del signo aparezca ante los fieles con mayor claridad, son admitidos a la Comunión bajo las dos especies también los fieles laicos, en los casos indicados en los libros litúrgicos, con la debida catequesis previa y en el mismo momento, sobre los principios dogmáticos que en esta materia estableció el Concilio Ecuménico Tridentino[186].

101. Para administrar a los fieles laicos la sagrada Comunión bajo las dos especies, se deben tener en cuenta, convenientemente, las circunstancias, sobre las que deben juzgar en primer lugar los

Obispos diocesanos. Se debe excluir totalmente cuando exista peligro, incluso pequeño, de profanación de las sagradas especies[187]. Para una mayor coordinación, es necesario que la Conferencia de Obispos publique normas, con la aprobación de la Sede Apostólica, por medio de la Congregación para el Culto Divino y la Disciplina de los Sacramentos, especialmente lo que se refiere "al modo de distribuir a los fieles la sagrada Comunión bajo las dos especies y a la extensión de la facultad"[188].

102. No se administre la Comunión con el cáliz a los fieles laicos donde sea tan grande el número de los que van a comulgar[189] que resulte difícil calcular la cantidad de vino para la Eucaristía y exista el peligro de que "sobre demasiada cantidad de Sangre de Cristo, que deba sumirse al final de la celebración"[190]; tampoco donde el acceso ordenado al cáliz sólo sea posible con dificultad, o donde sea necesaria tal cantidad de vino que sea difícil poder conocer su calidad y su proveniencia, o cuando no esté disponible un número suficiente de ministros sagrados ni de ministros extraordinarios de la sagrada Comunión que tengan la formación adecuada, o donde una parte importante del pueblo no quiera participar del cáliz, por diversas y persistentes causas, disminuyendo así, en cierto modo, el signo de unidad.

103. Las normas del Misal Romano admiten el principio de que, en los casos en que se administra la sagrada Comunión bajo las dos especies, "la sangre del Señor se puede tomar bebiendo directamente del cáliz, o por *intinción,* o con una pajilla, o una cucharilla"[191]. Por lo que se refiere a la administración de la Comunión a los fieles laicos, los Obispos pueden excluir, en los lugares donde no sea costumbre, la Comunión con pajilla o con cucharilla, permaneciendo siempre, no obstante, la opción de distribuir la Comunión por *intinción.* Pero si se emplea esta forma, utilícense hostias que no sean ni demasiado delgadas ni demasiado pequeñas, y el comulgante reciba del sacerdote el sacramento, solamente en la boca[192].

104. No se permita al comulgante mojar por sí mismo la hostia en el cáliz, ni recibir en la mano la hostia mojada. Por lo que se refiere a la hostia que se debe mojar, esta debe hacerse de materia válida y estar consagrada; está absolutamente prohibido el uso de pan no consagrado o de otra materia.

105. Si no es suficiente un cáliz, para la distribución de la Comunión bajo las dos especies a los sacerdotes concelebrantes o a los fieles, nada impide que el sacerdote celebrante utilice varios cálices[193]. Recuérdese, no obstante, que todos los sacerdotes que celebran la santa Misa tienen que realizar la Comunión bajo las dos especies. Empléese laudablemente, por razón del signo, un cáliz principal más grande, junto con otros cálices más pequeños.

106. Sin embargo, se debe evitar completamente, después de la consagración, echar la Sangre de Cristo de un cáliz a otro, para excluir cualquier cosa de pueda resultar un agravio de tan gran misterio. Para contener la Sangre del Señor nunca se utilicen frascos, vasijas u otros recipientes que no respondan plenamente a las normas establecidas.

107. Según la normativa establecida en los cánones, "quien arroja por tierra las especies consagradas, o las lleva o retiene con una finalidad sacrílega, incurre en excomunión *latae sententiae* reservada a la Sede Apostólica; el clérigo puede ser castigado además con otra pena, sin excluir la expulsión del estado clerical"[194]. En este caso se debe considerar incluida cualquier acción, voluntaria y grave, de desprecio a las sagradas especies. De donde si alguno actúa contra las normas arriba indicadas, por ejemplo, arrojando las sagradas especies en el lavabo de la sacristía, o en un lugar indigno, o por el suelo, incurre en las penas establecidas[195]. Además, recuerden todos que al terminar la distribución de la sagrada Comunión, dentro de la celebración de la Misa, hay que observar lo que prescribe el Misal Romano, y sobre todo que el sacerdote o, según las normas, otro ministro, de inmediato debe sumir en el altar, íntegramente, el vino consagrado que quizá haya quedado; las hostias consagradas que han sobrado, o las consume el sacerdote en el altar o las lleva al lugar destinado para la reserva de la Eucaristía[196].

CAPÍTULO V
OTROS ASPECTOS QUE SE REFIEREN A LA EUCARISTÍA

1. EL LUGAR DE LA CELEBRACIÓN DE LA SANTA MISA

108. "A celebración eucarística se ha de hacer en lugar sagrado, a no ser que, en un caso particular, la necesidad exija otra cosa; en este caso, la celebración debe realizarse en un lugar digno"[197]. De

la necesidad del caso juzgará, habitualmente, el Obispo diocesano para su diócesis.

109. Nunca es lícito a un sacerdote celebrar la Eucaristía en un templo o lugar sagrado de cualquier religión no cristiana.

2. DIVERSOS ASPECTOS RELACIONADOS CON LA SANTA MISA

110. "Los sacerdotes, teniendo siempre presente que en el misterio del Sacrificio eucarístico se realiza continuamente la obra de la redención, deben celebrarlo frecuentemente; es más, se recomienda encarecidamente la celebración diaria, la cual, aunque no pueda tenerse con asistencia de fieles, es una acción de Cristo y de la Iglesia, en cuya realización los sacerdotes cumplen su principal ministerio"[198].

111. En la celebración o concelebración de la Eucaristía, "admítase a celebrar a un sacerdote, aunque el rector de la iglesia no lo conozca, con tal de que presente cartas comendaticias" de la Sede Apostólica, o de su Ordinario o de su Superior, dadas al menos en el año, las enseñe "o pueda juzgarse prudentemente que nada le impide celebrar"[199]. El Obispo debe proveer para que desaparezcan las costumbres contrarias.

112. La Misa se celebra o bien en lengua latina o bien en otra lengua, con tal de que se empleen textos litúrgicos que hayan sido aprobados, según las normas del derecho. Exceptuadas las celebraciones de la Misa que, según las horas y los momentos, la autoridad eclesiástica establece que se hagan en la lengua del pueblo, siempre y en cualquier lugar es lícito a los sacerdotes celebrar el santo sacrificio en latín[200].

113. Cuando una Misa es concelebrada por varios sacerdotes, al pronunciar la Plegaria Eucarística, utilícese la lengua que sea conocida por todos los sacerdotes concelebrantes y por el pueblo congregado. Cuando suceda que entre los sacerdotes haya algunos que no conocen la lengua de la celebración y, por lo tanto, no pueden pronunciar debidamente las partes propias de la Plegaria Eucarística, no concelebren, sino que preferiblemente asistan a la celebración revestidos de hábito coral, según las normas[201].

114. "En las Misas dominicales de la parroquia, como 'comunidad eucarística', es normal que se encuentren los grupos, movimientos, asociaciones y las pequeñas comunidades religiosas presentes en ella"[202]. Aunque es lícito celebrar la Misa, según las normas del derecho, para grupos particulares[203], estos grupos de ninguna manera están exentos de observar fielmente las normas litúrgicas.

115. Se reprueba el abuso de que sea suspendida de forma arbitraria la celebración de la santa Misa en favor del pueblo, bajo el pretexto de promover el "ayuno de la Eucaristía", contra las normas del Misal Romano y la sana tradición del Rito romano.

116. No se multipliquen las Misas, contra la norma del derecho, y sobre los estipendios obsérvese todo lo que manda el derecho[204].

3. LOS VASOS SAGRADOS

117. Los vasos sagrados, que están destinados a recibir el Cuerpo y la Sangre del Señor, se deben fabricar, estrictamente, conforme a las normas de la tradición y de los libros litúrgicos[205]. Las Conferencias de Obispos tienen la facultad de decidir, con la aprobación de la Sede Apostólica, si es oportuno que los vasos sagrados también sean elaborados con otros materiales sólidos. Sin embargo, se requiere estrictamente que este material, según la común estimación de cada región, sea verdaderamente noble[206], de manera que con su uso se tribute honor al Señor y se evite absolutamente el peligro de debilitar, a los ojos de los fieles, la doctrina de la presencia real de Cristo en las especies eucarísticas. Por lo tanto, se reprueba cualquier uso por el que son utilizados para la celebración de la Misa vasos comunes o de escaso valor, en lo que se refiere a la calidad, o carentes de todo valor artístico, o simples cestos, u otros vasos de cristal, arcilla, creta y otros materiales, que se rompen fácilmente. Esto vale también de los metales y otros materiales, que se corrompen fácilmente[207].

118. Los vasos sagrados, antes de ser utilizados, son bendecidos por el sacerdote con el rito que se prescribe en los libros litúrgicos[208]. Es laudable que la bendición sea impartida por el Obispo diocesano, que juzgará si los vasos son idóneos para el uso al cual están destinados.

119. El sacerdote, vuelto al altar después de la distribución de la Comunión, de pie junto al altar o en la credencia, purifica la patena

o la píxide sobre el cáliz; después purifica el cáliz, como prescribe el Misal, y seca el cáliz con el purificador. Cuando está presente el diácono, este regresa al altar con el sacerdote y purifica los vasos. También se permite dejar los vasos para purificar, sobre todo si son muchos, sobre el corporal y oportunamente cubiertos, en el altar o en la credencia, de forma que sean purificados por el sacerdote o el diácono, inmediatamente después de la Misa, una vez despedido el pueblo. Del mismo modo, el acólito debidamente instituido ayuda al sacerdote o al diácono en la purificación y arreglo de los vasos sagrados, ya sea en el altar, ya sea en la credencia. Ausente el diácono, el acólito litúrgicamente instituido lleva los vasos sagrados a la credencia, donde los purifica, seca y arregla, de la forma acostumbrada[209].

120. Cuiden los pastores que los paños de la sagrada mesa, especialmente los que reciben las sagradas especies, se conserven siempre limpios y se laven con frecuencia, conforme a la costumbre tradicional. Es laudable que se haga de esta manera: que el agua del primer lavado, hecho a mano, se vierta en un recipiente apropiado de la iglesia o sobre la tierra, en un lugar adecuado. Después de esto, se puede lavar nuevamente del modo acostumbrado.

4. LAS VESTIDURAS LITÚRGICAS

121. "La diversidad de los colores en las vestiduras sagradas tiene como fin expresar con más eficacia, aun exteriormente, tanto las características de los misterios de la fe que se celebran como el sentido progresivo de la vida cristiana a lo largo del año litúrgico"[210]. También la diversidad "de ministerios se manifiesta exteriormente, al celebrar la Eucaristía, en la diversidad de las vestiduras sagradas". Pero estas "vestiduras deben contribuir al decoro de la misma acción sagrada"[211].

122. "El alba" está "ceñida a la cintura con el cíngulo, a no ser que esté confeccionada de tal modo que se adhiera al cuerpo sin cíngulo. Antes de ponerse el alba, si no cubre totalmente el vestido común alrededor del cuello, empléese el amito"[212].

123. "La vestidura propia del sacerdote celebrante, en la Misa y en otras acciones sagradas que directamente se relacionan con ella, es la casulla o planeta, si no se indica otra cosa, revestida sobre el alba y la estola"[213]. Igualmente, el sacerdote que se reviste con la casulla, conforme a las rúbricas, no deje de ponerse la estola.

Todos los Ordinarios vigilen para que sea extirpada cualquier costumbre contraria.

124. En el Misal Romano se da la facultad de que los sacerdotes que concelebran en la Misa, excepto el celebrante principal, que siempre debe llevar la casulla del color prescrito, puedan omitir "la casulla o planeta y usar la estola sobre el alba", cuando haya una justa causa, por ejemplo el gran número de concelebrantes y la falta de ornamentos[214]. Sin embargo, en el caso de que esta necesidad se pueda prever, en cuanto sea posible, provéase. Los concelebrantes, a excepción del celebrante principal, pueden también llevar la casulla de color blanco, en caso de necesidad. Obsérvense, en lo demás, las normas de los libros litúrgicos.

125. La vestidura propia del diácono es la dalmática, puesta sobre el alba y la estola. Para conservar la insigne tradición de la Iglesia, es recomendable no usar la facultad de omitir la dalmática[215].

126. Sea reprobado el abuso de que los sagrados ministros realicen la santa Misa, incluso con la participación de sólo un asistente, sin llevar las vestiduras sagradas, o con sólo la estola sobre la cogulla monástica, o el hábito común de los religiosos, o la vestidura ordinaria, contra lo prescrito en los libros litúrgicos[216]. Los Ordinarios cuiden de que este tipo de abusos sean corregidos rápidamente y haya, en todas las iglesias y oratorios de su jurisdicción, un número adecuado de ornamentos litúrgicos, confeccionados según las normas.

127. En los libros litúrgicos se concede la facultad especial, para los días más solemnes, de usar vestiduras sagradas festivas o de mayor dignidad, aunque no sean del color del día[217]. Esta facultad, que también se aplica adecuadamente a los ornamentos fabricados hace muchos años, a fin de conservar el patrimonio de la Iglesia, es impropio extenderla a las innovaciones, para que así no se pierdan las costumbres transmitidas y el sentido de estas normas de la tradición no sufra menoscabo, por el uso de formas y colores según la inclinación de cada uno. Cuando sea un día festivo, los ornamentos sagrados de color dorado o plateado pueden sustituir a los de otros colores, pero no a los de color morado o negro.

128. La santa Misa y las otras celebraciones litúrgicas, que son acción de Cristo y del pueblo de Dios jerárquicamente constituido, sean organizadas de tal manera que los sagrados ministros y

los fieles laicos, cada uno según su condición, participen claramente. Por eso es preferible que "los presbíteros presentes en la celebración eucarística, si no están excusados por una justa causa, ejerzan la función propia de su Orden, como habitualmente, y participen por lo tanto como concelebrantes, revestidos con las vestiduras sagradas. De otro modo, lleven el hábito coral propio o la sobrepelliz sobre la vestidura talar"[218]. No es apropiado, salvo los casos en que exista una causa razonable, que participen en la Misa, en cuanto al aspecto externo, como si fueran fieles laicos.

CAPÍTULO VI
LA RESERVA DE LA SANTÍSIMA EUCARISTÍA Y SU CULTO FUERA DE LA MISA

1. LA RESERVA DE LA SANTÍSIMA EUCARISTÍA

129. "La celebración de la Eucaristía en el Sacrificio de la Misa es, verdaderamente, el origen y el fin del culto que se le tributa fuera de la Misa. Las sagradas especies se reservan después de la Misa, principalmente con el objeto de que los fieles que no pueden estar presentes en la Misa, especialmente los enfermos y los de avanzada edad, puedan unirse a Cristo y a su sacrificio, que se inmola en la Misa, por la Comunión sacramental"[219]. Además, esta reserva permite también la práctica de tributar adoración a este gran Sacramento, con el culto de latría, que se debe a Dios. Por lo tanto, es necesario que se promuevan vivamente aquellas formas de culto y adoración, no sólo privada sino también pública y comunitaria, instituidas o aprobadas por la misma Iglesia[220].

130. "Según la estructura de cada iglesia y las legítimas costumbres de cada lugar, el Santísimo Sacramento será reservado en un sagrario, en la parte más noble de la iglesia, más insigne, más destacada, más convenientemente adornada" y también, por la tranquilidad del lugar, "apropiado para la oración", con espacio ante el sagrario, así como suficientes bancos o asientos y reclinatorios[221]. Atiéndase diligentemente, además, a todas las prescripciones de los libros litúrgicos y a las normas del derecho[222], especialmente para evitar el peligro de profanación[223].

131. Además de lo prescrito en el can. 934 § 1, se prohibe reservar el Santísimo Sacramento en los lugares que no están bajo la segura autoridad del Obispo diocesano o donde exista peligro de

profanación. Si esto ocurriera, el Obispo revoque inmediatamente la facultad, ya concedida, de reservar la Eucaristía[224].

132. Nadie lleve la Sagrada Eucaristía a casa o a otro lugar, contra las normas del derecho. Se debe tener presente, además, que sustraer o retener las sagradas especies con un fin sacrílego, o arrojarlas, constituye uno de los *"graviora delicta"*, cuya absolución está reservada a la Congregación para la Doctrina de la Fe[225].

133. El sacerdote o el diácono, o el ministro extraordinario, cuando el ministro ordinario esté ausente o impedido, que lleva al enfermo la Sagrada Eucaristía para la Comunión, irá directamente, en cuanto sea posible, desde el lugar donde se reserva el Sacramento hasta el domicilio del enfermo, excluyendo mientras tanto cualquier otra actividad profana, para evitar todo peligro de profanación y para guardar el máximo respeto al Cuerpo de Cristo. Además, sígase siempre el ritual para administrar la Comunión a los enfermos, como se prescribe en el *Ritual Romano*[226].

2. ALGUNAS FORMAS DE CULTO A LA SAGRADA EUCARISTÍA FUERA DE LA MISA

134. "El culto que se da a la Eucaristía fuera de la Misa es de un valor inestimable en la vida de la Iglesia. Dicho culto está estrechamente unido a la celebración del sacrificio Eucarístico"[227]. Por lo tanto, promuévase insistentemente la piedad hacia la santísima Eucaristía, tanto privada como pública, también fuera de la Misa, para que sea tributada por los fieles la adoración a Cristo, verdadera y realmente presente[228], que es "pontífice de los bienes futuros"[229] y Redentor del universo. "Corresponde a los sagrados Pastores animar, también con el testimonio personal, el culto eucarístico, particularmente la exposición del santísimo Sacramento y la adoración de Cristo presente bajo las especies eucarísticas"[230].

135. "La visita al santísimo Sacramento", los fieles, "no dejen de hacerla durante el día, puesto que el Señor Jesucristo, presente en el mismo, como una muestra de gratitud, prueba de amor y un homenaje de la debida adoración"[231]. La contemplación de Jesús, presente en el santísimo Sacramento, en cuanto es comunión espiritual, une fuertemente a los fieles con Cristo, como resplandece en el ejemplo de tantos Santos[232]. "La Iglesia en la que está reservada la santísima Eucaristía debe quedar abierta a los fieles, por

lo menos algunas horas al día, a no ser que obste una razón grave, para que puedan hacer oración ante el santísimo Sacramento"[233].

136. El Ordinario promueva intensamente la adoración eucarística con asistencia del pueblo, ya sea breve, prolongada o perpetua. En los últimos años, de hecho, en tantos "lugares la adoración del Santísimo Sacramento tiene cotidianamente una importancia destacada y se convierte en fuente inagotable de santidad", aunque también hay "sitios donde se constata un abandono casi total del culto de adoración eucarística"[234].

137. La exposición de la santísima Eucaristía hágase siempre como se prescribe en los libros litúrgicos[235]. Además, no se excluya el rezo del rosario, admirable "en su sencillez y en su profundidad"[236], delante de la reserva eucarística o del santísimo Sacramento expuesto. Sin embargo, especialmente cuando se hace la exposición, se evidencie el carácter de esta oración como contemplación de los misterios de la vida de Cristo Redentor y de los designios salvíficos del Padre omnipotente, sobre todo empleando lecturas sacadas de la sagrada Escritura[237].

138. Sin embargo, el santísimo Sacramento nunca debe permanecer expuesto sin suficiente vigilancia, ni siquiera por un tiempo muy breve. Por lo tanto, hágase de tal forma que, en momentos determinados, siempre estén presentes algunos fieles, al menos por turno.

139. Donde el Obispo diocesano dispone de ministros sagrados u otros que puedan ser designados para esto, es un derecho de los fieles visitar frecuentemente el santísimo sacramento de la Eucaristía para adorarlo y, al menos algunas veces en el transcurso de cada año, participar de la adoración ante la santísima Eucaristía expuesta.

140. Es muy recomendable que, en las ciudades o en los núcleos urbanos, al menos en los mayores, el Obispo diocesano designe una iglesia para la adoración perpetua, en la cual se celebre también la santa Misa, con frecuencia o, en cuanto sea posible, diariamente; la exposición se interrumpirá rigurosamente mientras se celebra la Misa[238]. Conviene que en la Misa, que precede inmediatamente a un tiempo de adoración, se consagre la hostia que se expondrá a la adoración y se coloque en la custodia, sobre el altar, después de la Comunión[239].

141. El Obispo diocesano reconozca y, en la medida de lo posible, aliente a los fieles en su derecho de constituir hermandades o asociaciones para practicar la adoración, incluso perpetua. Cuando esta clase de asociaciones tenga carácter internacional, corresponde a la Congregación para el Culto Divino y la Disciplina de los Sacramentos erigirlas o aprobar sus estatutos[240].

3. LAS PROCESIONES Y LOS CONGRESOS EUCARÍSTICOS

142. "Corresponde al Obispo diocesano dar normas sobre las procesiones, mediante las cuales se provea a la participación en ellas y a su decoro"[241] y promover la adoración de los fieles.

143. "Como testimonio público de veneración a la santísima Eucaristía, donde pueda hacerse a juicio del Obispo diocesano, téngase una procesión por las calles, sobre todo en la solemnidad del Cuerpo y Sangre de Cristo"[242], ya que la devota "participación de los fieles en la procesión eucarística de la solemnidad del Cuerpo y Sangre de Cristo es una gracia de Dios que cada año llena de gozo a quienes toman parte en ella"[243].

144. Aunque en algunos lugares esto no se pueda hacer, sin embargo, conviene no perder la tradición de realizar procesiones eucarísticas. Sobre todo, búsquense nuevas maneras de realizarlas, acomodándolas a los tiempos actuales, por ejemplo, en torno al santuario, en lugares de la Iglesia o, con permiso de la autoridad civil, en parques públicos.

145. Sea considerada de gran valor la utilidad pastoral de los Congresos Eucarísticos, que "son un signo importante de verdadera fe y caridad"[244]. Prepárense con diligencia y realícense conforme a lo establecido[245], para que los fieles veneren de tal modo los sagrados misterios del Cuerpo y la Sangre del Hijo de Dios, que experimenten los frutos de la redención[246].

CAPÍTULO VII
MINISTERIOS EXTRAORDINARIOS DE LOS FIELES LAICOS

146. El sacerdocio ministerial no se puede sustituir en ningún modo. En efecto, si falta el sacerdote en la comunidad, esta carece del ejercicio y la función sacramental de Cristo, Cabeza y Pastor,

que pertenece a la esencia de la vida misma de la comunidad[247]. Puesto que "sólo el sacerdote válidamente ordenado es ministro capaz de confeccionar el sacramento de la Eucaristía, actuando *in persona Christi*"[248].

147. Sin embargo, donde la necesidad de la Iglesia así lo aconseje, faltando los ministros sagrados, pueden los fieles laicos suplir algunas tareas litúrgicas, conforme a las normas del derecho[249]. Estos fieles son llamados y designados para desempeñar unas tareas determinadas, de mayor o menor importancia, fortalecidos por la gracia del Señor. Muchos fieles laicos se han dedicado y se siguen dedicando con generosidad a este servicio, sobre todo en los países de misión, donde aún la Iglesia está poco extendida, o se encuentra en circunstancias de persecución[250], pero también en otras regiones afectadas por la escasez de sacerdotes y diáconos.

148. Sobre todo, debe considerarse de gran importancia la formación de los catequistas, que con grandes esfuerzos han dado y siguen dando una ayuda extraordinaria y absolutamente necesaria al crecimiento de la fe y de la Iglesia[251].

149. Muy recientemente, en algunas diócesis de antigua evangelización, son designados fieles laicos como "asistentes pastorales", muchísimos de los cuales, sin duda, han sido útiles para el bien de la Iglesia, facilitando la acción pastoral desempeñada por el Obispo, los presbíteros y los diáconos. Vigílese, sin embargo, que la determinación de estas tareas no se asimile demasiado a la forma del ministerio pastoral de los clérigos. Por lo tanto, se debe cuidar que los "asistentes pastorales" no asuman aquello que propiamente pertenece al servicio de los ministros sagrados.

150. La actividad del asistente pastoral se dirige a facilitar el ministerio de los sacerdotes y diáconos, a suscitar vocaciones al sacerdocio y al diaconado y, según las normas del derecho, a preparar cuidadosamente los fieles laicos, en cada comunidad, para las distintas tareas litúrgicas, según la variedad de los carismas.

151. Solamente por verdadera necesidad se recurra al auxilio de ministros extraordinarios, en la celebración de la Liturgia. Pero esto, no está previsto para asegurar una plena participación a los laicos, sino que, por su naturaleza, es suplementario y provisional[252]. Además, donde por necesidad se recurra al servicio de los ministros extraordinarios, multiplíquense especiales y fervientes peticiones para que el Señor envíe pronto un sacerdote para el

servicio de la comunidad y suscite abundantes vocaciones a las sagradas órdenes[253].

152. Por lo tanto, estos ministerios de mera suplencia no deben ser ocasión de una deformación del mismo ministerio de los sacerdotes, de modo que estos descuiden la celebración de la santa Misa por el pueblo que les ha sido confiado, la personal solicitud hacia los enfermos, el cuidado del bautismo de los niños, la asistencia a los matrimonios, o la celebración de las exequias cristianas, que ante todo conciernen a los sacerdotes, ayudados por los diáconos. Así pues, no suceda que los sacerdotes, en las parroquias, cambien indiferentemente con diáconos o laicos las tareas pastorales, confundiendo de esta manera lo específico de cada uno.

153. Además, nunca es lícito a los laicos asumir las funciones o las vestiduras del diácono o del sacerdote, u otras vestiduras similares.

1. EL MINISTRO EXTRAORDINARIO DE LA SAGRADA COMUNIÓN

154. Como ya se ha recordado, "sólo el sacerdote válidamente ordenado es ministro capaz de confeccionar el sacramento de la Eucaristía, actuando *in persona Christi*"[254]. De donde el nombre de "ministro de la Eucaristía" sólo se refiere, propiamente, al sacerdote. También, en razón de la sagrada Ordenación, los ministros ordinarios de la sagrada Comunión son el Obispo, el presbítero y el diácono[255], a los que corresponde, por lo tanto, administrar la sagrada Comunión a los fieles laicos, en la celebración de la santa Misa. De esta forma se manifiesta adecuada y plenamente su tarea ministerial en la Iglesia, y se realiza el signo del sacramento.

155. Además de los ministros ordinarios, está el acólito instituido ritualmente, que por la institución es ministro extraordinario de la sagrada Comunión, incluso fuera de la celebración de la Misa. Todavía, si lo aconsejan razones de verdadera necesidad, conforme a las normas del derecho[256], el Obispo diocesano puede delegar también otro fiel laico como ministro extraordinario, ya sea para ese momento, ya sea para un tiempo determinado, recibida en la manera debida la bendición. Sin embargo, este acto de designación no tiene necesariamente una forma litúrgica, ni de ningún modo, si tiene lugar, puede asemejarse la sagrada Ordenación. Sólo en casos especiales e imprevistos, el sacerdote que preside la celebración eucarística puede dar un permiso *ad actum*[257].

156. Este ministerio se entienda conforme a su nombre en sentido estricto, este es ministro extraordinario de la sagrada Comunión, pero no "ministro especial de la sagrada Comunión", ni "ministro extraordinario de la Eucaristía", ni "ministro especial de la Eucaristía"; con estos nombres es ampliado indebida e impropiamente su significado.

157. Si habitualmente hay número suficiente de ministros sagrados, también para la distribución de la sagrada Comunión, no se pueden designar ministros extraordinarios de la sagrada Comunión. En tales circunstancias, los que han sido designados para este ministerio, no lo ejerzan. Repruébese la costumbre de aquellos sacerdotes que, a pesar de estar presentes en la celebración, se abstienen de distribuir la comunión, encomendando esta tarea a laicos[258].

158. El ministro extraordinario de la sagrada Comunión podrá administrar la Comunión solamente en ausencia del sacerdote o diácono, cuando el sacerdote está impedido por enfermedad, edad avanzada, o por otra verdadera causa, o cuando es tan grande el número de los fieles que se acercan a la Comunión, que la celebración de la Misa se prolongaría demasiado[259]. Pero esto debe entenderse de forma que una breve prolongación sería una causa absolutamente insuficiente, según la cultura y las costumbres propias del lugar.

159. Al ministro extraordinario de la sagrada Comunión nunca le está permitido delegar en ningún otro para administrar la Eucaristía, como, por ejemplo, los padres o el esposo o el hijo del enfermo que va a comulgar.

160. El Obispo diocesano examine de nuevo la praxis en esta materia durante los últimos años y, si es conveniente, la corrija o la determine con mayor claridad. Donde por una verdadera necesidad se haya difundido la designación de este tipo de ministros extraordinarios, corresponde al Obispo diocesano, teniendo presente la tradición de la Iglesia, dar las directrices particulares que establezcan el ejercicio de esta tarea, según las normas del derecho.

2. LA PREDICACIÓN

161. Como ya se ha dicho, la homilía, por su importancia y naturaleza, dentro de la Misa está reservada al sacerdote o al diácono[260]. Por lo que se refiere a otras formas de predicación, si concurren

especiales necesidades que lo requieran, o cuando en casos particulares la utilidad lo aconseje, pueden ser admitidos fieles laicos para predicar en una iglesia u oratorio, fuera de la Misa, según las normas del derecho[261]. Lo cual puede hacerse solamente por la escasez de ministros sagrados en algunos lugares, para suplirlos, sin que se pueda convertir, en ningún caso, la excepción en algo habitual, ni se debe entender como una auténtica promoción del laicado[262]. Además, recuerden todos que la facultad para permitir esto, en un caso determinado, se reserva a los Ordinarios del lugar, pero no concierne a otros, incluso presbíteros o diáconos.

3. CELEBRACIONES PARTICULARES QUE SE REALIZAN EN AUSENCIA DEL SACERDOTE

162. La Iglesia, en el día que se llama "domingo", se reúne fielmente para conmemorar la resurrección del Señor y todo el misterio pascual, especialmente por la celebración de la Misa[263]. De hecho, "ninguna comunidad cristiana se edifica si no tiene su raíz y quicio en la celebración de la santísima Eucaristía"[264]. Por lo que el pueblo cristiano tiene derecho a que sea celebrada la Eucaristía en su favor, los domingos y fiestas de precepto, o cuando concurran otros días festivos importantes, y también diariamente, en cuanto sea posible. Por esto, donde el domingo haya dificultad para la celebración de la Misa, en la iglesia parroquial o en otra comunidad de fieles, el Obispo diocesano busque las soluciones oportunas, juntamente con el presbiterio[265]. Entre las soluciones, las principales serán llamar para esto a otros sacerdotes o que los fieles se trasladen a otra iglesia de un lugar cercano, para participar del misterio eucarístico[266].

163. Todos los sacerdotes, a quienes ha sido entregado el sacerdocio y la Eucaristía "para" los otros[267], recuerden su encargo para que todos los fieles tengan oportunidad de cumplir con el precepto de participar en la Misa del domingo[268]. Por su parte, los fieles laicos tienen derecho a que ningún sacerdote, a no ser que exista verdadera imposibilidad, rechace nunca celebrar la Misa en favor del pueblo, o que esta sea celebrada por otro sacerdote, si de diverso modo no se puede cumplir el precepto de participar en la Misa, el domingo y los otros días establecidos.

164. "Cuando falta el ministro sagrado u otra causa grave hace imposible la participación en la celebración eucarística"[269], el pueblo cristiano tiene derecho a que el Obispo diocesano, en lo

posible, procure que se realice alguna celebración dominical para esa comunidad, bajo su autoridad y conforme a las normas de la Iglesia. Pero esta clase de celebraciones dominicales especiales, deben ser consideradas siempre como absolutamente extraordinarias. Por lo tanto, ya sean diáconos o fieles laicos, todos los que han sido encargados por el Obispo diocesano para tomar parte en este tipo de celebraciones, "considerarán como cometido suyo el mantener viva en la comunidad una verdadera "hambre" de la Eucaristía, que lleve a no perder ocasión alguna de tener la celebración de la Misa, incluso aprovechando la presencia ocasional de un sacerdote que no esté impedido por el derecho de la Iglesia para celebrarla"[270].

165. Es necesario evitar, diligentemente, cualquier confusión entre este tipo de reuniones y la celebración eucarística[271]. Los Obispos diocesanos, por lo tanto, valoren con prudencia si se debe distribuir la sagrada Comunión en estas reuniones. Conviene que esto sea determinado, para lograr una mayor coordinación, por la Conferencia de Obispos, de modo que alcanzada la resolución, la presentará a la aprobación de la Sede Apostólica, mediante la Congregación para el Culto Divino y la Disciplina de los Sacramentos. Además, en ausencia del sacerdote y del diácono, será preferible que las diversas partes puedan ser distribuidas entre varios fieles, en vez de que uno sólo de los fieles laicos dirija toda la celebración. No conviene, en ningún caso, que se diga de un fiel laico que "preside" la celebración.

166. Así mismo, el Obispo diocesano, a quien solamente corresponde este asunto, no conceda con facilidad que este tipo de celebraciones, sobre todo si en ellas se distribuye la sagrada Comunión, se realicen en los días feriales y, sobretodo en los lugares donde el domingo precedente o siguiente se ha podido o se podrá celebrar la Eucaristía. Se ruega vivamente a los sacerdotes que, a ser posible, celebren diariamente la santa Misa por el pueblo, en una de las iglesias que les han sido encomendadas.

167. "De manera parecida, no se puede pensar en reemplazar la santa Misa dominical con celebraciones ecuménicas de la Palabra o con encuentros de oración en común con cristianos miembros de dichas [. . .] comunidades eclesiales, o bien con la participación en su servicio litúrgico"[272]. Si por una necesidad urgente, el Obispo diocesano permitiera ad actum la participación de los católicos, vigilen los pastores para que entre los fieles católicos no se

produzca confusión sobre la necesidad de participar en la Misa de precepto, también en estas ocasiones, a otra hora del día[273].

4. DE AQUELLOS QUE HAN SIDO APARTADOS DEL ESTADO CLERICAL

168. "El clérigo que, de acuerdo con la norma del derecho, pierde el estado clerical", "se le prohíbe ejercer la potestad de orden"[274]. A este, por lo tanto, no le está permitido celebrar los sacramentos bajo ningún pretexto, salvo en el caso excepcional establecido por el derecho[275]; ni los fieles pueden recurrir a él para la celebración, si no existe una justa causa que lo permita, según la norma del canon 1335[276]. Además, estas personas no hagan la homilía[277], ni jamás asuman ninguna tarea o ministerio en la celebración de la sagrada Liturgia, para evitar la confusión entre los fieles y que sea oscurecida la verdad.

CAPÍTULO VIII
LOS REMEDIOS

169. Cuando se comete un abuso en la celebración de la sagrada Liturgia, verdaderamente se realiza una falsificación de la liturgia católica. Ha escrito Santo Tomás: "incurre en el vicio de falsedad quien de parte de la Iglesia ofrece el culto a Dios, contrariamente a la forma establecida por la autoridad divina de la Iglesia y su costumbre"[278].

170. Para que se dé una solución a este tipo de abusos, lo "que más urge es la formación bíblica y litúrgica del pueblo de Dios, pastores y fieles"[279], de modo que la fe y la disciplina de la Iglesia, en lo que se refiere a la sagrada Liturgia, sean presentadas y comprendidas rectamente. Sin embargo, donde los abusos persistan, debe procederse en la tutela del patrimonio espiritual y de los derechos de la Iglesia, conforme a las normas del derecho, recurriendo a todos los medios legítimos.

171. Entre los diversos abusos hay algunos que constituyen objetivamente los *graviora delicta,* los actos graves, y también otros que con no menos atención hay que evitar y corregir. Teniendo presente todo lo que se ha tratado, especialmente en el Capítulo I de esta Instrucción, conviene prestar atención a cuanto sigue.

1. GRAVIORA DELICTA

172. Los *graviora delicta* contra la santidad del sacratísimo Sacramento y Sacrificio de la Eucaristía y los sacramentos, son tratados según las "Normas sobre los *graviora delicta,* reservados a la Congregación para la Doctrina de la Fe"[280], esto es:

a) sustraer o retener con fines sacrílegos, o arrojar las especies consagradas[281];

b) atentar la realización de la liturgia del Sacrificio eucarístico o su simulación[282];

c) concelebración prohibida del Sacrificio eucarístico juntamente con ministros de Comunidades eclesiales que no tienen la sucesión apostólica, ni reconocen la dignidad sacramental de la ordenación sacerdotal[283];

d) consagración con fin sacrílego de una materia sin la otra, en la celebración eucarística, o también de ambas, fuera de la celebración eucarística[284].

2. LOS ACTOS GRAVES

173. Aunque el juicio sobre la gravedad de los actos se hace conforme a la doctrina común de la Iglesia y las normas por ella establecidas, como actos graves se consideran siempre, objetivamente, los que ponen en peligro la validez y dignidad de la santísima Eucaristía, esto es, contra lo que se explicó más arriba, en los nn. 48–52, 56, 76–77, 79, 91–92, 94, 96, 101–102, 104, 106, 109, 111, 115, 117, 126, 131–133, 138, 153 y 168. Prestándose atención, además, a otras prescripciones del Código de Derecho Canónico, y especialmente a lo que se establece en los cánones 1364, 1369, 1373, 1376, 1380, 1384, 1385, 1386 y 1398.

3. OTROS ABUSOS

174. Además, aquellas acciones, contra lo que se trata en otros lugares de esta Instrucción o en las normas establecidas por el derecho, no se deben considerar de poca importancia, sino incluirse entre los otros abusos a evitar y corregir con solicitud.

175. Como es evidente, lo que se expone en esta Instrucción no recoge todas las violaciones contra la Iglesia y su disciplina, que en los cánones, en las leyes litúrgicas y en otras normas de la

Iglesia, han sido definidas por la enseñanza del Magisterio y la sana tradición. Cuando algo sea realizado mal, corríjase, conforme a las normas del derecho.

4. EL OBISPO DIOCESANO

176. El Obispo diocesano, "por ser el dispensador principal de los misterios de Dios, ha de cuidar incesantemente de que los fieles que le están encomendados crezcan en la gracia por la celebración de los sacramentos, y conozcan y vivan el misterio pascual"[285]. A este corresponde, "dentro de los límites de su competencia, dar normas obligatorias para todos, sobre materia litúrgica"[286].

177. "Dado que tiene obligación de defender la unidad de la Iglesia universal, el Obispo debe promover la disciplina que es común a toda la Iglesia, y por tanto exigir el cumplimiento de todas las leyes eclesiásticas. Ha de vigilar para que no se introduzcan abusos en la disciplina eclesiástica, especialmente acerca del ministerio de la palabra, la celebración de los sacramentos y sacramentales, el culto de Dios y de los Santos"[287].

178. Por lo tanto, cuantas veces el Ordinario, sea del lugar sea de un Instituto religioso o Sociedad de vida apostólica tenga noticia, al menos probable, de un delito o abuso que se refiere a la santísima Eucaristía, infórmese prudentemente, por sí o por otro clérigo idóneo, de los hechos, las circunstancias y de la culpabilidad.

179. Los delitos contra la fe y también los *graviora delicta* cometidos en la celebración de la Eucaristía y de los otros sacramentos, sean comunicados sin demora a la Congregación para la Doctrina de la Fe, la cual "examina y, en caso necesario, procede a declarar o imponer sanciones canónicas a tenor del derecho, tanto común como propio"[288].

180. De otro modo, el Ordinario proceda conforme a la norma de los sagrados cánones, aplicando, cuando sea necesario, penas canónicas y recordando de modo especial lo establecido en el canon 1326. Si se trata de hechos graves, hágase saber a la Congregación para el Culto Divino y la Disciplina de los Sacramentos.

5. LA SEDE APOSTÓLICA

181. Cuantas veces la Congregación para el Culto Divino y la Disciplina de los Sacramentos tenga noticia, al menos probable, de un delito o abuso que se refiere a la santísima Eucaristía, se lo hará saber al Ordinario, para que investigue el hecho. Cuando resulte un hecho grave, el Ordinario envíe cuanto antes, a este Dicasterio, un ejemplar de las actas de la investigación realizada y, cuando sea el caso, de la pena impuesta.

182. En los casos de mayor dificultad, el Ordinario, por el bien de la Iglesia universal, de cuya solicitud participa por razón de la misma ordenación, antes de tratar la cuestión, no omita solicitar el parecer de la Congregación para el Culto Divino y la Disciplina de los Sacramentos. Por su parte, esta Congregación, en vigor de las facultades concedidas por el Romano Pontífice, ayuda al Ordinario, según el caso, concediendo las dispensas necesarias[289] o comunicando instrucciones y prescripciones, las cuales deben seguirse con diligencia.

6. QUEJA POR ABUSOS EN MATERIA LITÚRGICA

183. De forma muy especial, todos procuren, según sus medios, que el santísimo sacramento de la Eucaristía sea defendido de toda irreverencia y deformación, y todos los abusos sean completamente corregidos. Esto, por lo tanto, es una tarea gravísima para todos y cada uno, y, excluida toda acepción de personas, todos están obligados a cumplir esta labor.

184. Cualquier católico, sea sacerdote, sea diácono, sea fiel laico, tiene derecho a exponer una queja por un abuso litúrgico, ante el Obispo diocesano o el Ordinario competente que se le equipara en derecho, o ante la Sede Apostólica, en virtud del primado del Romano Pontífice[290]. Conviene, sin embargo, que, en cuanto sea posible, la reclamación o queja sea expuesta primero al Obispo diocesano. Pero esto se haga siempre con veracidad y caridad.

CONCLUSIÓN

185. "A los gérmenes de disgregación entre los hombres, que la experiencia cotidiana muestra tan arraigada en la humanidad a causa del pecado, se contrapone la fuerza generosa de unidad del

cuerpo de Cristo. La Eucaristía, construyendo la Iglesia, crea, precisamente por ello, comunidad entre los hombres"[291]. Por tanto, esta Congregación para el Culto Divino y la Disciplina de los Sacramentos desea que también mediante la diligente aplicación de cuanto se recuerda en esta Instrucción, la humana fragilidad obstaculice menos la acción del santísimo Sacramento de la Eucaristía y, eliminada cualquier irregularidad, desterrado cualquier uso reprobable, por intercesión de la Santísima Virgen María, "mujer eucarística"[292], resplandezca en todos los hombres la presencia salvífica de Cristo en el Sacramento de su Cuerpo y de su Sangre.

186. Todos los fieles participen en la santísima Eucaristía de manera plena, consciente y activa, en cuanto es posible[293]; la veneren con todo el corazón en la piedad y en la vida. Los Obispos, presbíteros y diáconos, en el ejercicio del sagrado ministerio, se pregunten en conciencia sobre la autenticidad y sobre la fidelidad en las acciones que realizan en nombre de Cristo y de la Iglesia, en la celebración de la sagrada Liturgia. Cada uno de los ministros sagrados se pregunte también con severidad si ha respetado los derechos de los fieles laicos, que se encomiendan a él y le encomiendan a sus hijos con confianza, en la seguridad de que todos desempeñan correctamente las tareas que la Iglesia, por mandato de Cristo, desea realizar en la celebración de la sagrada Liturgia, para los fieles[294]. Cada uno recuerde siempre que es servidor de la sagrada Liturgia[295].

Sin que obste nada en contrario.

Esta Instrucción, preparada por mandato del Sumo Pontífice Juan Pablo II por la Congregación para el Culto Divino y la Disciplina de los Sacramentos, en colaboración con la Congregación para la Doctrina de la Fe, el mismo Pontífice la aprobó el día 19 del mes de marzo, solemnidad de San José, del año 2004, disponiendo que sea publicada y observada por todos aquellos a quienes corresponde.

En Roma, en la Sede de la Congregación para el Culto Divino y la Disciplina de los Sacramentos, en la solemnidad de la Anunciación del Señor, 25 de marzo del 2004.

Francis Cardenal Arinze
Prefecto

Domenico Sorrentino
Arzobispo Secretario

CITAS

1. Cf. *Missale Romanum, ex decreto sacrosancti Oecumenici Concilii Vaticani II instauratum, auctoritate Pauli Pp. VI promulgatum, Ioannis Pauli Pp. II cura recognitum*, editio typica tertia, día 20 de abril del 2000, Typis Vaticanis, 2002, Missa votiva de Dei misericordia, oratio super oblata, p. 1159.
2. Cf. 1 Corintios 11, 26; *Missale Romanum*, Prex Eucharistica, acclamatio post consecrationem, p. 576; Juan Pablo II, Carta Encíclica, *Ecclesia de Eucharistia*, día 17 de abril del 2003, nn. 5, 11, 14, 18: AAS 95 (2003) pp. 436, 440–441, 442, 445.
3. Cf. *Isaías* 10, 33; 51, 22; *Missale Romanum*, In sollemnitate Domini nostri Iesu Christi, universorum Regis, Praefatio, p. 499.
4. Cf. 1 Corintios 5, 7; Concilio Ecuménico Vaticano II, Dec. sobre el ministerio y la vida de los presbíteros, *Presbyterorum ordinis*, día 7 de diciembre de 1965, n. 5; Juan Pablo II, Exhortación Apostólica, *Ecclesia in Europa*, día 28 de junio del 2003, n. 75: AAS 95 (2003) pp. 649–719, esto p. 693.
5. Cf. Concilio Ecuménico Vaticano II, Constitución dogm. sobre la Iglesia, *Lumen gentium*, día 21 de noviembre de 1964, n. 11.
6. Cf. Juan Pablo II, Carta Encíclica, *Ecclesia de Eucharistia*, día 17 de abril del 2003, n. 21: AAS 95 (2003) p. 447.
7. Cf. ibidem: AAS 95 (2003) pp. 433–475.
8. Cf. ibidem, n. 52: AAS 95 (2003) p. 468.
9. Cf. ibidem.
10. Ibidem, n. 10: AAS 95 (2003) p. 439.
11. Ibidem; cf. Juan Pablo II, Carta Apostólica, *Vicesimus quintus annus*, día 4 de diciembre de 1988, nn. 12–13: AAS 81 (1989) pp. 909–910; cf. también Concilio Ecuménico Vaticano II, Const. sobre la s. Liturgia, *Sacrosanctum Concilium*, día 4 de diciembre de 1963, n. 48.
12. *Missale Romanum*, Prex Eucharistica III, p. 588; cf. 1 Corintios 12, 12–13; Efesios 4,4.
13. Cf. Filipenses 2,5.
14. Juan Pablo II, Carta Encíclica, *Ecclesia de Eucharistia*, n. 10: AAS 95 (2003) p. 439.
15. Ibidem, n. 6: AAS 95 (2003) p. 437; cf. Lucas 24,31.
16. Cf. Romanos 1,20.
17. Cf. *Missale Romanum*, Praefatio I de Passione Domini, p. 528.
18. Cf. Juan Pablo II, Carta Encíclica, *Veritatis splendor*, día 6 de agosto de 1993, n. 35: AAS 85 (1993) pp. 1161–1162; Homilía en el Camden Yards, día 9 de octubre de 1995, n. 7: *Insegnamenti di Giovanni Paolo II, XVII, 2 (1995)*, Libreria Editrice Vaticana, 1998, p. 788.
19. Cf. Juan Pablo II, Carta Encíclica, *Ecclesia de Eucharistia*, n. 10: AAS 95 (2003) p. 439.

20. Concilio Ecuménico Vaticano II, Const. sobre la s. Liturgia, *Sacrosanctum Concilium,* n. 24; cf. Congr. Culto Divino y Disc Sacramentos, Instr., *Varietates legitimae,* día 25 de enero de 1994, nn. 19 y 23: AAS 87 (1995) pp. 295–296, 297.

21. Concilio Ecuménico Vaticano II, Const. sobre la s. Liturgia, *Sacrosanctum Concilium,* n. 33.

22. Cf. S. Ireneo, *Adversus Haereses,* III, 2: SCh., 211, 24–31; S. Agustín, *Epistula ad Ianuarium,* 54, I: PL 33, 200: "Illa autem quae non scripta, sed tradita custodimus, quae quidem toto terrarum orbe servantur, datur intellegi vel ab ipsis Apostolis, vel plenariis conciliis, quorum est in Ecclesia saluberrima auctoritas, commendata atque statuta retineri"; Juan Pablo II, Carta Encíclica, *Redemptoris missio,* día 7 de diciembre de 1990, nn. 53–54: AAS 83 (1991) pp. 300–302; Congr. Doctrina Fe, Carta a los obispos de la Iglesia católica, sobre algunos aspectos de la Iglesia como comunión *Communionis notio,* día 28 de mayo de 1992, nn. 7–10: AAS 85 (1993) pp. 842–844; Congr. Culto Divino y Disc. Sacramentos, Instr., *Varietates legitimae,* n. 26: AAS 87 (1995) pp. 298–299.

23. Cf. Concilio Ecuménico Vaticano II, Const. sobre la s. Liturgia, *Sacrosanctum Concilium,* n. 21.

24. Cf. Pío XII, Const. Apostólica, *Sacramentum Ordinis,* día 30 de noviembre de 1947: AAS 40 (1948) p. 5; Congr. Doctrina de la Fe, Declaración, *Inter insigniores,* día 15 de octubre de 1976, parte IV: AAS 69 (1977) pp. 107–108; Congr. Culto Divino y Disc Sacramentos, Instr., *Varietates legitimae,* n. 25: AAS 87 (1995) p. 298.

25. Cf. Pío XII, Carta Encíclica, *Mediator Dei,* día 20 de noviembre de 1947: AAS 39 (1947) p. 540.

26. Cf. S. Congr. Culto Divino y Disc Sacramentos, Instr., *Inaestimabile donum,* día 3 de abril de 1980: AAS 72 (1980) p. 333.

27. Juan Pablo II, Carta Encíclica, *Ecclesia de Eucharistia,* n. 52: AAS 95 (2003) p. 468.

28. Cf. Concilio Ecuménico Vaticano II, Const. sobre la s. Liturgia, *Sacrosanctum Concilium,* nn. 4, 38; Decreto sobre las Iglesias Orientales Católicas, *Orientalium Ecclesiarum,* día 21 de noviembre de 1964, nn. 1, 2, 6; Pablo VI, Const. Apostólica, *Missale Romanum:* AAS 61 (1969) pp. 217–222; *Missale Romanum,* Institutio Generalis, n. 399; Congr. Culto Divino y Disc Sacramentos, Instr., *Liturgiam authenticam,* día 28 de marzo del 2001, n. 4: AAS 93 (2001) pp. 685–726, esto p. 686.

29. Cf. Juan Pablo II, Exhortación Apostólica, *Ecclesia in Europa,* n. 72: AAS 95 (2003) pp. 692.

30. Cf. Juan Pablo II, Carta Encíclica, *Ecclesia de Eucharistia,* n. 23: AAS 95 (2003) pp. 448-449; S Congr. Ritos, Instr., *Eucharisticum mysterium,* día 25 de mayo de 1967, n. 6: AAS 59 (1967) p. 545.

31. Cf. S. Congr. Culto Divino y Disc Sacramentos, Instr., *Inaestimabile donum:* AAS 72 (1980) pp. 332–333.

32. Cf. 1 Corintios 11,17–34; Juan Pablo II, Carta Encíclica, *Ecclesia de Eucharistia,* n. 52: AAS 95 (2003) pp. 467–468.

33. Cf. *Código de Derecho Canónico,* día 25 de enero de 1983, c. 1752.

34. Concilio Ecuménico Vaticano II, Const. sobre la s. Liturgia, *Sacrosanctum Concilium*, n. 22 § 1. Cf. *Código de Derecho Canónico*, c. 838 § 1.

35. *Código de Derecho Canónico*, c. 331; cf. Concilio Ecuménico Vaticano II, Const. dogmática sobre la Iglesia, *Lumen gentium*, n. 22.

36. Cf. *Código de Derecho Canónico*, c. 838 § 2.

37. Juan Pablo II, Const. Apostólica, *Pastor bonus*, día 28 de junio de 1988: AAS 80 (1988) pp. 841–924; esto arts. 62, 63 y 66, pp. 876–877.

38. Cf. Juan Pablo II, Carta Encíclica, *Ecclesia de Eucharistia*, n. 52: AAS 95 (2003) p. 468.

39. Cf. Concilio Ecuménico Vaticano II, Decreto sobre el ministerio pastoral de los Obispos, *Christus Dominus*, día 28 de octubre de 1965, n. 15; cf. también, Const. sobre la s. Liturgia, *Sacrosanctum Concilium*, n. 41; *Código de Derecho Canónico*, c. 387.

40. Oración de la consagración episcopal en rito bizantino: *Euchologion to mega*, Roma 1873, p. 139.

41. Cf. S. Ignacio de Antioquía, *Ad Smyrn.* 8, 1: ed. F. X. Funk I, p. 282.

42. Concilio Ecuménico Vaticano II, Const. dogmática sobre la Iglesia, *Lumen gentium*, n. 26; cf. S. Congr. Ritos, Instr., *Eucharisticum mysterium*, n. 7: AAS 59 (1967) p. 545; cf. también Juan Pablo II, Exhortación Apostólica, *Pastores gregis*, día 16 de octubre del 2003, nn. 32–41: *L'Osservatore romano*, día 17 de octubre del 2003, pp. 6–8.

43. Cf. Concilio Ecuménico Vaticano II, Const. sobre la s. Liturgia, *Sacrosanctum Concilium*, n. 41; cf. S. Ignacio de Antioquía, *Ad Magn.* 7; *Ad Philad.* 4; *Ad Smyr.* 8: ed. F. X. Funk, I, pp. 236, 266, 281; *Missale Romanum*, Institutio Generalis, n. 22; cf. también *Código de Derecho Canónico*, c. 389.

44. Concilio Ecuménico Vaticano II, Const. dogmática sobre la Iglesia, *Lumen gentium*, n. 26.

45. *Código de Derecho Canónico*, c. 838 § 4.

46. Cf. Consilium Ad Exseq. Const. Litur., Dubium: *Notitiae* 1 (1965) p. 254.

47. Cf. *Hechos* 20, 28; Concilio Ecuménico Vaticano II, Const. dogmática sobre la Iglesia, *Lumen gentium*, nn. 21 y 27; Decreto sobre el ministerio pastoral de los Obispos, *Christus Dominus*, n. 3.

48. Cf. S. Congr. Culto Divino, Instr., *Liturgicae instaurationes*, día 5 de septiembre de 1970: AAS 62 (1970) p. 694.

49. Cf. Concilio Ecuménico Vaticano II, Const. dogmática sobre la Iglesia, *Lumen gentium*, n. 21; Decreto sobre el ministerio pastoral de los Obispos, *Christus Dominus*, n. 3.

50. Cf. *Caeremoniale Episcoporum ex decreto sacrosancti Oecumenici Concilii Vaticani II instauratum, auctoritate Ioannis Pauli Pp. II promulgatum, editio typica*, día 14 de septiembre de 1984, Typis Polyglottis Vaticanis, 1985, n. 10.

51. Cf. *Missale Romanum*, Institutio Generalis, n. 387.

52. Cf. ibidem, n. 22.

53. Cf. S. Congr. Culto Divino, Instr., *Liturgicae instaurationes*: AAS 62 (1970) p. 694.

54. Concilio Ecuménico Vaticano II, Const. dogmática sobre la Iglesia, *Lumen gentium,* n. 27; cf. 2 Corintios 4,15.

55. Cf. *Código de Derecho Canónico,* cc. 397 § 1; 678 § 1.

56. Cf. ibidem, c. 683 § 1.

57. Cf. ibidem, c. 392.

58. Cf. Juan Pablo II, Carta Apostólica, *Vicesimus quintus annus,* n. 21: AAS 81 (1989) p. 917; Concilio Ecuménico Vaticano II, Const. sobre la s. Liturgia, *Sacrosanctum Concilium,* nn. 45–46; Pío XII, Carta Encíclica, *Mediator Dei:* AAS 39 (1947) p. 562.

59. Cf. Juan Pablo II, Carta Apostólica, *Vicesimus quintus annus,* n. 20: AAS 81 (1989) p. 916.

60. Cf. ibidem.

61. Cf. Concilio Ecuménico Vaticano II, Const. sobre la s. Liturgia, *Sacrosanctum Concilium,* n. 44; Congr. Obispos, Carta *Praesidibus Episcoporum Conferentiarum missa nomine quoque Congr. pro Gentium Evangelizatione,* día 21 de junio de 1999, n. 9: AAS 91 (1999) p. 999.

62. Cf. S. Congr. Culto Divino, Instr., *Liturgicae instaurationes,* n. 12: AAS 62 (1970) pp. 692–704, esto p. 703.

63. Cf. Congr. Culto Divino, *Declarationem circa Preces eucharisticae et experimenta liturgica,* día 21 de marzo de 1988: *Notitiae* 24 (1988) pp. 234–236.

64. Cf. S. Congr. Culto Divino y Disc Sacramentos, Instr., *Varietates legitimae:* AAS 87 (1995) pp. 288–314.

65. Cf. *Código de Derecho Canónico,* c. 838 § 3; S. Congr. Ritos, Instr., *Inter Oecumenici,* día 26 de septiembre de 1964, n. 31: AAS 56 (1964) p. 883; S. Congr. Culto Divino y Disc. Sacramentos, Instr., *Liturgiam authenticam,* n. 79–80: AAS 93 (2001) pp. 711–713.

66. Cf. Concilio Ecuménico Vaticano II, Decr. sobre el ministerio y vida de los presbíteros, *Presbyterorum ordinis,* día 7 de diciembre de 1965, n. 7; *Pontificale Romanum,* ed. 1962: Ordo consecrationis sacerdotalis, in Praefatione; *Pontificale Romanum ex decreto sacrosancti Oecumenici Concilii Vaticani II renovatum, auctoritate Pauli Pp. VI editum, Ioannis Pauli Pp. II cura recognitum: De Ordinatione Episcopi, presbyterorum et diaconorum,* editio typica altera, día 29 de junio de 1989, Typis Polyglottis Vaticanis, 1990, cap. II, De Ordin. presbyterorum, Praenotanda, n. 101.

67. Cf. S. Ignacio de Antioquía, *Ad Philad.,* 4: ed. F. X. Funk, I, p. 266; S. Cornelio I, Papa, en S. Cipipriano, *Epist.* 48, 2: ed. G. Hartel, III, 2, p. 610.

68. Concilio Ecuménico Vaticano II, Const. dogmática sobre la Iglesia, *Lumen gentium,* n. 28.

69. Ibidem.

70. Juan Pablo II, Carta Encíclica, *Ecclesia de Eucharistia,* n. 52; cf. n. 29: AAS 95 (2003) pp. 467–468; 452–453.

71. *Pontifacale Romanum,* De Ordinatione Episcopi, presbyterorum et diaconorum, editio typica altera: *De Ordinatione presbyterorum,* n. 124; cf. *Missale Romanum,* Feria V in Hebdomada Sancta: Ad Missam chrismatis, Renovatio promissionum sacerdotalium, p. 292.

72. Cf. Concilio Ecuménico Tridentino, sesión VII, día 3 de marzo de 1547, Decreto De Sacramentis, can. 13: DS 1613; Concilio

Ecuménico Vaticano II, Const. sobre la s. Liturgia, *Sacrosanctum Concilium,* n. 22; Pío XII, Carta Encíclica, *Mediator Dei:* AAS 39 (1947) pp. 544, 546–547, 562; *Código de Derecho Canónico,* c. 846 § 1; *Missale Romanum,* Institutio Generalis, n. 24.

73. S. Ambrosio, *De Virginitate,* n. 48: PL 16, 278.

74. *Código de Derecho Canónico,* c. 528 § 2.

75. Concilio Ecuménico Vaticano II, Decr. sobre el ministerio y vida de los presbíteros, *Presbyterorum ordinis,* n. 5.

76. Cf. Juan Pablo II, Carta Encíclica, *Ecclesia de Eucharistia,* n. 5: AAS 95 (2003) p. 436.

77. Concilio Ecuménico Vaticano II, Const. dogmática sobre la Iglesia, *Lumen gentium,* n. 29; cf. *Constitutiones Ecclesiae Aegypticae,* III, 2: ed. F. X. Funk, *Didascalia,* II, p. 103; *Statuta Ecclesiae Ant.,* 37–41: ed. D. Mansi, 3, 954.

78. Cf. Hechos 6,3.

79. Cf. Juan 13,35.

80. Mateo 20,28.

81. Lucas 22,27.

82. Cf. *Caeremoniale Episcoporum,* nn. 9, 23. Cf. Concilio Ecuménico Vaticano II, Const. dogmática sobre la Iglesia, *Lumen gentium,* n. 29.

83. Cf. *Pontificale Romanum, De Ordinatione Episcopi, presbyterorum et diaconorum,* editio typica altera, cap. III, *De Ordinatione diaconorum,* n. 199.

84. Cf. 1 Timoteo 3,9.

85. Cf. Pontifacale Romanum, De Ordinatione Episcopi, presbyterorum et diaconorum, editio typica altera, cap. III, *De Ordinatione diaconorum,* n. 200.

86. Concilio Ecuménico Vaticano II, Const. sobre la s. Liturgia, *Sacrosanctum Concilium,* n. 10.

87. Cf. ibidem, n. 41; Concilio Ecuménico Vaticano II, Const. dogmática sobre la Iglesia, *Lumen gentium,* n. 11; Decr. sobre el ministerio y vida de los presbíteros, *Presbyterorum ordinis,* nn. 2, 5, 6; Decr. sobre el ministerio pastoral de los Obispos, *Christus Dominus,* n. 30; Decr. sobre el ecumenismo, *Unitatis redintegratio,* día 21 de noviembre de 1964, n. 15; S. Congr. Ritos, Instr., *Eucharisticum mysterium,* nn. 3 y 6: AAS 59 (1967) pp. 542, 544–545; *Missale Romanum,* Institutio Generalis, n. 16.

88. Cf. Concilio Ecuménico Vaticano II, Const. sobre la sagrada Liturgia, *Sacrosanctum Concilium,* n. 26; *Missale Romanum,* Institutio Generalis, n. 91.

89. 1 Pedro 2,9; cf. 2,4–5.

90. *Missale Romanum,* Institutio Generalis, n. 91; cf. Concilio Ecuménico Vaticano II, Const. sobre la sagrada Liturgia, *Sacrosanctum Concilium,* n. 14.

91. Concilio Ecuménico Vaticano II, Const. dogmática sobre la Iglesia, *Lumen gentium,* n. 10.

92. Cf. Santo Tomás de Aquino, *Summa Theol.,* III, q. 63, a. 2.

93. Cf. Concilio Ecuménico Vaticano II, Const. dogmática sobre la Iglesia, *Lumen gentium,* n. 10; cf. Juan Pablo II, Carta Encíclica, *Ecclesia de Eucharistia,* n. 28: AAS 95 (2003) p. 452.

94. Cf. Hechos 2,42–47.

95. Cf. Romanos 12,1.

96. Cf. 1 Pedro 3,15; 2,4–10.

97. Cf. Juan Pablo II, Carta Encíclica, *Ecclesia de Eucharistia,* nn. 12–18: AAS 95 (2003) pp. 441–445;

Juan Pablo II, Carta, *Dominicae Cenae,* día 24 de febrero de 1980, n. 9: AAS 72 (1980) pp. 129–133.

98. Juan Pablo II, Carta Encíclica, *Ecclesia de Eucharistia,* n. 10: AAS 95 (2003) p. 439.

99. Cf. Concilio Ecuménico Vaticano II, Const. sobre la sagrada Liturgia, *Sacrosanctum Concilium,* nn. 30–31.

100. Cf. S. Congr. Culto Divino, Instr., *Liturgicae instaurationes,* n. 1: AAS 62 (1970) p. 695.

101. Cf. *Missale Romanum,* Feria secunda post Dominica V in Quadragesima, Collecta, p. 258.

102. Juan Pablo II, Carta Apostólica, *Novo Millennio ineunte,* día 6 de enero del 2001, n. 21: AAS 93 (2001) p. 280; cf. Juan 20, 28.

103. Cf. Pío XII, Carta Encíclica, *Mediator Dei:* AAS 39 (1947) p. 586; cf. también Concilio Ecuménico Vaticano II, Const. dogmática sobre la Iglesia, *Lumen gentium,* n. 67; Pablo VI, Exhortación Apostólica, *Marialis cultus,* día 11 de febrero de 1974, n. 24: AAS 66 (1974) pp. 113–168, esto p. 134; Congr. Culto Divino y Disc. Sacramentos, *Directorio sobre la piedad popular y la Liturgia,* día 17 de diciembre del 2001.

104. Cf. Juan Pablo II, Carta Apostólica, *Rosarium Virginis Mariae,* día 16 de octubre del 2002: AAS 95 (2003) pp. 5–36.

105. Pío XII, Carta Encíclica, *Mediator Dei:* AAS 39 (1947) p. 586–587.

106. Cf. Congr. Culto Divino y Disc Sacramentos, Instr., *Varietates legitimae,* n. 22: AAS 87 (1995) p. 297.

107. Cf. Pío XII, Carta Encíclica, *Mediator Dei:* AAS 39 (1947) p. 553.

108. Juan Pablo II, Carta Encíclica, *Ecclesia de Eucharistia,* n. 29: AAS 95 (2003) p. 453; cf. Concilio Ecuménico Lateranense IV, días 11–30 de noviembre de 1215, cap. 1: DS 802; Concilio Ecuménico Tridentino, Sesión XXIII, día 15 de julio de 1563, Doctrina y cánones de sacra ordinationis, cap. 4: DS 1767–1770; Pío XII, Carta Encíclica, *Mediator Dei:* AAS 39 (1947) p. 553.

109. Cf. *Código de Derecho Canónico,* c. 230 § 2; cf. también *Missale Romanum,* Institutio Generalis, n. 97.

110. Cf. *Missale Romanum,* Institutio Generalis, n. 109.

111. Cf. Pablo VI, Carta Apostólica "motu proprio datae", *Ministeria quaedam,* día 15 de agosto de 1972, nn. VI–XII: *Pontificale Romanum ex decreto sacrosancti Oecumenici Concilii Vaticani II instauratum, auctoritate Pauli Pp. VI promulgatum,* De institutione lectorum et acolythorum, de admissione inter candidatos ad diaconatum et presbyteratum, de sacro caelibatu amplectendo, editio typica, día 3 de diciembre de 1972, Typis Polyglottis Vaticanis, 1973, p. 10: AAS 64 (1972) pp. 529–534, esto pp. 532–533; *Código de Derecho Canónico,* c. 230 § 1; *Missale Romanum,* Institutio Generalis, nn. 98–99, 187–193.

112. Cf. *Missale Romanum,* Institutio Generalis, nn. 187–190, 193; *Código de Derecho Canónico,* c. 230 §§ 2–3.

113. Cf. Concilio Ecuménico Vaticano II, Const. sobre la sagrada Liturgia, *Sacrosanctum Concilium,* n. 24; S. Congr. Sacramentos y Culto Divino, Instr., *Inaestimabile donum,* nn. 2 y 18: AAS 72 (1980) pp. 334, 338; *Missale*

Romanum, Institutio Generalis, nn. 101, 194–198; *Código de Derecho Canónico*, c. 230 §§ 2–3.

114. Cf. *Missale Romanum*, Institutio Generalis, nn. 100–107.

115. Ibidem, n. 91; cf. Concilio Ecuménico Vaticano II, Const. sobre la sagrada Liturgia, *Sacrosanctum Concilium*, n. 28.

116. Cf. Juan Pablo II, Alocución a la Conferencia de Obispos de las Antillas, día 7 de mayo del 2002, n. 2: AAS 94 (2002) pp. 575–577; Exhortación Apostólica postsinodal, *Christifideles laici*, día 30 de diciembre de 1988, n. 23: AAS 81 (1989) pp. 393–521, esto pp. 429–431; Congr. Clero y otras, Instr., *Ecclesiae de mysterio*, día 15 de agosto de 1997, Principios teológicos, n. 4: AAS 89 (1997) pp. 860–861.

117. Cf. Concilio Ecuménico Vaticano II, Const. sobre la sagrada Liturgia, *Sacrosanctum Concilium*, n. 19.

118. Cf. S. Congr. De la Disciplina de los Sacramentos, Instr., *Immensae caritatis*, día 29 de enero de 1973: AAS 65 (1973) p. 266.

119. Cf. S. Congr. Ritos, Instr., *De Musica sacra*, día 3 de septiembre de 1958, n. 93c: AAS 50 (1958) p. 656.

120. Cf. Pont. Consejo para la Interp. De los Tex. Legislativos, Respuesta ad propositum dubium, día 11 de julio de 1992: AAS 86 (1994) pp. 541–542; Congr. Culto Divino y Disc. Sacramentos, Carta a los Presidentes de las Conferencias de Obispos sobre el servicio litúrgico de los laicos, día 15 de marzo de 1994: *Notitae* 30 (1994) pp. 333–335, 347–348.

121. Cf. Juan Pablo II, Constitución Apostólica, *Pastor bonus*, art. 65: AAS 80 (1988) p. 877.

122. Cf. Pont. Consejo para la Interp. De los Tex. Legislativos, Respuesta ad propositum dubium, día 11 de julio de 1992: AAS 86 (1994) pp. 541–542; Congr. Culto Divino y Disc Sacramentos, Carta a los Presidentes de las Conferencias de Obispos sobre el servicio litúrgico de los laicos, día 15 de marzo de 1994: *Notitae* 30 (1994) pp. 333–335, 347–348; Carta a un Obispo, día 27 de julio del 2001: *Notitae* 38 (2002) pp. 46–54.

123. Cf. *Código de Derecho Canónico*, c. 924 § 2; *Missale Romanum*, Institutio Generalis, n. 320.

124. Cf. S. Congr. Disciplina Sacramentos, Instr., *Dominus Salvator noster*, día 26 de marzo de 1929, n. 1: AAS 21 (1929) pp. 631–642, esto p. 632.

125. Cf. ibidem, n. II: AAS 21 (1929) p. 635.

126. Cf. *Missale Romanum*, Institutio Generalis, n. 321.

127. Cf. Lucas 22, 18; *Código de Derecho Canónico*, c. 924 §§ 1, 3; *Missale Romanum*, Institutio Generalis, n. 322.

128. Cf. *Missale Romanum*, Institutio Generalis, n. 323.

129. Juan Pablo II, Carta Apostólica, *Vicesimus quintus annus*, n. 13: AAS 81 (1989) p. 910.

130. S. Congr. Sacramentos y Culto Divino, Instr., *Inaestimabile donum*, n. 5: AAS 72 (1980) p. 335.

131. Cf. Juan Pablo II, Carta Encíclica, *Ecclesia de Eucharistia*, n. 28: AAS 95 (2003) p. 452; *Missale Romanum*, Institutio Generalis, n. 147; S. Congr. Culto Divino, Instr., *Liturgicae instaurationes*, n. 4: AAS 62 (1970) p. 698; S. Congr. Sacramentos y Culto Divino, Instr., *Inaestimabile*

donum, n. 4: AAS 72 (1980) p. 334.

132. *Missale Romanum,* Institutio Generalis, n. 32.

133. Ibidem, n. 147; cf. Juan Pablo II, Carta Encíclica, *Ecclesia de Eucharistia,* n. 28: AAS 95 (2003) p. 452; cf. también Congr. Sacramentos y Culto Divino, Instr., *Inaestimabile donum,* n. 4: AAS 72 (1980) pp. 334–335.

134. Juan Pablo II, Carta Encíclica, *Ecclesia de Eucharistia,* n. 39: AAS 95 (2003) p. 459.

135. Cf. S. Congr. Culto Divino, Instr., *Liturgicae instaurationes,* n. 2b: AAS 62 (1970) p. 696.

136. Cf. *Missale Romanum,* Institutio Generalis, nn. 356–362.

137. Cf. Concilio Ecuménico Vaticano II, Const. sobre la s. *Liturgia, Sacrosanctum Concilium,* n. 51.

138. *Missale Romanum,* Institutio Generalis, n. 57; cf. Juan Pablo II, Carta Apostólica, *Vicesimus quintus annus,* n. 13: AAS 81 (1989) p. 910; Congr. Doctrina de la Fe, Declaración sobre la unicidad y universalidad salvífica de Jesucristo y de la Iglesia, *Dominus Iesus,* día 6 de agosto del 2000: AAS 92 (2000) pp. 742–765.

139. *Missale Romanum,* Institutio Generalis, n. 60.

140. Cf. ibidem, nn. 59–60.

141. Cf. v.gr. *Missale Romanum, ex decreto sacrosancti Oecumenici Concilii Vaticani II renovatum, auctoritate Pauli Pp. VI editum Ioannis Pauli Pp. II cura recognitum:* Ordo celebrandi Matrimonium, editio typica altera, día 19 de marzo de 1990, Typis Polyglottis Vaticanis, 1991, n. 125; *Missale Romanum, ex decreto sacrosancti Oecumenici Concilii Vaticani II instauratum, auctoritate Pauli Pp. VI promulgatum:* Ordo Unctionis infirmorum eorumque pastoralis curae, editio typica, día 7 de diciembre de 1972, Typis Polyglottis Vaticanis, 1972, n. 72.

142. Cf. *Código de Derecho Canónico,* c. 767 § 1.

143. Cf. *Missale Romanum,* Institutio Generalis, n. 66; cf. también *Código de Derecho Canónico,* c. 6 §§ 1, 2; y c. 767 § 1, a lo que se refiere también la ya citada Congr. Clero y otras, Instr., *Ecclesiae de mysterio,* Disposiciones Prácticas, art. 3 § 1: AAS 89 (1997) p. 865.

144. *Missale Romanum,* Institutio Generalis, n. 66; cf. también *Código de Derecho Canónico,* c. 767 § 1.

145. Cf. Congr. Clero y otras, Instr., *Ecclesiae de mysterio,* Disposiciones Prácticas, art. 3 § 1: AAS 89 (1997) p. 865; cf. también *Código de Derecho Canónico,* c. 6 §§ 1, 2; Pont. Comisión para la Interp. Autética del Cod. Der. Canónico, Respuesta ad propositum dubium, día 20 de junio de 1987: AAS 79 (1987) p. 1249.

146. Cf. Congr. Clero y otras, Instr., *Ecclesiae de mysterio,* Disposiciones Prácticas, art. 3 § 1: AAS 89 (1997) pp. 864–865.

147. Cf. Concilio Ecuménico Tridentino, Sesión XXII, día 17 de septiembre de 1562, De Ss. Missae Sacrificio, cap. 8: DS 1749; *Missale Romanum,* Institutio Generalis, n. 65.

148. Cf. Juan Pablo II, Alocución a los Obispos de los Estados Unidos de América, venidos a Roma en visita "ad limina Apostolorum", día 28 de mayo de 1993, n. 2: AAS 86 (1994) p. 330.

149. Cf. *Código de Derecho Canónico,* c. 386 § 1.

150. Cf. *Missale Romanum,* Institutio Generalis, n. 73.

151. Cf. ibidem, n. 154.

152. Cf. ibidem, nn. 82, 154.

153. Ibidem, n. 83.

154. Cf. S. Congr. Culto Divino, Instr., *Liturgicae instaurationes,* n. 5: AAS 62 (1970) p. 699.

155. Cf. *Missale Romanum,* Institutio Generalis, nn. 83, 240, 321.

156. Cf. CONGR. CLERO y otras, Instr., *Ecclesiae de mysterio,* Disposiciones prácticas, art. 3 § 2: AAS 89 (1997) p. 865.

157. Cf. especialmente, *Institutio generalis de Liturgia Horarum,* nn. 93–98; *Rituale Romanum, ex decreto sacrosancti Oecumenici Concilii Vaticani II instauratum, auctoritate Ioannis Pauli Pp. II promulgatum:* De Benedictionibus, editio typica, día 31 de mayo de 1984, Typis Poliglottis Vaticanis, 1984, Praenotanda n. 28; Ordo coronandi imaginem beatae Mariae Virginis, editio typica, día 25 de marzo de 1981, Typis Poliglottis Vaticanis, 1981, nn. 10 y 14, pp. 10–11; S. Congr. Culto Divino, Instr., sobre las Misas con grupos particulares, *Actio pastoralis,* día 15 de mayo de 1969: AAS 61 (1969) pp. 806–811; Directorio de las Misas con niños, *Pueros baptizatos,* día 1 de noviembre de 1973: AAS 66 (1974) pp. 30–46; *Missale Romanum,* Institutio Generalis, n. 21.

158. Cf. Juan Pablo II, Carta Apostólica "motu proprio datae", *Misericordia Dei,* día 7 abril del 2002, n. 2: AAS 94 (2002) p. 455; cf. Congr. Culto Divino y Disciplina Sacramentos, Respuesta ad dubia proposita: *Notitiae* 37 (2001) pp. 259–260.

159. Cf. S. Congr. Culto Divino, Instr., *Liturgicae instaurationes,* n. 9: AAS 62 (1970) p. 702.

160. Concilio Ecuménico Tridentino, Sesión XIII, día 11 de octubre de 1551, Decr. de Ss. Eucharistia, cap. 2: DS 1638; cf. Sesión XXII, día 17 de septiembre de 1562, De Ss. Missae Sacrificio, caps. 1–2: DS 1740, 1743; S Congr. Ritos, Instr., *Eucharisticum mysterium,* n. 35: AAS 59 (1967) p. 560.

161. Cf. *Missale Romanum,* Ordo Missae, n. 4, p. 505.

162. *Missale Romanum,* Institutio Generalis, n. 51.

163. Cf. 1 Corintios 11, 28.

164. Cf. *Código de Derecho Canónico,* c. 916; Concilio Ecuménico Tridentino, Sesión XIII, día 11 de octubre de 1551, Decr. de Ss. Eucharistia, cap. 7: DS 1646–1647; Juan Pablo II, Carta Encíclica, *Ecclesia de Eucharistia,* n. 36: AAS 95 (2003) pp. 457–458; S. Congr. Ritos, Instr., *Eucharisticum mysterium,* n. 35: AAS 59 (1967) p. 561.

165. Juan Pablo II, Carta Encíclica, *Ecclesia de Eucharistia,* n. 42: AAS 95 (2003) p. 461.

166. Cf. *Código de Derecho Canónico,* c. 844 § 1; Juan Pablo II, Carta Encíclica, *Ecclesia de Eucharistia,* nn. 45-46: AAS 95 (2003) pp. 463–464; cf. también, Pont. Consejo para la Promoción de la Unidad de los Cristianos, Direct. para la aplicación de los principios y las normas sobre el ecumenismo, *La recherche de l'unité,* día 25 de marzo de 1993, nn. 130–131: AAS 85 (1993) pp. 1039–1119, esto p. 1089.

167. Cf. Juan Pablo II, Carta Encíclica, *Ecclesia de Eucharistia,* n. 46: AAS 95 (2003) pp. 463–464.

168. Cf. S. Congr. Ritos, Instr., *Eucharisticum mysterium*, n. 35: AAS 59 (1967) p. 561.

169. Cf. *Código de Derecho Canónico*, c. 914; S. Congr. Disciplina Sacramentos, Declaración, *Sanctus Pontifex*, día 24 de mayo de 1973: AAS 65 (1973) p. 410; S. Congr. Sacramentos y Culto Divino y S. Congr. Clero, Carta a los Presidentes de las Conferencias de Obispos, *In quibusdam*, día 31 de marzo de 1977: *Enchiridion Documentorum Instaurationis Liturgicae*, II, Roma, 1988, pp. 142–144; S. Congr. Sacramentos y Culto Divino y S. Congr. Clero, Respuesta *ad propositum dubium*, día 20 de mayo de 1977: AAS 69 (1977) p. 427.

170. Cf. Juan Pablo II, Carta Apostólica, *Dies Domini*, día 31 de mayo del 1998, nn. 31–34: AAS 90 (1998) pp. 713–766, esto pp. 731–734.

171. Cf. *Código de Derecho Canónico*, c. 914.

172. Cf. Concilio Ecuménico Vaticano II, Const. sobre la s. Liturgia, *Sacrosanctum Concilium*, n. 55.

173. Cf. S Congr. Ritos, Instr., *Eucharisticum mysterium*, n. 31: AAS 59 (1967) p. 558; Pont. Comis. Para la Interp. Auténtica del Código de Derecho Canónico, Respuesta *ad propositum dubium*, día 1 de junio de 1988: AAS 80 (1988) p. 1373.

174. *Missale Romanum*, Institutio Generalis, n. 85.

175. Cf. Concilio Ecuménico Vaticano II, Const. sobre la s. Liturgia, *Sacrosanctum Concilium*, n. 55; S CONGR. RITOS, Instr., *Eucharisticum mysterium*, n. 31: AAS 59 (1967) p. 558; *Missale Romanum*, Institutio Generalis, nn. 85, 157, 243.

176. Cf. *Missale Romanum*, Institutio Generalis, n. 160.

177. *Código de Derecho Canónico*, c. 843 § 1; cf. c. 915.

178. Cf. *Missale Romanum*, Institutio Generalis, n. 161.

179. Congr. Culto Divino y Disc. Sacramentos, Dubium: *Missale Romanum* 35 (1999) pp. 160–161.

180. Cf. *Missale Romanum*, Institutio Generalis, n. 118.

181. Ibidem, n. 160.

182. *Código de Derecho Canónico*, c. 917; cf. Pont. Comis. Para la Interp. Auténtica del Código de Derecho Canónico, Respuesta *ad propositum dubium*, día 11 de julio de 1984: AAS 76 (1984) p. 746.

183. Cf. Concilio Ecuménico Vaticano II, Const. sobre la s. Liturgia, *Sacrosanctum Concilium*, n. 55; *Missale Romanum*, Institutio Generalis, nn. 158–160, 243–244, 246.

184. Cf. *Missale Romanum*, Institutio Generalis, nn. 237–249; cf. también nn. 85, 157.

185. Cf. ibidem, n. 283a.

186. Cf. Concilio Ecuménico Tridentino, Sesión XXI, día 16 de julio de 1562, Decr. De communione eucharistica, caps. 1–3: DS 1725–1729; Concilio Ecuménico Vaticano II, Const. sobre la s. Liturgia, *Sacrosanctum Concilium*, n. 55; *Missale Romanum*, Institutio Generalis, nn. 282–283.

187. Cf. *Missale Romanum*, Institutio Generalis, n. 283.

188. Cf. ibidem.

189. Cf. S. Congr. Culto Divino, Instr., *Sacramentali Communione*, día 29 de junio de 1970: AAS 62 (1970) p. 665; Instr., *Liturgicae*

instaurationes, n. 6a: AAS 62 (1970) p. 699.

190. *Missale Romanum,* Institutio Generalis, n. 285a.

191. Ibidem, n. 245.

192. Cf. ibidem, nn. 285b y 287.

193. Cf. ibidem, nn. 207 y 285a.

194. Cf. *Código de Derecho Canónico,* c. 1367.

195. Cf. Pont. Consejo para la Interp. De los Tex. Legislativos, Respuesta *ad propositum dubium,* día 3 de julio de 1999: AAS 91 (1999) p. 918.

196. *Missale Romanum,* Institutio Generalis, nn. 163, 284.

197. *Código de Derecho Canónico,* c. 932 § 1; cf. S. Congr. Culto Divino, Instr., *Liturgicae instaurationes,* n. 9: AAS 62 (1970) p. 701.

198. *Código de Derecho Canónico,* c. 904; cf. Concilio Ecuménico Vaticano II, Const. dogmática sobre la Iglesia, *Lumen gentium,* n. 3; Decr. sobre el ministerio y vida de los presbíteros, *Presbyterorum ordinis,* n. 13; cf. también Concilio Ecuménico Tridentino, Sesión XXII, día 17 de septiembre de 1562, De Ss. Missae Sacrificio, cap. 6: DS 1747; Pablo VI, Carta Encíclica, *Mysterium fidei,* día 3 de septiembre de 1965: AAS 57 (1965) pp. 753–774, esto, pp. 761–762; cf. Juan Pablo II, Carta Encíclica, *Ecclesia de Eucharistia,* n. 11: AAS 95 (2003) pp. 440–441; S Congr. Ritos, Instr., *Eucharisticum mysterium,* n. 44: AAS 59 (1967) p. 564; *Missale Romanum,* Institutio Generalis, n. 19.

199. Cf. *Código de Derecho Canónico,* c. 903; *Missale Romanum,* Institutio Generalis, n. 200.

200. Cf. Concilio Ecuménico Vaticano II, Const. sobre la s. Liturgia, *Sacrosanctum Concilium,* n. 36 § 1; *Código de Derecho Canónico,* c. 928.

201. Cf. *Missale Romanum,* tercera ed. típica, Institutio Generalis, n. 114.

202. Juan Pablo II, Carta Apostólica, *Dies Domini,* n. 36: AAS 90 (1998) p. 735; cf. también S. Congr. Ritos, Instr., *Eucharisticum mysterium,* n. 27: AAS 59 (1967) p. 556.

203. Cf. Juan Pablo II, Carta Apostólica, *Dies Domini,* especialmente n. 36: AAS 90 (1998) pp. 735–736; S. Congr. Culto Divino, Instr., *Actio pastoraslis:* AAS 61 (1969) pp. 806–811.

204. Cf. *Código de Derecho Canónico,* cc. 905, 945–958; CONGR. CLERO, Decreto, *Mos iugiter,* día 22 de febrero de 1991: AAS 83 (1991) pp. 443–446.

205. Cf. *Missale Romanum,* Institutio Generalis, nn. 327–333.

206. Cf. ibidem, n. 332.

207. Cf. ibidem, n. 332; S. Congr. Sacramentos y Culto Divino, Instr., *Inaestimabile donum,* n. 16: AAS 72 (1980) p. 338.

208. Cf. *Missale Romanum,* Institutio Generalis, n. 333; Apéndice IV. *Ordo benedictionis calicis et patenae intra Missam adhibendus,* pp. 1255–1257; *Pontificale Romanum ex decreto sacrosancti Oecumenici Concilii Vaticani II instauratum, auctoritate Pauli Pp. VI promulgatum,* Ordo Dedicationis ecclesiae et altaris, editio typica, día 29 de mayo de 1977, Typis Polyglottis Vaticanis, 1977, cap. VII, pp. 125–132.

209. Cf. *Missale Romanum,* Institutio Generalis, nn. 163, 183, 192.

210. Ibidem, n. 345.

211. Ibidem, n. 335.

212. Cf. ibidem, n. 336.

213. Cf. ibidem, n. 337.

214. Cf. ibidem, n. 209.

215. Cf. ibidem, n. 338.

216. Cf. S. Congr. Culto Divino, Instr., *Liturgicae instaurationes,* n. 8c: AAS 62 (1970) p. 701.

217. Cf. *Missale Romanum,* Institutio Generalis, n. 346g.

218. Ibidem, n. 114, cf. nn. 16–17.

219. S. Congr. Culto Divino, Decr., *Eucharistiae sacramentum,* día 21 de junio de 1973: AAS 65 (1973) 610.

220. Cf. ibidem.

221. Cf. S. Congr. Ritos, Instr., *Eucharisticum mysterium,* n. 54: AAS 59 (1967) p. 568; Instr., *Inter Oecumenici,* día 26 de septiembre de 1964, n. 95: AAS 56 (1964) pp. 877–900, esto p. 898; *Missale Romanum,* Institutio Generalis, n. 314.

222. Cf. Juan Pablo II, Carta, *Dominicae Cenae,* n. 3: AAS 72 (1980) pp. 117–119; S. Congr. Ritos, Instr., *Eucharisticum mysterium,* n. 53: AAS 59 (1967) p. 568; *Código de Derecho Canónico,* c. 938 § 2; *Rituale Romanum,* De sacra Communione et de cultu Mysterii eucharistici extra Missam, Praenotanda, n. 9; *Missale Romanum,* Institutio Generalis, nn. 314–317.

223. Cf. *Código de Derecho Canónico,* c. 938 §§ 3–5.

224. S. Congr. Disc. Sacramentos, Instr., *Nullo unquam,* día 26 de mayo de 1938, n. 10d: AAS 30 (1938) pp. 198–207, esto p. 206.

225. Cf. Juan Pablo II, Carta Apostólica "motu proprio datae," *Sacramentorum sanctitatis tutela,* día 30 de abril del 2001: AAS 93 (2001) pp. 737–739; Congr. Doctrina de la Fe, Carta ad totius Catholicae Ecclesiae Episcopos aliosque Ordinarios et Hierarchas quorum interest: de delictis gravioribus eidem Congregationi pro Doctrina Fidei reservatis: AAS 93 (2001) p. 786.

226. Cf. *Rituale Romanum,* De sacra Communione et de cultu Mysterii eucharistici extra Missam, nn. 26–78.

227. Juan Pablo II, Carta Encíclica, *Ecclesia de Eucharistia,* n. 25: AAS 95 (2003) pp. 449–450.

228. Cf. Concilio Ecuménico Tridentino, Sesión XIII, día 11 de octubre de 1551, Decr. De Ss. Eucharistia, cap. 5: DS 1643; Pío XII, Carta Encíclica, *Mediator Dei:* AAS 39 (1947) p. 569; Pablo VI, Carta Encíclica, *Mysterium Fidei,* día 3 de septiembre de 1965: AAS 57 (1965) pp. 753–774, esto pp. 769–770; S CONGR. RITOS, Instr., *Eucharisticum mysterium,* n. 3f: AAS 59 (1967) p. 543; S. Congr. Sacramentos y Culto Divino, Instr., *Inaestimabile donum,* n. 20: AAS 72 (1980) p. 339; Juan Pablo II, Carta Encíclica, *Ecclesia de Eucharistia,* n. 25: AAS 95 (2003) pp. 449–450.

229. Cf. Hebreos 9,11; Juan Pablo II, Carta Encíclica, *Ecclesia de Eucharistia,* n. 3: AAS 95 (2003) p. 435.

230. Juan Pablo II, Carta Encíclica, *Ecclesia de Eucharistia,* n. 25: AAS 95 (2003) p. 450.

231. Pablo VI, Carta Encíclica, *Mysterium Fidei:* AAS 57 (1965) p. 771.

232. Cf. Juan Pablo II, Carta Encíclica, *Ecclesia de Eucharistia,* n. 25: AAS 95 (2003) pp. 449-450.

233. *Código de Derecho Canónico,* c. 937.

234. Juan Pablo II, Carta Encíclica, *Ecclesia de Eucharistia,* n. 10: AAS 95 (2003) p. 439.

235. Cf. *Rituale Romanum,* De sacra Communione et de cultu Mysterii eucharistici extra Missam, nn. 82-100; *Missale Romanum,* Institutio Generalis, n. 317; *Código de Derecho Canónico,* c. 941 § 2.

236. Juan Pablo II, Carta Apostólica, *Rosarium Virginis Mariae,* día 16 de octubre del 2002: AAS 95 (2003) pp. 5-36, esto en n. 2, p. 6.

237. Cf. Congr. Culto Divino y Disc. Sacramentos, Carta de la Congregación, día 15 de enero de 1998: *Notitiae* 34 (1998) pp. 506-510; Penitenciaría Apostólica, Carta ad quemdam sacerdotem, día 8 de marzo de 1996: *Notitiae* 34 (1998) p. 511.

238. Cf. S. Congr. Ritos, Instr., *Eucharisticum mysterium,* n. 61: AAS 59 (1967) p. 571; *Rituale Romanum,* De sacra Communione et de cultu Mysterii eucharistici extra Missam, n. 83; *Missale Romanum,* Institutio Generalis, n. 317; *Código de Derecho Canónico,* c. 941 § 2.

239. Cf. *Rituale Romanum,* De sacra Communione et de cultu Mysterii eucharistici extra Missam, n. 94.

240. Cf. Juan Pablo II, Const. Apostólica, *Pastor bonus,* art. 65: AAS 80 (1988) p. 877.

241. *Código de Derecho Canónico,* c. 944 § 2; cf. *Rituale Romanum,* De sacra Communione et de cultu Mysterii eucharistici extra Missam, Praenotanda, n. 102; *Missale Romanum,* Institutio Generalis, n. 317.

242. *Código de Derecho Canónico,* c. 944 § 1; *Rituale Romanum,* De sacra Communione et de cultu Mysterii eucharistici extra Missam, Praenotanda, nn. 101-102; *Missale Romanum,* Institutio Generalis, n. 317.

243. Juan Pablo II, Carta Encíclica, *Ecclesia de Eucharistia,* n. 10: AAS 95 (2003) p. 439.

244. Cf. *Rituale Romanum,* De sacra Communione et de cultu Mysterii eucharistici extra Missam, Praenotanda, n. 109.

245. Cf. ibidem, nn. 109-112.

246. Cf. *Missale Romanum,* In sollemnitate sanctissimi Corporis et Sanguinis Christi, Collecta, p. 489.

247. Cf. Congr. Clero y otras, Instr., *Ecclesiae de mysterio,* Principios teológicos, n. 3: AAS 89 (1997) p. 859.

248. *Código de Derecho Canónico,* c. 900 § 1; cf. Concilio Ecuménico Lateranense IV, días 11-30 de noviembre de 1215, cap. 1: DS 802; Clemente VI, Carta a Mekhitar, Catholicos de los Armenios, *Super quibusdam,* día 29 de septiembre de 1351: DS 1084; Concilio Ecuménico Tridentino, Sesión XXIII, día 15 de julio de 1563, Doctrina et canones de sacramento ordinis, cap. 4: DS 1767-1770; PÍO XII, Carta Encíclica, *Mediator Dei:* AAS 39 (1947) p. 553.

249. Cf. *Código de Derecho Canónico,* c. 230 § 3; Juan Pablo II, Alocución en el Simposio "de laicorum cooperatione in ministerio pastorali presbyterorum", día 22 de abril de 1994, n. 2: *L'Osservatore Romano,* 23 de abril 1994; Congr. Clero y otras, Instr., *Ecclesiae de*

mysterio, Proemio: AAS 89 (1997) pp. 852–856.

250. Cf. Juan Pablo II, Carta Encíclica, *Redemptoris missio,* nn. 53–54: AAS 83 (1991) pp. 300–302; Congr. Clero y otras, Instr., *Ecclesiae de mysterio,* Proemio: AAS 89 (1997) pp. 852–856.

251. Cf. Concilio Ecuménico Vaticano II, Decreto sobre la actividad misionera de la Iglesia, *Ad gentes,* día 7 de diciembre de 1965, n. 17; Juan Pablo II, Carta Encíclica, *Redemptoris missio,* n. 73: AAS 83 (1991) p. 321.

252. Cf. Congr. Clero y otras, Instr., *Ecclesiae de mysterio,* Disposiciones prácticas, art. 8 § 2: AAS 89 (1997) p. 872.

253. Cf. Juan Pablo II, Carta Encíclica, *Ecclesia de Eucharistia,* n. 32: AAS 95 (2003) p. 455.

254. *Código de Derecho Canónico,* c. 900 § 1.

255. Cf. ibid., c. 910 § 1; cf. también Juan Pablo II, Carta, *Dominicae Cenae,* n. 11: AAS 72 (1980) p. 142; Congr. Clero y otras, Instr., *Ecclesiae de mysterio,* Disposiciones prácticas, art. 8 § 1: AAS 89 (1997) pp. 870–871.

256. Cf. *Código de Derecho Canónico,* c. 230 § 3.

257. Cf. S. Congr. de la Disciplina de los Sacramentos, Instr., *Immensae caritatis,* proemio: AAS 65 (1973) p. 264; Pablo VI, Carta Apostólica "motu proprio datae", *Ministeria quaedam,* día 15 de agosto de 1972: AAS 64 (1972) p. 532; *Missale Romanum,* Appendix III: Ritus ad deputandum ministrum sacrae Communionis ad actum distribuendae, p. 1253; Congr. Clero y otras, Instr., *Ecclesiae de mysterio,* Disposiciones prácticas, art. 8 § 1: AAS 89 (1997) p. 871.

258. Cf. S. Congr. Sacramentos y Culto Divino, Instr., *Inaestimabile donum,* n. 10: AAS 72 (1980) p. 336; Pont. Comis. Para la Interp. Auténtica del Código de Derecho Canónico, Respuesta ad propositum dubium, día 11 de julio de 1984: AAS 76 (1984) p. 746.

259. Cf. S. Congr. Disciplina Sacramentos, Instr., *Immensae caritatis,* n. 1: AAS 65 (1973) pp. 264–271, espec. pp. 265–266; Pont. Comis. Para la Interp. Auténtica del Código de Derecho Canónico, Respuesta ad propositum dubium, día 1 de junio de 1988: AAS 80 (1980) p. 1373; Congr. Clero y otras, Instr., *Ecclesiae de mysterio,* Disposiciones prácticas, art. 8 § 2: AAS 89 (1997) p. 871.

260. Cf. *Código de Derecho Canónico,* c. 767 § 1.

261. Cf. *Código de Derecho Canónico,* c. 766.

262. Cf. Congr. Clero y otras, Instr., *Ecclesiae de mysterio, Disposiciones* prácticas, art. 2 §§ 3–4: AAS 89 (1997) p. 865.

263. Cf. Juan Pablo II, Carta Apostólica, *Dies Domini,* espec. nn. 31–35: AAS 90 (1998) pp. 713–766, esto pp. 731–746; Juan Pablo II, Carta Apostólica, *Novo Millennio ineunte,* día 6 de enero del 2001, nn. 35–36: AAS 93 (2001) pp. 290–292; Juan Pablo II, Carta Encíclica, *Ecclesia de Eucharistia,* n. 41: AAS 95 (2003) pp. 460–461.

264. Concilio Ecuménico Vaticano II, Decr. sobre el ministerio y vida de los presbíteros, *Presbyterorum ordinis,* n. 6; cf. Juan Pablo II, Carta Encíclica, *Ecclesia de Eucharistia,* nn. 22, 33: AAS 95 (2003) pp. 448, 455–456.

265. Cf. S. Congr. Ritos, Instr., *Eucharisticum mysterium*, n. 26: AAS 59 (1967) pp. 555–556; Congr. Culto Divino, Directorio para las celebraciones dominicales en ausencia de presbítero, *Christi Ecclesia*, día 2 de junio de 1988, nn. 5 y 25: *Notitiae* 24 (1988) pp. 366–378, esto pp. 367, 372.

266. Cf. Congr. Culto Divino, Directorio para las celebraciones dominicales en ausencia de presbítero, *Christi Ecclesia*, n. 18: *Notitiae* 24 (1988) p. 370.

267. Cf. Juan Pablo II, Carta, *Dominicae Cenae*, n. 2: AAS 72 (1980) p. 116.

268. Cf. Juan Pablo II, Carta Apostólica, *Dies Domini*, n. 49: AAS 90 (1998) p. 744; Carta Encíclica, *Ecclesia de Eucharistia*, n. 41: AAS 95 (2003) pp. 460–461; *Código de Derecho Canónico*, cc. 1246–1247.

269. *Código de Derecho Canónico*, c. 1248 § 2; cf. Congr. Culto Divino, Directorio para las celebraciones dominicales en ausencia de presbítero, *Christi Ecclesia*, nn. 1–2: *Notitiae* 24 (1988) p. 366.

270. Juan Pablo II, Carta Encíclica, *Ecclesia de Eucharistia*, n. 33: AAS 95 (2003) pp. 455–456.

271. Cf. Congr. Culto Divino, Directorio para las celebraciones dominicales en ausencia de presbítero, *Christi Ecclesia*, n. 22: *Notitiae* 24 (1988) p. 371.

272. Juan Pablo II, Carta Encíclica, *Ecclesia de Eucharistia*, n. 30: AAS 95 (2003) pp. 453–454; cf. también Pont. Consejo para la Promoción de la Unidad de los Cristianos, Direct. para la aplicación de los principios y las normas sobre el ecumenismo, *La recherche de l'unité*, día 25 de marzo de 1993, n. 115: AAS 85 (1993) pp. 1039–1119, esto p. 1085.

273. Cf. Pont. Consejo para la Promoción de la Unidad de los Cristianos, Direct. para la aplicación de los principios y las normas sobre el ecumenismo, *La recherche de l'unité*, n. 115: AAS 85 (1993) p. 1085.

274. *Código de Derecho Canónico*, c. 292; cf. Pont. Consejo para la Interp. De los Tex. Legislativos, *Declaración de la recta interpretación del c. 1335, segunda parte, C.I.C.*, día 15 de mayo de 1997, n. 3: AAS 90 (1998) p. 64.

275. Cf. *Código de Derecho Canónico*, cc. 976; 986 § 2.

276. Cf. Pont. Consejo para la Interp. De los Tex. Legislativos, *Declaración de la recta interpretación del can. 1335, segunda parte, C.I.C.*, día 15 de mayo de 1997, nn. 1–2: AAS 90 (1998) pp. 63–64.

277. Lo que se refiere a sacerdotes que han obtenido la despensa del celibato, cf. S. Congr. Doctrina de la Fe, Normas de dispensa del celibato sacerdotal, a instancia de la parte, *Normae substantiales*, día 14 de octubre de 1980, art. 5; cf. también Congr. Clero y otras, Instr., *Ecclesiae de mysterio*, Disposiciones prácticas, art. 3 § 5: AAS 89 (1997) p. 865.

278. S. Tomás de Aquino, *Summa Theol.*, II, 2, q. 93, a. 1.

279. Cf. Juan Pablo II, Carta Apostólica, *Vicesimus quintus annus*, n. 15: AAS 81 (1989) p. 911; cf. también Concilio Ecuménico Vaticano II, Const. de s. Liturgia, *Sacrosanctum Concilium*, nn. 15–19.

280. Cf. Juan Pablo II, Carta Apostólica motu propio, *Sacramentorum sanctitatis tutela:* AAS 93 (2001) pp. 737–739; cf. Congr.

Doctrina de la Fe, Carta a todos los Obispos de la Iglesia Católica y a los otros Ordinarios y Jerarcas a los que interese: *de delictis gravioribus eidem Congregationi pro Doctrina Fidei reservatis:* AAS 93 (2001) p. 786.

281. Cf. *Código de Derecho Canónico,* c. 1367; Pont. Consejo para la Interp. De los Tex. Legislativos, Respuesta ad propositum dubium, día 3 de julio de 1999: AAS 91 (1999) p. 918; Congr. Doctrina de la Fe, Carta a todos los Obispos de la Iglesia Católica y a los otros Ordinarios y Jerarcas a los que interese: *de delictis gravioribus eidem Congregationi pro Doctrina Fidei reservatis:* AAS 93 (2001) p. 786.

282. Cf. *Código de Derecho Canónico,* cc. 1378 § 2 n. 1 y 1379; Congr. Doctrina de la Fe, Carta a todos los Obispos de la Iglesia Católica y a los otros Ordinarios y Jerarcas a los que interese: *de delictis gravioribus eidem Congregationi pro Doctrina Fidei reservatis:* AAS 93 (2001) p. 786.

283. Cf. *Código de Derecho Canónico,* cc. 908 y 1365; Conr. Doctrina de la Fe, Carta a todos los Obispos de la Iglesia Católica y a los otros Ordinarios y Jerarcas a los que interese: *de delictis gravioribus eidem Congregationi pro Doctrina Fidei reservatis:* AAS 93 (2001) p. 786.

284. Cf. *Código de Derecho Canónico,* c. 927; Congr. Doctrina de la Fe, Carta a todos los Obispos de la Iglesia Católica y a los otros Ordinarios y Jerarcas a los que interese: *de delictis gravioribus eidem Congregationi pro Doctrina Fidei reservatis:* AAS 93 (2001) p. 786.

285. *Código de Derecho Canónico,* c. 387.

286. Ibidem, c. 838 § 4.

287. Ibidem, c. 392.

288. Juan Pablo II, Constitución Apostólica, *Pastor bonus,* art. 52: AAS 80 (1988) p. 874.

289. Cf. ibidem, n. 63: AAS 80 (1988) p. 876.

290. Cf. *Código de Derecho Canónico,* c. 1417 § 1.

291. Juan Pablo II, Carta Encíclica, *Ecclesia de Eucharistia,* n. 24: AAS 95 (2003) p. 449.

292. Cf. ibidem, nn. 53-58: AAS 95 (2003) pp. 469–472.

293. Cf. Concilio Ecuménico Vaticano II, Constitución sobre la s. Liturgia *Sacrosanctum Concilium,* n. 14; cf. también nn. 11, 41 y 48.

294. Cf. Santo Tomás de Aquino, Summa Theol., III, q. 64, a. 9 ad primum.

295. Cf. *Missale Romanum,* Institutio Generalis, n. 24.

INDEX

ÍNDICE TEMÁTICO

EE: Ecclesia de Eucharistia
RS: Redemptionis Sacramentum